IS ANYONE OUT THERE?

IS ANYONE OUT THERE?

*The Scientific Search
for EXTRATERRESTRIAL
INTELLIGENCE*

FRANK DRAKE
and DAVA SOBEL

**Delacorte
Press**

Published by
Delacorte Press
Bantam Doubleday Dell Publishing Group, Inc.
666 Fifth Avenue
New York, New York 10103

Library of Congress Cataloging-in-Publication Data

Drake, Frank
    Is anyone out there? : the scientific search for extraterrestrial
intelligence / by Frank Drake and Dava Sobel.
        p.   cm.
    Includes bibliographical references (p.   ) and index.
    ISBN 0-385-30532-X
    1. Life on other planets.   2. Drake, Frank   3. Astronomers—
United States—Biography.   I. Sobel, Dava.   II. Title.
QB54.D72   1992
591.9099—dc20   92-3884   CIP

Manufactured in the United States of America
Published simultaneously in Canada

October 1992

10   9   8   7   6   5   4   3   2   1
RRH

Hold fast to dreams,
Let them stay with you forever.
Don't let them die.
You might fly up in the sky
On a silver unicorn's back,
Dreaming of the ocean,
Listening to the dolphins sing.
Dreams, hold on to them forever.

—NADIA DRAKE, age 9 (1989)

Acknowledgments

Our thanks to Dick Teresi and Art Klein for encouraging us to undertake this project, to Michael Carlisle and Marcy Posner of the William Morris Agency for representing it, and to Brian DeFiore of Delacorte Press for providing it a welcome home.

We are also grateful to John Billingham, Bernard Oliver, Thomas Pierson, Carl Sagan, and Jill Tarter for reading the entire manuscript very carefully and providing many useful comments, additions, and corrections.

Contents

Preface

From a distance of a hundred yards at twilight, you might almost mistake them for human. They'll have their heads at the tops of their bodies, I suspect, and their eyes in their heads, not far from their mouths. I think they'll walk on two legs, too, as we do, but I suppose that, more often than not, intelligent extraterrestrials will have four arms instead of two. Two just aren't enough, as far as I'm concerned. Four make for a much better design.

My scientific colleagues raise their eyebrows when I speculate on the appearance of extraterrestrials. But about 99.9 percent of them agree wholeheartedly that other intelligent life-forms do exist—and furthermore that there may be large populations of them throughout our galaxy and beyond.

Personally, I find nothing more tantalizing than the thought that radio messages from alien civilizations in space are passing through our offices and homes, right now, like a whisper we can't quite hear. In fact, we have the technology to detect such signals *today*, if only we knew where to point our radio telescopes, and the right frequency for listening.

I have been scanning the stars in search of extraterrestrial intelligence (an activity now abbreviated as SETI, and pronounced *SET-ee*) for more than thirty years. I engineered the first such effort in 1959, at the National Radio Astronomy Observatory in Green Bank, West Virginia. I named it "Project Ozma," after a land far away, difficult to reach, and populated by strange and exotic beings. I used what would now be considered crude equipment to listen for signals from two nearby, Sunlike stars. It took two months to complete the job. With the marvelous technological advances we have made in the intervening years, we could repeat the whole of Project Ozma today in a fraction of a second. We could scan for signals from a *million* stars or more at a time, at distances of at least a *thousand* light-years from Earth.

Such a search is not only possible, it is also all planned out, poised, and ready to begin at the time this book is published. In its first few days of operation, it will outstrip *all* current and previous search efforts combined.

Until the late 1980s, the fact that we had not yet found another civilization, despite continued global efforts and better equipment, simply meant we had not looked long enough or hard enough. No knowledgeable person was disappointed by our inability to detect alien intelligence, as this in no way proved that extraterrestrials did not exist. Rather, our failure simply confirmed that our efforts were puny in relation to the enormity of the task—somewhat like hunting for a needle in a cosmic haystack of inconceivable size. The way we were going about it, with our small-scale attempts, was like looking for the needle by strolling past the haystack every now and then. We weren't embarked on a search that had any real chance of success.

Then many people began to grasp the nature and scope of the challenge, the consequent investment required to succeed, and the importance of success to all humanity. They pushed relentlessly for a serious search. And won. The National Aeronautics and Space Administration (NASA) committed $100 million to a formal SETI mission spanning the decade of the 1990s, making the work a priority for the space agency and guaranteeing that coveted telescope time will be devoted to the search.

Now, after all our efforts over the past three decades, I am standing with my colleagues at last on the brink of discovery. This book is the behind-the-scenes story of the search for extraterrestrial intelligence as I have lived it, with all my reminiscences and impressions of the events, and especially the people involved. But it is not simply the chronicle of an interesting chapter in the history of science. I am telling my story because I see a pressing need to prepare thinking adults for the outcome of the present search activity—the imminent detection of signals from an extraterrestrial civilization. This discovery, which I fully expect to witness before the year 2000, will profoundly change the world.

The point of this book, as of my life's work, is that interstellar contact will enrich our lives immeasurably. In all likelihood, any civilization we can detect will be more advanced than our own, providing us with a glimpse of what Earth's future could be. For the first time we will witness the history of the future, not just of the past.

I want to nurture people's yearning curiosity about the beings who will no doubt contact us. At the same time, I want to quell the misleading myths about extraterrestrials, from the mistaken belief that they have visited us in the past, to the terrifying idea that they will wrest the future from our hands.

I want to show that we need not be afraid of interstellar contact, for unlike the primitive civilizations on Earth that were overpowered by more advanced technological societies, we cannot be exploited or enslaved. The extraterrestrials aren't going to come and eat us; they are too far away to pose a threat. Even back-and-forth conversation with them is highly unlikely, since radio signals, traveling at the speed of light, take *years* to reach the nearest stars, and many *millennia* to get to the farthest ones, where advanced civilizations may reside. But one-way communication is a different story. Just as our radio and television transmissions leak out into space, carrying the news of our existence far and wide, so similar information from the planets of other stars has no doubt been quietly arriving at Earth for perhaps billions of years. Even more exciting is the likelihood of *intentional* messages beamed to Earth for our particular benefit. As we know from our own efforts at composing for a pangalactic audience, reams of information about a planet's culture, history, and technology—the entire thirty-seven-volume set, if you will, of the "Encyclopedia Galactica"—could be transmitted (and received) easily and cheaply.

As a scientist, I'm driven by curiosity, of course. I want to know what's out there. But as a human being, I persevere in this pursuit because SETI promises answers to our most profound questions about who we are and where we stand in the universe. SETI is at once the most technical of scientific subjects, and also the most human. Every tactical problem in the search endeavor rests on some age-old philosophical conundrum: *Where did we come from? Are we unique? What does it mean to be a human being?*

SETI makes the starry sky reverberate with our self-wonder. In this book, as in the search itself, we address deeply emotional issues with far-reaching ramifications:

- What evidence do we have that intelligent life is common in the universe?
- Where might we look for extraterrestrial civilizations more advanced than we are?
- What do we stand to gain from interstellar contact?
- Which facts about ourselves do we want to communicate to extraterrestrials?
- Who among us should undertake the task of searching? Of sharing information?
- Will extraterrestrials try to make contact with us? How? And when?
- Are we at risk?
- What would it mean if we could not find them?
- How will we respond to a signal from an extraterrestrial civilization?

These thoughts led me to attempt Project Ozma in 1959. No doubt when I initiated that effort—when I proposed using the newest, largest radio telescope at a premier national research facility to search for intelligent signals from space—I was risking my professional reputation and future employment, not to mention public ridicule. At that time, no scientist talked seriously about extraterrestrial life. Percival Lowell's speculations about Mars had tainted the subject. And I had only just begun to establish myself as a scientist: I had discovered Van Allen radiation belts, just like Earth's, around Jupiter, created radio maps of the galactic center, and made observations of the radio spectrum of Venus that proved our sister planet's extremely high atmospheric temperature was really due to heat—and not some unknown phenomenon or glitch in the measurements. Still, I was a novice, and had a long way to go before my career was anything approaching secure.

If Project Ozma failed to detect a sign of extraterrestrial intelligence, it did succeed in identifying our group at Green Bank as people who were committed to SETI. It also portrayed SETI to other scientists and to the world at large for the first time as a legitimate and doable scientific endeavor. And the project stimulated activity among others who shared our interest but had been afraid to act or had lacked the means to search.

Today I have security and credibility as an established scientist. SETI is considered mainstream science. I can stick my neck out without fear of professional repercussions. Having lived with the subject as long as I have, I tend to take more risks—to speculate a little more—than my SETI peers. I claim, for example, according to the "Drake Equation," which I developed soon after Project Ozma, that there are approximately ten thousand advanced extraterrestrial civilizations in our Milky Way Galaxy alone. I believe that what they have to tell us is of supreme importance. I feel certain we can find them now, at a cost that would make this discovery the greatest bargain in history. And therefore I maintain it is worth doing everything in our power to ensure that we receive their signal at the earliest possible moment.

—Frank Drake
University of California, Santa Cruz

▲
▲
▲

CHAPTER 1

Intimations of an Infinitely Populated Universe

To consider the Earth as the only populated world in infinite space is as absurd as to assert that in an entire field of millet, only one grain will grow.

—METRODORUS,
Greek philosopher of
the fourth century B.C.

Forty years as an astronomer have not quelled my enthusiasm for lying outside after dark, staring up at the stars. It isn't only the beauty of the night sky that thrills me. It's the sense I have that some of those points of light—*which* ones I can't even guess—are the home stars of beings not so different from us, daily cares and all, who look across space with wonder, just as we do.

My predecessors in this business of stargazing imagined they saw animals and heroes outlined in the patterns of the stars. Those heavenly characters—Cygnus, Ursa Major, Hercules—still survive in the names of the familiar constellations. But there is more of real life than of legend among the stars, I'm certain.

Directly over my head now is Orion, the Hunter. Orion is my particular favorite, with his three-star belt, his three-star sword cutting a jaunty angle with the belt, and a red-hot star for his left shoulder. All Orion's stars are young and bright. Every one of them has burst out of a glowing green cloud in his sword within the past half-million years. With a small telescope, or even a good pair of binoculars, you can see that green cloud where, even now, new stars are still being born.

I have one more, very special, celestial favorite in addition to Orion, though I don't know its location. It is an old star, nearing death. It is so dense with age after aeons of burning that it is no longer visible to the naked eye. But in its heyday it was a giant. And once, about five billion years ago, it exploded with an unimaginable display of fireworks. Burning gas and dust shot into the heavens, mixing with the residue of previous stellar explosions. Then all this debris slowly coalesced to form a nebula something like the one we can see tonight in Orion's sword. It spawned a new crop of smaller stars and their companions. Among them was our Sun, surrounded by the planets of our Solar System. The explosion also seeded the new nebula with the chemical elements that live today in every plant and animal on the face of the Earth.

"I believe a leaf of grass is no less than the journeywork of the stars," Walt Whitman wrote, and he was right. We are children of the stars. We trace our roots to ancient suns that formed at the dawn of time. And although our science of astronomy has forced us to accept the fact that we are not the center of the universe, or even of the Solar System, that same science is now helping us reach across the void to kinsmen we didn't even know we had.

I have been waiting for this moment nearly all my life. Indeed, if there is anything unusual about my otherwise normal childhood, it is that I started tracing my ties to alien civilizations of intelligent life in the universe at age eight. I did this in spite of my family's fundamentalist religious beliefs and despite their scorn for fantastic ideas. Although those parental attitudes didn't stop my mind from straying into space, they did make me hold my tongue on the topic until I became a grown man.

Certainly the other facts of my early years were ordinary enough. I was born in Chicago on May 28, 1930. I grew up in a neighborhood called South Shore, in the first-floor apartment of a two-family house my parents owned. The second floor was rented out to tenants.

My father, Richard Carvel Drake, worked all his adult life as a chemical engineer for the city of Chicago. He was in charge of a laboratory that tested everything the city considered buying, from concrete and asphalt for paving streets to fire hydrants and fire engines. I remember he used to test parking meters by first putting samples of the various models up on the roof of the building for a year to weather them. Then he'd hand out hammers to a group of teenagers, and send them up to try to break into the meters. The last to break was the one that won his approval. When it was time to purchase police paddy wagons, he rounded up a bunch of really mean guys from inside the city jail and turned them loose on the collected models from all the manufacturers; the winning vehicle was the one that required the largest number of inmates to turn it over. I always chuckle when I think of some of his strategies, but my father implemented them without humor or irony. He was one of the most serious men I have ever known. Neither he nor my mother seemed to have any idea of how to have fun—at least in my opinion.

Father met my mother, Winifred Pearl Thompson, when the two of them were students at the University of Illinois. After they married, she worked as a housewife and a mother. She played the piano well, but never publicly or professionally. What she liked to do most was craftwork for church benefits—doll clothes, doilies, needlework, quilts, bedspreads, holiday ornaments—and she turned out enormous quantities of these items every time there were funds to be raised.

My sister, Alma, was born when I was three. Alma has managed to follow in both my parents' footsteps—first my father's, by becoming a biochemist and working for DuPont in the testing of materials for toxicity, and then my mother's, by leaving science for marriage and a family.

I grew up and left home before my brother, Robert, twelve years younger than I, was even a thinking person. I know him much better now, as a leading economist at the Los Alamos National Laboratory in New Mexico.

All through my childhood, my family made a big safari every Sunday to our church, the Hyde Park Baptist Church, which was right on the campus of the University of Chicago. It was about a four-mile drive from our house, and the drive itself was the main element of family togetherness. Once arrived, Father dropped us off and left us. He never went to church; he didn't like it. He was not a religious man, but he was very strict about upholding the rules of Baptist morality: no drinking, no smoking, no dancing, no partying. He took all of that to heart, but only rarely chose to set foot inside the church building. On most Sundays he'd go visit for two hours or so with some old friends of his who lived nearby, and pick us up later.

My mother was not devoutly religious either, although she had faith. Mostly she liked the social aspects of churchgoing, and the creative outlet of making all those crafts for the fairs. Alma and I (and later Robert, too) went to church at our parents' insistence to attend Sunday school.

At that time, in the mid- to late 1930s, the University of Chicago, which had been founded by Baptists, was still strongly influenced by the Baptist Church. In later years, the Baptist roots came to be considered a negative point, and the administration backed away from any visible sign of religious affiliation. But the special connection between the church and the university held strong sway during my Sunday school education. Indeed, our religious instruction was provided by professors from the university's renowned Oriental Institute.

My Sunday school teachers included Walter Havighurst and other eminent Egyptologists from the institute. Some of these men were among the foremost Middle East archaeologists of their time. They filled their lectures about the Hittites and ancient Damascus with archaeological evidence to prove that the Bible was factually accurate. They even took the fifteen eight-year-olds in my Sunday school class to visit the Oriental Institute—in a great big building only a block away from the church, where we saw the Egyptian mummies and other startling relics housed there. But none of the professors' efforts convinced me of the correctness of fundamentalist dogma. If anything, the lectures had the opposite effect. The topics seemed remote from the twentieth-century world I knew, with little light to shed on the serious questions of life that faced me, concerning clean living, morals, and ethics for eight-year-olds. I was not the only child in my group to veer away from organized religion as a result of those Sunday morning sessions.

Looking back, I think the teachers believed they were doing the right thing by trying to give us more religious education than most kids received. They wanted to prepare us to understand the real basis of religion. And in fact they achieved that for me, although I assume they would consider my case a failure. The fact is, I *did* come to understand the real basis of religion in those classes. I saw that religious history, as described to us, had to do with the particular history of one small region, and certain people's conclusions and supposed insights. It was an artificially narrow history, because it ignored the many different ways of life and ways of belief there were in the world. Our way was presented as the right way, of course, and our values and standards correct. But this view was really quite arbitrary. The weekly lessons, far from being the sole source of *truth*, seemed more and more like some imagined truths being foisted on us as *the* truth. There began inside me, at that very early age, a quiet rebellion against the church.

If religion was arbitrary, and I believed it was, then perhaps humanity, too, was arbitrary—was just one truth among many possible truths. I could see no reason to think that humankind was the only example of civilization, unique in all the universe. I imagined there could well be other forms of intelligent life elsewhere. But I never breathed a word of these ideas to anyone in my family, for fear of sounding like a foolish kid. Nor did I find support for such thoughts in church or school. Nevertheless, I was able to develop and expand them in another large institution that stood just a few blocks from the university campus. This was the Museum of Science and Industry. To a young boy, it was a gateway to all manner of wonders in science and engineering, and I found myself drawn there repeatedly.

All through grade school and high school, I often rode my bike to the museum with my best friend, Ralph Bransky. He and I were very interested in science. We made little electric motors and tiny radios and did a lot of amateurish experiments with a toy chemistry set. (Later, as teenagers, we tinkered with car engines together and got interested in girls. Ralph even dated my sister for a while, but wound up marrying someone else.) We received a good science education from school, and beefed it up through the exhibits at the museum, where we spent so much of our time. We explored every square inch of that place, over and over.

There was no elementary curriculum in astronomy when I was a child, so it was in the museum that I discovered the Sun to be just one star among billions of other stars in the Milky Way Galaxy. Not only was it one of many, it also was unspectacular. It was as average a star as you could find. The grand Milky Way itself, whose glowing white veil I had seen in the great dome of the Adler Planetarium on Lake Michigan, was but one galaxy among billions that studded a vast and awesome universe. It seemed more than likely to me then that many stars besides the Sun could have solar systems of their own, and hospitable planets, peopled with different species of intelligent creatures. I began to think ever more seriously about extraterrestrials and to wonder what "they" might be like. Not being much of a science fiction buff, I didn't fuel my fancy with stories. To me, the idea of alien intelligence was a distinct possibility in the real world. Or the real *universe*, I should say.

My interest in science continued to grow all through high school, where I had some excellent teachers. The school provided no college or career guidance to speak of, however, and I took it into my head that I wanted a career in airplane design. I really didn't know anything about that profession, but the idea of it was attractive to me. And so I decided to go to a college where I could learn how to design airplanes. I also wanted to attend an Ivy League college. I didn't know what that meant, precisely, though I'd heard somewhere along the line that those schools were good schools. In Chicago generally in 1947, and at my public high school in particular, "Ivy League" was an unknown concept. Most of the kids I knew went to the state university—the University of Illinois, where my parents had gotten their degrees—or to Purdue. But I made it my business to find out which colleges were Ivy League, and got their catalogs to see which ones taught airplane design. A year's tuition was only $600 then, and besides, I'd won a scholarship from the Naval Reserve Officers Training Corps (NROTC) that covered tuition and living expenses, so money was no object.

When I got the catalogs I discovered right away that most Ivy League colleges did not accept girls, which bothered me, and that only two of them taught anything resembling airplane design. I applied to these two—to all-male Princeton, which offered a formal program in aeronautical engineering, and to Cornell, which had a less aeronautically oriented engineering program but did boast a coeducational student body. Princeton never responded to my application; I'd picked Cornell as my first choice in any case because it had girls.

In preparation for my future in airplane design, I took a job that summer with TWA—as a baggage handler at Chicago Midway Airport. It's a good thing I was only seventeen, because the work was an exercise in building strength and endurance. There were no forklifts. We baggage handlers climbed up and down ladders all day to the cargo bays of DC-3's and Constellations, loading and unloading suitcases. However, I got much closer to the top echelons of the company than you would think from my job description. I even had what might be called an intimate encounter with the owner of the company, Howard Hughes, who was being pursued by the federal government over an antitrust issue.

Hughes's strategy was to stay airborne, setting down just long enough to switch planes, making it impossible for anyone to serve him a subpoena. Inevitably, he arrived at Midway one afternoon. I was instructed to board his incoming plane with an extra pair of white coveralls, like the ones I wore, for him to don as a disguise. I led him off the plane to the baggage handlers' locker room, where we spent about half an hour together—in silence, of course—before his next flight.

The following fall, as a Cornell student in Ithaca, New York, I soon discovered that airplane design wasn't at all what I had imagined it to be. I did not even find it interesting. This realization might have crushed me had I not simultaneously developed a genuine fascination for another field of engineering: electronics. I switched to the hardest curriculum in the school, engineering physics, where I found only twenty-eight students in my class.

As an engineering physics major, I was required to take a basic electronics course given by the legendary Alexander Barry Credle, reputed to be a ruthless, superdemanding monster. The course, infamous on campus, was known to be extremely difficult, with tons of homework and tough exams. Students looked on it as one of the great obstacles on the path to graduation. But I got a grade of 100 in that course. It was the first time anyone had done that. And true to form, Professor Credle did not acknowledge me or my achievement in any way. Nevertheless, I was inspired by my own facility for the subject, and I switched from airplane design to electronics.

All the while I was still thinking about extraterrestrial life and the nature of the universe, wondering whether the Earth was special, or whether there were possibilities for life elsewhere. And, of course, I was still keeping these long-secret thoughts to myself. But in my sophomore year I tried to nourish them by enrolling in an elementary astronomy course.

I am ever indebted to my first astronomy professor, R. William Shaw, for his stirring lectures and for giving me the chance, as he gave all his students, to make real astronomical observations. He had charge of an old fifteen-inch telescope in a building close to campus, where part of his course was conducted. I remember going up there after dark. And I will never forget seeing the planet Jupiter through that telescope like some kind of revelation. I saw it for the first time as another world, with stunningly beautiful colors and clouds, surrounded by its own four large moons, the Galilean satellites. Everything I had read or heard about astronomy suddenly became three-dimensional. At that moment, I was smitten. Literally starstruck. I felt the same kind of thrill I imagine Galileo himself must have experienced when he looked through his own small telescope to discover mountains on the Moon, spots on the Sun, rings around Saturn, and moons circling Jupiter.

To this day, I try to repeat that moment for students in the courses I teach at the University of California in Santa Cruz. I always schedule a field trip to the Lick Observatory, and I try to do it when Jupiter is up. We use a telescope that was the world's largest about a hundred years ago. One at a time, the students get to look through the eyepiece at Jupiter, and about half of them instantly drop the snide or blasé attitudes they have in class. All they can say is *WOW!* or *COOL!* And I'm quiet but happy, because I know what they're feeling, and how important it may be to them, too.

When I went home for summer vacation after my freshman year, I proceeded to build a six-inch telescope in my basement in Chicago, grinding the mirror myself. I loved every minute of the work. I still have that telescope, in fact, in a storage shed outside the house where I live now in Aptos, California. I built another, better instrument and telescope mount before I finished college. But I simply could not part with the first one, or forget what it meant to me.

Professor Shaw never broached the subject of extraterrestrial life, nor did it come up in the more advanced courses I pursued in astronomy. I continued to feel that I dare not mention my ideas aloud. It was nothing that serious astronomers discussed. Or so it seemed until 1951, in the fall of my junior year, when the great astrophysicist Otto Struve visited the campus to give a prestigious series of endowed talks called the Messenger Lectures.

Struve, then fifty-four, was imperiously tall and impeccably well mannered. While most astronomers in those days looked and dressed like elegant gentlemen, Struve really was one. He came from an aristocratic German family—a dynasty, really, of distinguished astronomers. His great-grandfather had moved the family to St. Petersburg, in Russia, where he was the equivalent of astronomer royal to Czar Nicholas I. Struve's grandfather, father, and uncle were also astronomers, and all gained international acclaim as directors of some of the world's greatest observatories, including the Berlin Observatory and the Pulkova Observatory in St. Petersburg. The Otto Struve who came to Cornell in 1951 thus represented the fourth generation of this incredible family. He had already earned his own reputation as director of the Yerkes and McDonald observatories of the University of Chicago, and had recently left the chairmanship of Chicago's astronomy department to teach astrophysics at the University of California at Berkeley.

Struve's discoveries were even more impressive than his credentials and his personal history. He could take the same observational data available to every other astronomer, and squeeze from them whole new dimensions of information. He had an uncanny ability to hatch bold new theories—and find evidence to support them. He was considered the father of modern astrophysics and one of the finest astronomers of the twentieth century.

I attended all three of his talks, which were held every other day over the course of a week. I was awed by his genius. Sitting spellbound as I did, I could not possibly imagine that I would meet again with Struve eight years later, when he would play a crucial role in helping me initiate the search for extraterrestrial intelligence.

Struve's area of expertise was the evolution and structure of stars, which he studied by analyzing their spectra. The spectrum of a star, I had come to learn, is its dossier. Everything we can hope to know about that star, from our vantage point on Earth, comes from the small amount of starlight reaching us through the telescope. Another instrument, the spectrograph, takes that starlight collected by the telescope and acts like a prism, separating the light into the rainbow of its component colors, then making a photographic record of it. These are long, narrow pictures. All up and down their length, the ribbons of variegated light are striped with bright and dark lines, some broad, some narrow, like the lines in a bar code on a supermarket item. By reading the pattern of these lines and understanding their significance, astronomers can deduce vital information about the star itself.

One of the first puzzles solved through photographic spectroscopy was the one posed in the children's nursery rhyme *Twinkle, twinkle, little star. How I wonder what you are.* The answer—that a star is a hot, luminous ball of gaseous elements—came from comparing the patterns of the bar codes from space with bar codes in the spectra of hot gases in laboratories on Earth. The characteristic patterns of the lines of hydrogen, say, or of helium or carbon, proved to be readily identifiable in the stellar spectra.

Every such line or group of lines that astronomers had detected since the 1800s, when the spectrograph was invented, corresponded to a known element or a combination of elements that existed on Earth. There wasn't one that could not be identified—although some elements, particularly helium (from the Greek *helios* for Sun), were detected first on the Sun, and only later on Earth. This meant that even the giant stars at enormous distances were made of familiar material. There was a physical truth in the words "on Earth as it is in Heaven." The stars were not materially different from the Earthly realm, as the ancients had believed. Nor were they made of exceedingly strange substances, as some science fiction writers had supposed. No. The stars, the planets, and every living and nonliving thing on Earth, it turned out, had the same elements in common. To me, these findings were additional evidence that life, like the elements themselves, would one day prove to be common throughout the universe.

There was just one discernible difference between spectral lines from sources on Earth and those from celestial sources, and it had nothing to do with chemical composition. Because the stars were all moving at high speed, their light was "Doppler-shifted" by their motion. It was pushed toward the red or blue end of the spectrum, just as the scream of a siren is raised or lowered in pitch as the motion of the speeding ambulance carries it toward or away from us.

Until Struve did his pioneering work, astronomers used spectroscopy mainly to determine the precise list of ingredients in a given star. From that they could tell its temperature, its age, and chemical abundances. Bright stars with sparse spectral lines—made up of almost pure hydrogen and helium—were old stars, born early in the life of the Galaxy. Stars like the Sun, on the other hand, were relatively young. Their spectra contained thousands of closely packed lines indicating the presence of carbon, iron, and other heavy elements—materials the young stars had inherited at birth from the stellar debris of an increasingly complex universe. As a student I had to memorize the standard classes of stars, each one indicated by a letter of the alphabet, in the descending order of their stellar temperatures: O, B, A, F, G, K, M, R, N, S. (Sexist as it sounds today, the standard mnemonic for astronomy students was, "Oh, be a fine girl, kiss me right now, sweetheart!")

Then came Struve. He raised the practice of stellar spectroscopy to an art form. It seemed as though the spectra spoke to him. He discerned new meaning in the brightness of bright lines, or the width of broad lines. Every nuance revealed some secret about the universe, and these insights were the topics of his first two Messenger lectures. I remember his discussion of stars with two or more sets of spectral lines—and some sets *blue*-shifted, as though the star were coming toward us instead of moving away. (In our expanding universe, most stars are receding from us, so their light is red-shifted.) From these observations, Struve deduced that such stars were in fact blowing off great envelopes of gas that spread through space. The portion of the expelled envelope moving toward us created the blue-shifted lines.

Struve also discovered double stars in orbit around each other, which looked to the telescope's eye like single stars. To Struve's eye, subtle red shifts and blue shifts signaled that the spectrum indicated the interplay of two sources of starlight. Although companion stars in close proximity to one another were already known to astronomers, Struve discovered many new examples of these "binary stars" purely by their spectra; such binary systems are called spectroscopic binaries, because their spectra disclosed their true nature even though the telescope could not resolve them as separate entities. In some of Struve's double-star systems, he deduced that material was being pulled out of one star by the gravitational force of the other. These conclusions took heroic observational stamina and interpretive skill, because the spectrum of such star systems would change from hour to hour, challenging Struve to account for their many different aspects with one plausible explanation. His research greatly enriched the whole subject of astronomy.

It was in the last of his Messenger lectures that Struve presented the most startling findings of all. These had to do with the rotations of stars. Just as the Earth spins on its axis as it orbits the Sun, giving us day and night, the stars also spin. Their spin speed, Struve showed, could be deduced from the width of their spectral lines, which were spread out by the rotation. This was because the spinning star, seen from afar, was in a sense both coming and going: Part of the star was moving toward us, while part of it was moving away. As a result, the spectrum was both red-shifted and blue-shifted at once, broadening the spectral lines in a distinctly characteristic way. Struve saw in the width of those lines a speedometer for clocking the period of the star's rotation. He showed us elegant charts of his data. Remarkably, all the massive hot stars—the O, B, A, and F types—were whirling like dervishes, while all the stars of the Sun's size or smaller—the more numerous "solar-type" G, K, and M stars—were spinning slowly. There was a sharp cutoff point between the two groups that chopped a big chunk out of the line on his graphs. It seemed clear that on the stellar carousel, speeds were either breakneck or leisurely, with no middle ground. Struve thought he knew why.

The massive hot stars spin fast because they spin alone, he concluded. The solar-type stars, which account for a substantial fraction of the stars in the Galaxy, spin more slowly because they have unseen companions—faint stars or planets—that also spin.* If the Sun were not accompanied by its Solar System, he showed in carefully constructed mathematical equations, it would now be spinning faster. His numerical results were correct and compelling.

In the space of a few moments in the lecture hall, Struve had raised the number of planets in the Galaxy from the nine we knew to more than ninety-nine billion. But he didn't stop there. He went on to say that the presence of all those planets clearly indicated that life could exist in many corners of the cosmos.

It was an electric moment. All of a sudden I wasn't alone anymore. I had an ally in the person of this most preeminent astronomer who dared to speak aloud what I had only dreamed about. There he was, seriously proposing in a public forum, before some of the world's foremost scientists, that the universe was full of planetary systems and living things. No one laughed at him.

What I wanted to do more than anything then was to talk to Struve about the notion we shared. But he cut such an imposing figure at the podium, facing that huge audience, which included all the big names on campus; I was just a lowly undergraduate. I was

---

* The "spin," or angular momentum, of a protostellar cloud of gas and dust must be preserved. If the cloud condenses into a single star, then the star inherits the cloud's full spin. If the cloud condenses into a star and several planets, however, the spin is divided among the several new bodies.

too timid to pursue him. Soon after the applause ended, Struve returned to Berkeley, and I to my studies.

In 1952 I graduated with honors in engineering physics from Cornell, and although I was set on graduate school in astronomy, I had a promise to keep. The Navy had paid for my college education, in exchange for which I now had to spend three years on active duty. I was assigned to the engineering department of the U.S.S. *Albany*, a heavy cruiser out of Norfolk, Virginia. The ship's electronics officer was due to retire, and because of my background, I was the obvious choice to succeed him. I was sent immediately to naval electronics school on Treasure Island, in the middle of San Francisco Bay.

I lived and worked on Treasure Island for the next four months, immersed in concentrated training programs. The Navy's electronics courses were wonderful—better than any I'd had at Cornell. When I was through, I returned to the *Albany* as electronics officer. I was in charge of electronics maintenance for all the equipment on board. That was a great adventure in itself, because we had many prototypes of the latest inventions. We even had color television—the first color television. And nobody on that ship knew how to fix it but me.

When the *Albany* was in the Mediterranean, it was the flagship of the Sixth Fleet, which meant that we had Admiral Wooldridge and his staff on board for about three months. This was the same Admiral Wooldridge who had started the NROTC program, and he was a famous figure even then. The ship's executive officer, Richard Colbert, didn't want the admiral to think that the *Albany* was in any way ill taken care of, especially that color television and other electronic equipment. He would send for me at all hours of the day or night to fix whatever needed fixing. My life got to be so hectic that I took to carrying around an old burned-out magnetron in self-defense. This was a great big, heavy device that was the source of radar power in those days. I'd make sure I was seen, with a worried expression on my face, walking down the passageway clutching my defunct magnetron. It made me look as though I was already doing something important, and it slowed down, just a bit, any of Commander Colbert's aides who'd been sent to summon me. One of the other officers nicknamed me "Old Gitme" because any time a problem with electronics arose, the captain or second in command would say, "Git me Drake."

I recall that when we went into Gibraltar, there appeared on the dock a brand-new Austin sports car. An order was passed down to get the crane and load the car into the ship's hangar, alongside the helicopter we carried. I thought I might get to work on the sports car, too, but it just sat there in the hangar until we got back to Norfolk. Then one of the ship's officers quietly took it out of the hangar and drove off into the night. The customs agents never knew of the car's arrival.

With my discharge approaching in June 1955, I applied to graduate schools. I picked Harvard as my first choice among the various possibilities because the university offered the greatest variety of programs in astronomy. It had optical astronomy, of course, which was my great love, but it also had planetary, theoretical, and something called radio astronomy. I found that most of the graduate programs in astronomy at other universities were more limited.

Not having much money, I had also applied for a research assistantship. The chairman of the astronomy department was Barton J. Bok, a preeminent scientist and a prince of a person. He was particularly cordial to and supportive of his students, always looking out to see that they had enough money, that they were living decently, and that they got good jobs. Bok not only accepted me as a graduate student but also kindly agreed to arrange a summer job for me, to tide me over until classes started in the fall.

As it turned out, the job was not in the optical observatory but in the radio astronomy project. My Navy electronics experience made me uniquely qualified for this position. What's more, it was the only available opening. Although I didn't realize what was happening at the time, my fate was sealed with that summer job. I was not going to spend my life looking through an optical telescope at the moons of Jupiter or any other pretty sights in the night sky. I was destined by this coincidence to become a radio astronomer.

Radio astronomers don't concern themselves with the visible light from stars, but with the radio signals they emit. Visible light, although it's extremely important to human beings, is just one form of electromagnetic radiation, like one octave on a piano keyboard. Stars also give off radio waves, infrared waves, X rays, and gamma rays. The Earth's atmosphere screens out most of this radiation, except for a tiny window to the universe in the visible and infrared regions, and a much larger window in the radio region. X-ray and gamma-ray astronomy, which didn't exist when

I started at Harvard, have to be conducted from satellites, far above the Earth's surface.

Radio astronomers can study planets by shooting radar signals at their surfaces and seeing what bounces back. Just as the Navy employs radar to find enemy ships through fog, so astronomers use it to map the surface features of Venus, for example, right through that planet's dense cloud cover.*

A radio telescope looks like a TV satellite dish, only much bigger. It has nothing in common with the long-tube optical telescope made of lenses. It "sees" a spectacle your eyes would scarcely recognize. The moon and planets are barely visible, or even silhouetted against the brightly shining radio sky. Gone are all the familiar stars and constellations, replaced by a host of brilliant new radio sources and bright, hot clouds of interstellar dust. These share the perpetual night of radio astronomy with the radiant Milky Way, which appears far more dazzling in radio than in ordinary light.

The "perpetual night" of radio astronomy means that radio astronomers are not limited to observing after dark, as most optical astronomers are. Radio signals can be studied day or night, even through thick clouds and dust. In fact, some radio astronomers get so accustomed to working the day shift that they'd be hard-pressed to identify most constellations on a starry night.

Radio telescopes need big collecting dishes because cosmic radio sources shed so little power on Earth—even the strongest radio sources in the sky shed only a few watts. In fact, all the energy collected in the history of radio astronomy barely equals the energy released when a few snowflakes fall on the ground. (That's the energy released when the flakes hit, mind you; the energy lost as they melt is far greater.)

My induction into radio astronomy was an accident of circumstance, but so was the chance discovery of the discipline itself. In 1931, Bell Telephone Laboratories in Holmdel, New Jersey, assigned a young physicist named Karl Jansky to investigate static from the atmosphere that might interfere with radiotelegraphy. Jansky, then about twenty-five years old, built a contraption that looked like something the Wright brothers might have flown. It was an array of wire antennas with wood buttresses, crisscrossed

---

* In 1976, when *Viking I* became the first spacecraft to land on the surface of Mars, it settled down on a site chosen in part by Earth-based radio telescopes.

like the struts of a biplane, that rotated once every twenty minutes on wheels from a Model T Ford. Jansky's "merry-go-round," as it was called, immediately picked up a steady hissing sound of unknown origin. Through his headphones, Jansky heard a sound like ordinary radio static, or like steam escaping through a tiny hole, but he sensed it had some larger significance. When he tried to pin down its source, the noise seemed at first to be coming from the Sun. A year of his careful observations, however, showed that the noise hailed from the distant stars. Indeed, the source of the strongest radio emission was in the direction of the center of the Milky Way Galaxy, in the constellation Sagittarius. Jansky had tuned in to the music of the spheres. The hissing he detected was the remnant of the primordial fireball from which the universe evolved. Faint as this radio emission is, it comes to us from all directions in space, over a very broad band of frequencies.

Bell Labs pulled Jansky off radio astronomy soon afterward, however, since it was not really relevant to their interests, and building his proposed bigger antennas was judged far too expensive for the expected payoff.

The task of turning Jansky's accidental discovery into a real science fell to Grote Reber, a young radio engineer in Wheaton, Illinois. Reber was a radio fanatic who had communicated with ham operators all over the world by the time he was fifteen—on equipment he'd built himself. When I met him years later at Green Bank, he was the renowned Grote Reber, but he was still building all his own equipment. He would even insist on cutting out the sheet metal for the chassis—the metal boxes that held the receivers—and bend or hammer the pieces into shape. Grote was so hard of hearing that the din of the activity never bothered him, though it often left our ears ringing for hours.

In his backyard in Wheaton, working as a hobbyist and using only his own money, Reber single-handedly built the first real radio telescope between June and September 1937. Nowadays small replicas of it grace lawns in neighborhoods such as Reber's, as many people now install them to improve television reception. But at the time, Reber's neighbors gossiped that his dish was a device for collecting water and controlling the weather. With it, Reber detected cosmic radio emissions and plotted the first radio map of the sky. Although he was a total unknown who lacked the proper training and background, he submitted his findings for publication in the prestigious *Astrophysical Journal*.

The editor of that journal in 1940 was none other than Otto Struve, who simply did not know what to make of Reber's paper. Reber had no credentials, and his discoveries were without precedent. They were inexplicable, too, because the intensities of the emissions he recorded were millions of times stronger than conventional wisdom or any theory predicted. Years later, Reber's observations proved to be completely accurate, but at the moment they were untested. Struve sent the paper to several eminent astronomers for review. They were as baffled by it as Struve himself. But it was wartime, and few manuscripts were in hand, so in the end, Struve published it for expediency's sake: The *Journal* was not to appear thin while he was editor.

When I arrived at Harvard in 1955, the big challenge in radio astronomy was to keep the equipment running. In those early days, knowing how to operate the machinery was at least as important as knowledge of celestial mechanics and astrophysics. Everything consisted of vacuum-tube receivers and amplifiers that broke down constantly. Having just served as a naval electronics officer, fixing broken-down electronic equipment was second nature to me. In practically no time I was a key person in the department because I could make machines work. I must admit it was a big thrill to be the new kid on the block at Harvard, and to find myself so indispensable so fast.

Radio astronomy was so interesting, too. The field was still in its infancy, with news of amazing discoveries reaching us every few days from all over the world. I decided to stay with it.

That winter I did get a chance to do some optical observing. I had found a radio source with the new radio telescope at the university's observatory at Oak Ridge, and I wanted to see if I could identify it optically. A very bright radio source may look like a rather dull star in visible light, but you can learn a lot by comparing the two views to get a total picture of the source. This was my big moment—my first chance to make optical observations since arriving at Harvard the preceding summer.

I traveled to the town of Harvard, Massachusetts, where the observatory stood, some twenty-six miles from the city lights of Boston and from Harvard University in Cambridge, Massachusetts. It was called the George R. Agassiz Station then, although it has since been renamed the Oak Ridge Observatory.

I loaded a photographic plate in the telescope and climbed into the prime focus cage. To operate this big old reflecting telescope, the observing astronomer actually rode the instrument like a jockey, high in the air, constantly adjusting the telescope's movements to track the target star. It was an exhilarating but exhausting, cold ride that took at least five hours—the time required to expose properly the photographic plates of those days to the faint light from the star. I was spent and more than half frozen by morning, since the dome of the observatory was open all the while to the November New England night air. Radio astronomy looked more attractive than ever to me then, being a lot more comfortable in comparison. For better or for worse, technology has since changed the nature of optical observing. At most modern observatories, you sit in a nice warm room and look at the computer monitor. You never see the telescope. You're never out in the cold. It's as pleasant as radio astronomy now.

Aside from the excitement of being at the dawn of a new science, and the personal satisfaction of being an integral member of a research team, I was revved up about a heady notion that struck me during that first year at Harvard. I realized that a radio telescope was the prime instrument for detecting and even communicating with extraterrestrial beings. Indeed, a radio telescope with a radar (transmitting) capability could be used to beam message-laden signals into space, aiming them at specific stars; and if creatures with radio telescopes existed in the target star's planetary system, then they could receive such a message. As I learned more about the theory and capabilities of radio telescopes, I began to estimate what signals each one could detect, and from what distances.

I often entertained such thoughts at night, alone in the Agassiz Station. It was common, then, to operate the whole observatory oneself, without any assistants, as I did during my doctoral thesis work. I was using the sixty-foot radio telescope to observe the Pleiades star cluster and measure its radio spectrum.

My Pleiades observations had become almost routine—until the night I detected what appeared to be an intelligent signal from an extraterrestrial civilization.

It was a strikingly regular signal—too regular, in fact, to be of natural origin. I had never seen it before, though I had repeated the spectrum measurement countless times. Now, all of a sudden, the spectrum had sprouted this strong added signal that looked unusual and surely of intelligent design.

I was twenty-six years old that night. I'm past sixty now, and I still can't adequately describe my emotions at that moment. I could barely breathe from excitement, and soon after my hair started to turn white. (This may have been just my family tendency to gray early, but the shock would have sufficed, I'm sure. In any case, I was completely white-haired by age thirty.)

What I felt was not a normal emotion. It was probably the sensation people have when they see what to them is a miracle: You know that the world is going to be quite a different place—and you are the only one who knows.

On the electromagnetic spectrum, the signal was in the region of hydrogen line radiation, which would be a logical choice for broadcasting by aliens attempting to attract attention. This made sense to me, because hydrogen is the most abundant element in the universe. Any scientifically savvy civilization would know that, and would expect others to know it, too, so they might choose the hydrogen channel as an interplanetary common ground. What's more, the signal's frequency was offset in a way that exactly correlated with the high speed of the Pleiades. It had the same high velocity and the same Doppler shift; the Pleiades must be its source.

Now I was even more excited, if possible. I knew that the hydrogen line band was closed to use by terrestrial transmitters because of its importance to radio astronomy. No license can be given anywhere in the world to transmit in that band. Who, then, was broadcasting? I thought I knew the answer, but I had to prove it.

I tested the signal for extraterrestrial origin by moving the telescope off the star cluster. And to my great disappointment, the signal continued to come in loud and clear when the telescope was turned in a different direction. The signal was *not* emanating from a point in the sky, after all. It had to be some form of terrestrial interference, probably military. I sat down, sweating and shaking from the heady moments spent almost believing I'd been in touch with a distant and alien mind.

From then on, whenever I looked at a radio telescope, I would ask myself as an aside, "Could this one be used to search for life?" The answer was always "No," until I got to the National Radio Astronomy Observatory in Green Bank, West Virginia, where I was to be a staff astronomer and head of Telescope Operations and Scientific Services. Soon after my arrival in 1958, we built a radio telescope with a receiving dish that was eighty-five feet in diameter—definitely large enough, at last, for a serious search.

▲
▲
▲

CHAPTER 2

Lost Keys
Under a Streetlamp

The universe is infinitely wide.
Its vastness holds innumerable atoms. . . .
So it must be unthinkable that
Our sky and our round world are precious and
*   unique. . . .*
Out beyond our world there are, elsewhere,
Other assemblages of matter making other worlds.
Ours is not the only one in air's embrace.

—LUCRETIUS,
Roman philosopher of
the first century B.C.

I left Cambridge for Green Bank in April 1958, a bona fide radio astronomer, in a white '53 Ford loaded down with all my belongings. I never set eyes on Green Bank until I arrived for work, having been recruited and hired over the telephone. I had jumped at the chance, too, even though the job didn't pay quite as much as some of the other offers I had. There simply was no possibility more promising than joining the new National Radio Astronomy Observatory (NRAO).

Seeing it for the first time, I was struck by the spectacular beauty of the site. It lay in a picture-postcard valley in the Allegheny Mountains of West Virginia, surrounded by hillsides full of trees just putting out their leaves, with wildflowers poking up everywhere.

You could have gazed down at that valley, an area of about four square miles, and found nothing but two tiny hamlets and a bunch of abandoned farms. That's all that was there, really. But to me, looking at it in the lushness of the Appalachian spring, it didn't have the air of something long past its prime. It sparkled like the beginnings of an entity completely new and different—an untouched palette surrounded by an aura of opportunity. I remember thinking that anything might be possible there.

The NRAO's charter and generous funding primed it for pioneering work. It was to provide no less than the best instruments in the world to all American astronomers. Eventually it did, but at the moment I arrived, there was more *actual* groundbreaking at hand than what you might call groundbreaking research. Everything was at the planning stage. Construction hadn't even begun on the two enormous telescopes—the heart and soul of the observatory. The only finished structures on the site were about a dozen old farmhouses that the government had acquired with the land, and refurbished modestly for the staff. I rented one of the small ones for my living quarters. The business offices occupied another, truly tiny farmhouse. All the science and engineering activity went on in a larger, two-story farmhouse, where I worked with my colleagues, David Heeschen and John Findlay. The three of us made up the whole scientific staff at first. We didn't even have a director to tell us what to do.

Findlay, a man of about forty, was a distinguished British ionospheric physicist who had been made over into a radio astronomer. In those days, most radio astronomers were made-over something, attracted to the field by its novelty and promise. On the other hand, Heeschen and I, both in our twenties, were young enough to have been formally trained as radio astronomers. He had been the first graduate of the Harvard Ph.D. program in radio astronomy. I was probably the fifth or sixth. Heeschen had known me at Harvard and liked me, and it was he who called to invite me to join the staff at Green Bank. (Years later, he became the very successful director of the NRAO, building it into one of the world's truly great observatories, and is still affiliated with it today.)

Not only had Heeschen and I been cast in the Harvard mold, but so had our telescope designs. They were patterned on the ones built in Cambridge by our beloved mentor, Bart Bok. Bok himself was a made-over optical astronomer. Both the instruments he built for the Harvard radio astronomy project resembled traditional optical telescopes in one regard: They had polar mountings. In other words, they had complicated support structures that moved at the same speed as the Earth turns, but in the opposite direction, enabling the telescopes to track the stars.

The polar, or equatorial mounts, as they were also called, had worked fine for optical telescopes for over a century, and were the basis of the enormous instruments at Mount Wilson and Palomar Mountain in California, with their 100-inch and 200-inch mirrors.

But radio telescopes were a different story. They had to be much, much larger than optical telescopes, both to make sharp images and to collect a detectable amount of power from radio sources that were so faint and far away. The earliest ones, including Grote Reber's telescope, did not track at all, but used the Earth's rotation as a way to scan the sky. The first equatorial-mount radio telescope Bok built at Harvard, 25 feet in diameter, instantly became an international curiosity. He went on to build another, with a 60-foot dish, increasing the sensitivity of the observations by enlarging the size of the antenna. The two instruments planned for Green Bank were to have *huge* dish antennas—140 feet and 600 feet in diameter, respectively.

To put dishes of such gigantic proportions on polar mounts invited staggering engineering problems that threatened to delay construction while driving up the costs. When I arrived, the smaller of the two instruments, the one-hundred-forty-foot, was still on the drawing board—and threatening to stay there indefinitely. Mired as we were in the difficulties presented by the 140-foot antenna, we could hardly greet the challenge of the 600-foot to come. So there we were, the brand-new and much-touted NRAO, supposed to be the best radio observatory in the world, with no telescope, and no hope of having one for another five or six years. This was simply an untenable situation, both scientifically and politically.

It was clear we needed a less grandiose design that could get us up and running—something on the order of an 85-foot telescope, which could be built fairly cheaply, within a single year, by copying telescopes already designed and under construction elsewhere. That would enable us to begin making observations, as well as to test equipment and gain experience and momentum while we waited—who knew how long?—for the big telescopes to follow. This idea pleased our parent organization, Associated Universities,

Inc. (AUI, the same consortium that operated Brookhaven National Laboratory in New York), and won approval, with full funding, from the National Science Foundation.

Soon we could look out the windows of our offices and see the 85-foot telescope rising, sleek and silver and strikingly anachronistic in those verdant, primitive mountains around Green Bank.

I had extraterrestrial designs on the telescope the moment it was finished. As a result of my "close encounter" experience with the Pleiades at Harvard, I had often made calculations to determine how successfully we might search for extraterrestrial civilizations with this or that instrument. Because radio telescopes can transmit as well as receive, they could theoretically "communicate" with each other across space.

"Suppose," I said to myself, "that some alien civilization has a radio telescope just like ours. How close would they have to be to us for us to pick up their signals?" I assumed their transmitters were no more powerful than our best ones. I guess I could have credited the aliens with far more advanced systems, emitting signals so strong that even the smallest telescope would hear them over interstellar distances, but that seemed like unfounded speculation to me.

The 25-foot telescope I'd first used at Harvard, and the newer 60-foot instrument there, could not have detected their theoretical twins in the galaxy beyond a couple of light-years. But the new 85-foot telescope at Green Bank, by my reckoning, had put us over the critical edge.

It was not just the larger size of the telescope that had created this increase in sensitivity to radio signals. In the United States two new forms of radio receivers had just been invented, both of which were great improvements over the receivers we'd been using previously. One was the solid-state maser, invented at Harvard by Nicolas Bloembergen, who was later awarded the Nobel prize in Physics as a result. This device improved sensitivity a thousandfold, at least in theory; in practice, it required that its amplifiers be cooled to the temperature of liquid helium—something not readily available anywhere, and surely not in Green Bank. The other form of new radio receiver was the so-called parametric amplifier, which used semiconductor devices to produce large amplifications of signals while adding very little noise. The combination of this device with the 85-foot telescope would raise our sensitivity by a factor of more than one hundred. With that boost, we could detect an identical radio telescope as far as twelve light-years away. That was a respectable distance. There were several Sun-like stars in that vicinity. The implausible had suddenly become possible.

But I didn't say anything right away. So many sound projects in conventional astronomy begged for time on our exciting new instrument. I watched and waited for my moment.

Those early days at Green Bank shine in my memory—the exhilaration we felt for the experiments we were planning, the close relationship shared by all the staff members. We were friends as much as colleagues. We spent literally all our time together, work time and leisure time, although it was hard to tell which we enjoyed more. We were doing precisely what interested us most, in the best possible setting, at just the right moment in history—and we knew it, too.

At first we had only an absentee director. This was Lloyd Berkner, an ionospheric physicist with political *savoir-faire*, who, as head of Associated Universities, had been the driving force behind the establishment of the observatory. He visited us periodically while he searched for an official director to take over.

Berkner soon found the perfect candidate in the tall, gaunt figure of Joseph Pawsey, a very brilliant physicist from Australia. Pawsey, then in his late fifties, was a senior staff member at the CSIRO (Commonwealth Scientific and Industrial Research Organisation) Radiophysics Laboratory in Sydney, the site of much exciting research in radio astronomy. Pawsey was the coauthor, with Ronald Bracewell, of the first textbook on radio astronomy, published in 1955. We knew the book, of course, having read and reread it, and considered Pawsey and Bracewell the source of all wisdom. (My original copy is now so worn with use that you can barely read the title, *Radio Astronomy*, on the cover.)

Pawsey himself was known to have been a giant creative presence at CSIRO, spewing out ideas that led to major developments in the field. But the word was that he never tried to get credit for any of these insights. He was excited just to think up things, and then pass his ideas along for others to work on, letting them take full credit. He seemed to have no ego at all. He just wanted the work to be done well, and never mind by whom.

Pawsey first came to Green Bank alone for a one-month stay to meet with the staff, prepare planning documents, draft budgets, and the like. He intended to go back to Australia soon after this visit to sell his house, pack up his belongings, and move to the States with his wife.

In an era when established astronomers looked elegant and kept a remote distance from their peers, Pawsey struck us as a regular guy. He was a little more noble than most, perhaps, but extremely pleasant and a good listener. We all felt close to him right away, and looked forward to our daily meetings.

One morning when I went to see him, I found him sitting in his chair looking strangely uncomfortable.

"Hi, Joe," I said. "How are you?"

"You know, it's funny, Frank," he answered slowly. "I'm asymmetrical today. My right and left sides don't work the same." I went over to help him, and he was in fact partially paralyzed on the right side of his body. He was having difficulty moving his right leg and arm. He seemed a bit more agile by the afternoon, but the problem returned in a day or so. We called Lloyd Berkner, who arranged to have Pawsey flown to Washington, D.C., for medical tests. The outcome was grim. He had an extremely fast-growing malignant brain tumor.

Next came a major operation in New York, where one of the world's best neurosurgeons (an AUI trustee Berkner knew) spent five hours trying to remove every last little scrap of the malignancy. He told us candidly that no one had ever survived a glioblastoma, which was the type of tumor Pawsey had. But he wanted this to be the first success story.

None of the doctors told Joe himself, though, how slim his chances were. I suppose they wanted to give him the benefit of his own hope, while they did whatever they could to help him. As far as we could tell, he believed he would recover completely and return to his post at the observatory. He wrote us long letters and memos from the hospital, informing us of new ideas as they came to him, and issuing instructions. Even when Mrs. Pawsey arrived from Australia to stay with him during his convalescence, he kept up a steady stream of observatory directives. The two of them were working out the details of their move to America when the cancer recurred two months later. He died within a few weeks.

Pawsey's death was a terrible blow to us. He was a good person, and he was the best person to run the observatory. We didn't think we could replace him. Berkner came back to Green Bank to shepherd us through the next transition.

He found us badly shaken. We had spent several months knowing that Pawsey was going to die, but also knowing that Pawsey *didn't* know it. We'd received his written instructions, but couldn't implement anything that had to do with long-term projects. We'd had to put all that on hold and just keep our fingers crossed while we went ahead with the immediate task of getting the telescope built.

Half in desperation, half in the hope of rising above the general depression, I decided to talk to Berkner about my ideas on extraterrestrial life.

Berkner, Findlay, Heeschen, and I would often eat lunch together at a tiny roadside diner, which we sarcastically called "Pierre's" or "Antoine's," in the nearby hamlet of Boyer. It was there, over hamburgers and greasy french fries, that I suggested we might use our new telescope to detect intelligent radio signals from some nearby Sun-like stars.

Heeschen and Findlay said nothing. They just went mute. Normally, a lunch at Antoine's was a free-for-all of animated conversation about recent discoveries, about who was doing what where, and about how best to be competitive with our rivals at Caltech. But now the two of them just sat and listened. At that time I was particularly close to Dave Heeschen, who kept a race car in the NRAO garage. I used to help him tune the car and take it to races, and we had literally held each other's lives in our hands on ropes while exploring caves in the nearby hills, but he wasn't following me on this adventure, I could tell.

If Heeschen and Findlay didn't know what to make of my comments, Berkner floored me with his enthusiastic response. He had a reputation in science for being an optimistic gambler, and he loved the idea. In fact, before the waitress brought our check, he gave me authorization to proceed.

Now I had a project, and I wanted to give it a name. I called it Ozma, after the princess in L. Frank Baum's children's story *Ozma of Oz*. That book was part of the series that started with *The Wonderful Wizard of Oz*, which I had adored as a child. Like Baum, I, too, was dreaming of a land far away, peopled by strange and exotic beings.

For all my high-flying romantic notions, my technical plan of action was quite reasonable and mindful of economic realities and scientific public relations. I intentionally designed the receiver so it could be used for other work we were planning to do at the observatory. I decided we should search for signals at the 21-centimeter wavelength—the part of the electromagnetic spectrum where the hydrogen atom naturally radiates. It seemed as likely a place as any, and furthermore, it was the preferred region to look for the Zeeman effect.* This was one of the big goals in radio astronomy. To achieve it at Green Bank would be a real feather in the observatory's cap. No one could question the value of building equipment to conduct one of the hottest experiments of the day. And if that same equipment could serve another purpose, so much the better. That was a bargain. We certainly couldn't be accused of squandering federal grant money on frivolous pursuits. What's more, the whole Ozma enterprise wouldn't cost more than two thousand dollars from start to finish, which wasn't very much money for a research effort, even in those days.

No sooner had I begun building the receiver than an extraordinary thing happened: Otto Struve took over as director of the observatory. Struve, whose guest lectures at Cornell had rekindled my interest in extraterrestrial life, was now to be my immediate superior. I was stunned at the news. I was, of course, thrilled at the prospect of working so closely with the man who, as I've said, was widely regarded as the greatest astronomer of the twentieth century. What better champion could I have for Project Ozma? At the same time, I was dumbfounded, because as far as Heeschen and Findlay and I could determine, Struve had absolutely no experience, knowledge, or interest in radio astronomy.

This turned out to be true. Yet he had left the University of California at Berkeley to accept the NRAO director's position. As it

---

* The Zeeman effect—which had been predicted in theory then and observed optically, but not yet directly observed in the radio spectrum—was the expected effect of magnetic fields in space on radio spectra. No one knew for sure whether such fields existed, but it was thought that they might split the emission from various elements, especially hydrogen, into two closely spaced lines. If hydrogen atoms, for example, were immersed in such a field, their radiation would not appear as a single line at the 21-centimeter wavelength on the spectrum, but as two lines, one with a slightly shorter wavelength and another with a slightly longer wavelength. Detection of such a Zeeman effect would prove the existence of interstellar magnetic fields and allow their measurement.

happened, Struve served on the board of directors of Associated Universities, our governing body, and Berkner had prevailed on him to take over, at least temporarily, after Pawsey's death.

"Do it for the sake of astronomy," Berkner had urged him. And it was in that spirit—as a duty to the science—that Struve had agreed to run Green Bank. His loyalty to his beloved science was so great that he was prepared to make any sacrifice in the interest of astronomy. His action proved indeed to be a great personal sacrifice, for his passions lay with optical astronomy, the field in which he had so distinguished himself. He found radio astronomy primitive by comparison—"barren" was the word he used—and predicted the field would dry up quickly.

Although he had accepted the invitation to direct our new observatory as a duty, I doubt that even Struve anticipated just how unhappy he'd be in radio work. He was disheartened from his first day at Green Bank, when he found himself supervising what was still a construction site. He enjoyed a brief reprieve when the 85-foot telescope was completed and we started making observations. One of the first things I did with it was to create a radio map of the center of the Milky Way Galaxy, showing that it consisted of many different objects, including strange-looking rings of ionized material. (The Soviets lionized me in their scientific literature by calling these structures "Drake rings," but the name never caught on in any other language or country.)

Struve was thrilled to see the galactic center at last, and in such detail. Optical astronomers *never* see the center of the Galaxy because it's so littered with dust. But the dust becomes transparent at radio wavelengths, and you see clearly all the way to the center. Struve couldn't get over it. After a lifetime of being inhibited by dust that blotted out the things he most wanted to look at, he now had in his hands a picture of Never-Never-Land.

"You have paid for the entire construction of the telescope with this one observation, as far as I am concerned," Struve told me. But his excitement was short-lived. He soon began lamenting how limited we were in our observations of individual stars. He couldn't pick up our radio jargon. And he found our instruments as incomprehensible as alien spacecraft.

He thought he could predict the future of radio astronomy, and it looked bleak to him. He warned us that unless some exciting discovery turned up—something like a variable radio source that we could keep on watching forever—we would run out of things to observe in one year and then we'd all be out of work. (Our staff had now grown to include ten scientists, plus electronics technicians, telescope operators, secretaries, business staff, and maintenance workers.)

It's a pity Struve never caught our enthusiasm for the subject, or foresaw how it would grow and change—even without variable radio sources (although these were in fact discovered in 1967). It would have made his time at Green Bank so much happier.

Struve hired two astronomers he had known and liked at Berkeley, a married couple named Roger and Beverly Lynds. Both of them had their doctoral degrees and all their prior experience in optical astronomy, which was part of their appeal for Struve: He could engage them in long talks about optical studies going on at other observatories. Nevertheless, the Lyndses were fascinated with the radio work and jumped right into it.

Struve actually wanted Beverly Lynds more than Roger at Green Bank, because he considered her to be the better astronomer. But those were such male-chauvinist times that Struve offered the scientist's position to her husband. To Beverly he assigned the job of organizing the observatory library. When they arrived, Beverly really did set up the library, but soon she began observing and compiled what has since become a classic catalog of dark nebulae, called the Lynds Catalog. Roger, too, made very important observations and discoveries, and is now a duly elected member of the National Academy of Sciences.

The Lyndses' companionship and conversation provided one way for Struve to keep his spirits up. Another was to fly every couple of months to New York City, where he would spend three days straight going to one movie after another.

I got to know Struve, but I never knew him well. Nor did anyone else on the staff. Although he treated me kindly, he did not accept informality. He was always very formal and polite. He shook hands ceremoniously at every encounter. He dressed impeccably, in a coat and tie at all times. You never saw Struve in shirtsleeves or a sweater. He looked very much the aristocrat. That was his background, reflected at all times in his bearing, his demeanor, and his approach to things. He stood well over six feet, and walked with an almost military carriage, having served in his youth as a Russian artillery officer in World War I, and with the White Russian Army—the losing side in the Russian Revolution. He had escaped to Turkey, where he was captured, and contracted hepatitis in a

Turkish prison camp. At Green Bank, he was still suffering the aftereffects of that illness. On many days he would feel sickly and tired, and his face would puff up.

Struve's gray eyes looked in two different directions, so that neither I nor anyone else ever knew which one to fix on when talking to him. In any case, my conversations with him were typically brief and confined to the science and business of running the observatory. I never got beyond his wall of elegant reserve to tell him how much his lectures at Cornell had affected me personally, because Struve made it clear he did not discuss personal matters. Nor did he introduce any of us to his wife, Mary Lanning Struve, though she was at Green Bank with him. Our only contact with her was at a distance—we would see her from time to time, walking the back roads around the observatory in a long purple robe, like some mystical figure out of a Fellini movie.

After the map of the galactic center, Project Ozma was about the only thing going on at Green Bank that excited Struve's enthusiasm. He never became directly involved in its planning or execution. He just liked the idea of it.

I had resolved to keep Project Ozma a secret from start to finish, so as to avoid publicity and interference from the press. As far as I knew, my search project was unprecedented, and so singular that other astronomers might scoff at it. But in September 1959, several months after I'd gotten permission to search and had begun building my equipment, a startling paper appeared in the journal *Nature*. It was called "Searching for Interstellar Communications." Its authors were two Cornell physics professors, Giuseppe Cocconi and Philip Morrison, who had coincidentally made the same calculations I had. They pointed out for the first time in print that existing radio telescopes were sensitive enough to detect radio signals from distant stars—signals of the same type and strength that could be broadcast from Earth.

Struve and Lloyd Berkner and I had been convinced that human beings weren't the only intelligent life in the universe. Now we knew we weren't the only scientists who believed something should be done about it!

Cocconi and Morrison conceded in their article that searching for the signals would be extremely arduous and time-consuming. "The probability of success is difficult to estimate," they wrote, "but if we never search, the chance of success is zero." I couldn't wait to tell them that we were about to *raise* that chance of success.

The landmark paper created a whirlwind. All the newspapers carried the story that well-known scientists were proposing a search for extraterrestrial intelligence. I was encouraged at the reception the idea was enjoying. Struve, to my surprise, was enraged. He had been director of one observatory or another for enough years to know that getting credit in science was important. He was the opposite of Pawsey on this point. I remember how Struve stormed up and down the halls of the new administration building, railing how this idea had been born at Green Bank almost a year earlier, and now Cornell was going to win all the glory. We had missed the chance to gain prominence for the observatory.

Suddenly he stopped, seeing a way to turn the situation to our advantage. He was scheduled to give lectures at MIT in just a few weeks, he said, and he vowed to use that occasion to announce our project publicly. He would rewrite his text, devoting one whole lecture to the search for extraterrestrial intelligence as it was proceeding at the National Radio Astronomy Observatory in Green Bank, West Virginia.

I stayed home, of course, hard at work now under heavy pressure from Struve to bring Project Ozma on line. Heeschen, too, feeling the heat of the public eye, was pushing me to get on with it, though he was no more supportive of the project than he'd been from the first.

Not only had the *Nature* paper suggested doing what I was already doing, but also the authors recommended listening on the same frequency band I had chosen: the long-wavelength region near the hydrogen line. I had picked it because we needed to build equipment to study that region anyway, for other astronomy goals. I was just being frugal. But Cocconi and Morrison offered theoretical reasons for the choice—the fact that the most abundant and fundamental atoms of the universe, the hydrogen atoms, emitted in this region, and furthermore that a search would encounter very little radio interference here.

Their rationale reassured and heartened me, especially in the face of growing public attention focused on the project, not to mention Heeschen's and Findlay's continued coolness. They weren't actively opposed to my search for extraterrestrial intelligence, but they weren't exactly in favor of it, either. Findlay also had a real gripe with me for another reason: I had been put in charge of running a summer program for college students at the observatory, to which I admitted two women. Just two of the twelve students I had selected were female, and they unquestionably had the right credentials for the positions, but Findlay was furious.

"What are you *doing*, Drake, to do such a dumb thing?" he shouted. Findlay always called me "Drake" or "Young Drake." "This is a total waste of resources and contrary to all tradition!" I held my ground, though. I knew from personal experience that women could be excellent astronomers, and I couldn't go along with the chauvinistic attitudes that tried to exclude them from the field. My thesis adviser at Harvard had been Cecilia Payne-Geposchkin, the first great woman astrophysicist and also the first woman to secure a tenured position on the Harvard faculty. I remembered the toughness and courage she'd displayed to carve an outstanding career exploring the nature of stars. She was an inspiration to all her students. (One of the two women I selected, Ellen Gundermann, vindicated my judgment by going on to take her Ph.D. in astronomy at Harvard. She later joined in the discovery of the first molecule to be found in interstellar space, and helped establish the existence of molecular line astronomy, which is now a major field of study. Eventually, however, she did what Findlay predicted would happen: She got married and went on the mommy track.)

In spite of this revolutionary act on my part, I still had Findlay's and Heeschen's friendship, and I had a growing band of supporters and helpmates as well.

The first was Ross Meadows, an electrical engineer from Slough in England, who came to visit the observatory during his sabbatical year. I quickly stuck him with the dirty work of assembling the Ozma receiver. It had a fairly simple design, with a single signal channel through which Meadows and I hoped to hear our counterparts on another planet. We had to be sure the receiver output wasn't drifting up and down in voltage of its own accord, as receivers were wont to do in those days, or we would never be able to tell the difference between a real signal and random fluctuations in receiver gain. We picked a standard technique for keeping a constant check on the receiver: We would compare the signal channel, hooked up to the real antenna, to a reference channel, hooked up to another antenna pointing nowhere in particular. Any change in voltage that came through both antennas could be written off as a glitch in the receiver itself. But a change in voltage that came only via the main antenna had to be a true signal.

Soon after Meadows came Kochu Menon, whom Heeschen and I had known in the radio astronomy graduate program at Harvard. Menon expressed a vested interest in the building of the equipment: He was the one who was going to use it, once Project Ozma was finished, to investigate the Zeeman effect. In operation, the receiver would tune itself slowly, shifting frequency by about 100 hertz (cycles per second) every minute, so that it automatically scanned the region around the hydrogen line (1420 megahertz). This would enable me to track extraterrestrial messages sent on or about the hydrogen-line frequency, and let Menon hunt for slight deviations in that frequency caused by the Zeeman effect. Because we were investigating such a narrow band of frequencies, our receiver required very stable oscillators to stay precisely tuned. Stable oscillators were just becoming available then in the form of quartz crystals. (Menon did eventually proceed as planned with his experiment, but the telescope proved too small for the attempt, and the Zeeman effect remained undetected for another ten years.)

Struve's public announcement of Ozma at MIT recruited the support of Dana Atchley, Jr., then president of Microwave Associates, a sophisticated electronics firm near Boston. Atchley, an amateur radio buff at heart, just called up one day and offered me one of the best parametric amplifiers then in existence.* It was a prototype machine—a laboratory curiosity that had never been used on a real radio telescope. From Atchley's description, it sounded far superior to any device we might be able to purchase. With it, we would be able to boost significantly the receiving sensitivity of our radio antenna. I couldn't believe my good fortune. I even had trouble finding the words to thank him enough. But Atchley was only too happy to lend us his amplifier. He insisted on it. As an old radio ham himself, he couldn't wait to tune in to narrow-band signals from outer space.

The equipment was unique and so valuable that Atchley had it chauffeured to us in a private car driven by his chief engineer, Sam Harris. He also instructed Harris to stay at Green Bank until he had successfully installed the amplifier and taught me how to use it. I knew of Harris by reputation, for he was an electronics genius and

---

* The parametric amplifier exploited the properties of a newly invented semiconductor device called a "varactor," which could amplify signals without adding much noise to them.

a pioneer radio ham who regularly wrote important articles for the ham magazines.

Harris's actual arrival might have been anticlimactic after the generosity of the offer and the talks with Atchley, but it wasn't at all. Harris drove up to the observatory in an old Morgan sports car, made of real wood, with the top down and leather straps around the hood. He had a flowing red beard and wore an even redder tam-o'-shanter. The parametric amplifier was sitting next to him, in the passenger's seat. He had built it himself, and was the only person in the world who could make it work. He proved himself an able teacher, however, and when he was satisfied that I could operate the thing myself, he drove off, leaving it in my care. Now there were two people who could tune it. (In 1966, when I moved to Puerto Rico to become director of the Arecibo Observatory, I was delighted to find Sam Harris again, ensconced in the control room as chief radio receiver engineer!)

After Harris left, I drew more support from the team of telescope operators, and from the two female students, Ellen Gundermann and Margaret Hurley, who were captivated by the Ozma idea and volunteered to assist me. But Heeschen and Findlay kept hands off Project Ozma. They were not in the control room on April 8, 1960, when the observations started in earnest.

I had set my alarm for 3:00 A.M. that day, and made my way through the early-morning fog and cold to start the preparations. My two student assistants, true to their word, were already at the base of the telescope, giggling a little incredulously in the darkness. We knew—and yet we tittered because we thought we might be fooling ourselves to think so—that this was a historic moment.

The first thing I had to do was tune the parametric amplifier. This took some doing, because the amplifier sat inside a metal canister, supported on steel struts that rose out of the 85-foot dish. Even with the antenna dish tipped way over on its side, the cylinder holding the amplifier was still about five stories above the ground. I rode up to it on a telescoping tower (something like a cherry picker that moves straight up and down), opened the canister from the top, and climbed in. I must have spent at least forty-five minutes inside this glorified garbage can, lying on my side, tilted at the same odd angle as the dish, and twiddling the controls while Gundermann and Hurley called up to me for progress reports.

The task took a long time because the amplifier had four interactive tuning knobs, so that each time I tuned any one of them, I had to adjust the other three. Even as I worked, I could see myself repeating this whole laborious procedure several times over the course of the day, because the sunrise and then the growing midday heat would keep upsetting the tuning. At the moment, though, it was awfully cold, and I was struck by the irony of finding myself freezing in the dark again, like an optical astronomer in a prime focus cage.

By 5:00 A.M. I was in the control room with a hot cup of coffee, setting up the Ozma receiver. It had the simplest possible output device: a chart recorder, consisting of a pen that wiggled with each sound received from space, leaving squiggles describing those sounds on a moving strip of paper.

What we were doing was unprecedented, of course, and no one knew what to expect. Even I, in my fever of enthusiasm, couldn't assume we would really detect an intelligent signal. Nevertheless, I was loaded for bear. In addition to the chart recorder, I hooked up a regular audio tape recorder and a loudspeaker. If anything did come in, we were going to have the thrill of seeing it on paper *and* hearing it all at once.

Everything was ready. We pointed the telescope at Tau Ceti.* And then there was nothing to do but wait.

You will perhaps not be surprised to learn that we waited with breathless anticipation. It was as though we expected the aliens to speak to us at any moment. We were that hopeful, that excited. Menon and I hovered over the chart recorder, convinced that every time the pen began to move up, THIS WAS IT. But it wasn't, and we had to settle ourselves back down. Had the chart recorder been tracking our heartbeats, erratic signals would have been a dime a dozen.

We followed Tau Ceti—uneventfully, I might add—until it set in the west at noon. Then we aimed the telescope toward our second target, Epsilon Eridani. We set up the recorders again and readied ourselves for the long wait. But scarcely five minutes passed before the whole system erupted. WHAM! A burst of noise shot out of the

---

* Bright stars in every constellation are designated by letters of the Greek alphabet, according to their apparent brightness. Thus Tau Ceti is the nineteenth brightest star of Cetus, the Whale, and our second target, Epsilon Eridani, is the fifth brightest star in Eridanus, the River.

loudspeaker, the chart recorder started banging off the scale, and we were all jumping at once, wild with excitement.

Now we really had a signal—a strong, unique, pulsed signal. Precisely what you would expect from an extraterrestrial intelligence trying to attract attention—as though they'd just been waiting for us to tune them in. The squawking noises were blasting out of the loudspeaker eight times a second, and the pen on the chart recorder was trying to keep that pace, too. None of us had ever seen anything like it. We looked at each other wide-eyed. I felt I was reliving my encounter with the Pleiades all over again, only this time I wasn't alone, and I was actively searching. Could discovery be this easy?

All of a sudden everybody started talking at once, saying inane things such as, "What do we do now?" and "Better check the equipment!" We proceeded to do what I'd done at Harvard, which was to move the telescope off the star. The signal disappeared immediately—making it seem even more likely that Epsilon Eridani was its source. But then, when we repointed the telescope at the star a few moments later, the signal did not return. We couldn't tell if it had come from the star, or if it was some kind of terrestrial interference that just happened to quit the moment we moved the telescope. There was no way to know. And there was no useful way to channel our adrenaline. The rest of that day, hope and tune as we might, the signal did not come back.

When our observing period ended, one of the telescope operators telephoned a friend in Ohio to share what had happened. That person had connections at his local newspaper, and before we knew it, the press had picked up the story. We were deluged with inquiries about the mysterious signal. We tried to answer them, but we knew so little about what had happened that our half-baked answers sounded like evasive tactics.

"Have you really detected an alien civilization?"

"We're not sure. There's no way to know."

"But you did receive a message?"

"We heard a signal. We don't know what it was."

"When will you know?"

"We can't say. It's hard to tell." And so on.

The curious became convinced that we were hiding something, probably with government knowledge and approval. (The idea that we made a secret discovery on the first day of Project Ozma has never died, and I continue even today to be questioned and mis-quoted about it by UFO fans.)

The short-lived signal now lured us on like a siren's song. Every day we tried to find it again. As soon as Epsilon Eridani rose, we would tune the receiver to the exact frequency on which we had heard the signal in the first place. We would hold to that frequency for about half an hour, before we let the receiver return to its normal scanning mode. We also added one new piece of detection apparatus to our setup. This was an ordinary antenna horn, the kind that could pick up terrestrial interference, whether from a ham radio operator stumbling into a protected frequency, or some kind of military aircraft or radar. We stuck it out the window of the control room and wired it to its own recorder inside. An extrater-restrial signal would come to us via the Ozma receiver alone. Terrestrial signals would be received through both systems. That's how we would test the signal when—if—it ever returned.

After about five days, we could no longer sustain our high level of eager anxiety. We sat quietly in the control room as the loud-speaker hissed randomly. The tape recorders turned. The pen on the chart recorder drifted slowly up and down. The whole thing started to become, well, boring. People actually yawned. And we still had days ahead of us. I would find myself thinking almost fondly at times of retuning the parametric amplifier, as it would get me outdoors and give me something to do.

After another five days, while going through our observing rou-tine, we heard it again, HOORAY! just like the last time—big blasts of radio noise pulsing eight times a second. Only this time, the noise was coming in stereo. The recorder attached to the little antenna horn out the window was picking it up, too. And so it wasn't an extraterrestrial message after all. Scrutinizing the pat-terns then, with the sobriety that dashed hopes bring, we noticed how the bursts crescendoed and then faded. They were undoubt-edly coming from a passing plane.

The project design called for us to observe Tau Ceti and Epsilon Eridani for another two weeks, before taking a break for a month, to free the telescope for other observations. We would then rein-state Project Ozma for four additional weeks, or a total of two hundred hours' observing time. Meanwhile, we were busy enter-taining visitors who had come to call because of Project Ozma.

John Lear, science editor of *Saturday Review*, set up camp in a corner of the control room, expecting to observe history in the making. He made us feel at first as though we were doing science in a goldfish bowl, but he was such a fixture in his corner that we soon forgot all about him. He, at the same time, was converted to our cause, and wrote glowingly of the importance of the work we were doing.

Theodore M. Hesburgh, who had just assumed the presidency of the University of Notre Dame, came to ponder the religious significance of Project Ozma. Our mission in no way conflicted with his. Indeed, Hesburgh confided to me that the God he worshiped was surely powerful enough to have created an infinity of worlds, had that been His desire. As a priest and theologian, Hesburgh viewed the exploration of the universe as a means to better understand God. We got along just fine, and he stayed with us for several days.

Bernard M. Oliver, vice president for research of Hewlett-Packard Company in Silicon Valley, called after reading about us in *Time* magazine. He was in Washington, D.C., on business, with a day to kill between meetings, and wanted to run down and see for himself what we were up to. I would have loved to have him come, I said, but there was no way to get from Washington to Green Bank and back in one day.

"You underestimate me," he barked, in a way that I have since come to know as characteristic. Oliver had a private plane at his disposal, and soon dropped through a tiny hole in the cloud cover to tour the observatory. "Barney" Oliver had been waiting for Project Ozma most of his life. He had been weaned on good science fiction, especially Hugo Gernsback's *Amazing Stories.* He was already a very successful inventor, too, with vast expertise in physics and electronics. That combination of interests and abilities made Barney a marked man. He was destined to become involved in the search for extraterrestrial intelligence. And the search itself was looking more than ever like a defined goal with a community of interested supporters.

Project Ozma progressed and drew to completion without further incident. We never intercepted another strong signal. We filled thousands of yards of chart paper and recording tape with the signature and sound of hissing noise. Sifting through it, we could discern no trace of an intelligent signal, or any nonrandom noise of extraterrestrial origin. A pessimist might have presumed at that point that the experiment had been a failure and that aliens were not out there to be discovered. But that would have been a preposterously premature conclusion. Our search had been anything but conclusive.

We had set out looking for advanced alien civilizations the way a drunk searches for lost keys: by hunting under the light of a streetlamp, where the effort is easy, instead of in the dark places out of sight—where searching might yield results. Beyond the perimeter of the lamp glow, out beyond the reach of the 85-foot telescope, lay billions more stars to be explored before the question could be answered.

The 140-foot telescope, if we ever finished it, would be more sensitive because of its larger size, and would enable us to pick up signals only half as strong as the ones we were equipped to detect during Project Ozma. What if signals had been coming in from Tau Ceti or Epsilon Eridani all along, but at a level just below the threshold of our detection capability? If that were true, we might well hear them someday by repeating the attempt with the 140-foot telescope. And the prospect of still larger telescopes to come invited grandiose schemes for future searches.*

---

* We soon abandoned the idea of building the 600-foot telescope. Aside from continuing construction difficulties with the 140-foot, we watched the U.S. Navy fail in its attempt to build a 600-foot in nearby Sugar Grove. The Navy had planned to use this telescope for intelligence-gathering—to monitor the Soviets by observing radio communications of theirs that got reflected off the surface of the Moon. It had an alt-azimuth mount, which could track the stars with the aid of a computer, and was more stable than the old equatorial mounts. Nevertheless, unforeseen problems jacked the final price up to $300 million, which was too much, especially since satellites were promising a better way to gather intelligence. The Navy had already spent $200 million when the 600-foot at Sugar Grove was scrapped in favor of a 150-foot telescope.

At Green Bank, we considered ourselves lucky to have scrapped *our* 600-foot *before* construction began. We settled instead on a 300-foot design, called a transit instrument. Its very simple mount could not track stars, but used the Earth's rotation to scan the sky. We built it on the cheap for $1 million, and completed it in 1963—a full year before the 140-foot was finally finished. So the 85-foot telescope, which had not been part of the original NRAO plan, wound up serving as the observatory workhorse from 1959 to 1963. It's still there, now flanked by two additional 85-foot antennas, and the three of them function in concert as though they were one giant antenna several miles in diameter. The 300-foot collapsed with a big boom on a still night in 1989, like the house of cards it was. And the 140-foot, much to my delight, will soon become the first telescope at a national research center to be dedicated *full-time* to the search for extraterrestrial intelligence.

The negative findings of Project Ozma could not rule out the existence of life in the vicinity of Tau Ceti or Epsilon Eridani. Wasn't it at least possible that we had been looking at the right stars, and on the right frequency to detect extraterrestrials, but at the wrong time? Perhaps "their" transmitters had been down for repairs those two months, or simply pointed in another direction while engaged in other work. If we extended our current project, even for just one more day, we might yet find them. I put that thought out of my mind, however. I had used up my allotted telescope time. There was a lot of regular astronomy to occupy my attention. Project Ozma was over.

We had failed to detect a genuine alien signal, it was true, but we had succeeded in demonstrating that searching was a feasible and even reasonable thing to do. That was not just my conclusion, but also the reaction of the world at large. Although I had not gotten a lot of support from within the observatory at the outset, I never heard a single criticism of the project. No scientist denounced it outright, and no layperson objected to it enough to tell me so. Instead, I received dozens of letters from interested, excited people, who caught the spirit of adventure and hope for the future embodied in our efforts. (Letters have continued to come ever since, in ever increasing numbers.) The correspondents all seemed to agree that the most fascinating phenomenon one could find in the universe would not be another kind of star or galaxy, but another kind of life.

As the first attempt of its kind, Ozma taught us several important lessons and established precedents that are still followed today. For example, when I poked that extra feed horn out the control-room window, I showed the validity of using two feed horns as a way to distinguish bona fide signals from terrestrial interference. At first, the receiver was set up to switch periodically from a signal channel to a reference channel, to verify the receiver's own precision. After we received our surprise signal, we made the receiver switch between two signal channels as well, to determine whether incoming signals hailed from deep space or from somewhere much closer to home. Nearly all subsequent searches have incorporated some variation of this basic setup.

Ozma also proved that searches could be accomplished without huge outlays of money, and could be dovetailed with other projects and goals. In fact, search activities *had* to be combined with other studies—not only for research economy, but also to preserve the sanity of the searchers. I consider it a major finding of Project Ozma that the excitement of the hunt fades very quickly. All through the challenge of the project planning, when you set your goals and build your equipment, you are sustained by the hope that you may succeed, and the grand vision of what success might mean. Those first few hours or days in the control room are exquisitely tantalizing. But soon you are left with only the tedium of the daily operations. I learned then and there that any serious search for extraterrestrial intelligence needs to be combined with other astronomical research at the same time—something that yields real results and that keeps you from getting too discouraged, by tweaking your imagination to explain other findings.

Before, during, and after Project Ozma, I was engrossed in Solar System observations with the 85-foot telescope. A visiting Norwegian scientist named Hein Hvatum and I had found radiation belts, just like the Van Allen belts of Earth, around the planet Jupiter. On my own, I was also investigating the extraordinarily high surface temperature on the planet Venus, which was about 800 degrees Fahrenheit. And that was on the night side of the planet (the side facing the Earth when the two sisters are close to each other). To measure the day-side temperature, I had to observe Venus when it was on the far side of the Sun. It took eighty hours of telescope time to get that measurement, which remains, as far as I know, the longest observation ever made. The temperature turned out to be the same, day and night, suggesting that the atmosphere on Venus was about as dense as our ocean, so that heat stayed trapped and winds moved at a slow walking pace of just a few miles an hour. (These points have since been confirmed by satellite observations.)

As a result of the Venus work, I received a letter from a University of Chicago graduate student who said he was writing his doctoral dissertation about the atmosphere of Venus—a young man named Carl Sagan. We began to correspond, and soon found events conspiring to bring us together as lifelong colleagues.

In another important precedent, both Project Ozma and the Cocconi-Morrison paper identified the region around the hydrogen line as a primary hunting ground for interstellar signals. We are still covering that same ground today. The region has come to be known as the "waterhole" because it is bounded on one end by the hydrogen atom, H, which emits a natural radio signal with a wavelength of 21 centimeters, and on the other by the hydroxyl radical, or OH molecule, which emits a signal with a wavelength of 18 centimeters. In chemistry, H plus OH equals H_2O, or water. And water is a key component of all terrestrial life. Even though the H and the OH are not combined as water in this part of the electromagnetic spectrum, the name "waterhole" has stuck.

There's something aesthetically appealing about the idea of communicating with aliens at an interstellar waterhole, just the way so many species of animals have traditionally gathered at the waterholes of Earth, to share another vital resource. We suspect that water is very important to life elsewhere in the universe as well. What's more, the electromagnetic waterhole occupies a very quiet region, containing the least possible extraneous noise from the Galaxy (and the Earth's atmosphere). This fact makes it a logical choice as a frequency for transmitting signals over great distances. That is, it appears logical to *us*. Time will tell if the logic has truly universal appeal.

One last element of Project Ozma persists in modern search efforts, and that is its target star, Epsilon Eridani, which seemed at first blush to be signaling us. Akin to our own Sun in size, age, and temperature, Epsilon Eridani still looks like a good prospect for a targeted search. Its name appears on the current list of the thousand stars most likely to foster inhabited worlds. We took it to be a single star in 1960, but recent evidence suggests it has several small companions. Perhaps some of these will prove to be planets, and perhaps a civilization—invisible to us then, but detectable now—may thrive on one of them.

Epsilon Eridani lies in the constellation Eridanus, the River. (More water symbolism!) According to ancient mythology, this river is the one traveled by Jason and the crew of the *Argo* on their quest for the Golden Fleece. Here they found what they were looking for. And maybe someday we will, too.

CHAPTER 3

▲
▲
▲
▲

A Compounding of Uncertainties

Heaven and earth are large, yet in the whole of space they are but as a small grain of rice. . . . How unreasonable it would be to suppose that, besides the heaven and earth which we can see, there are no other heavens and no other earths.

—TENG MU,
Chinese philosopher of
the thirteenth century A.D.

In the afterglow of Project Ozma, I took the liberty of putting a sign on my office door that asked, "Is there intelligent life on Earth?" People would stop to read the sign, and then slowly smile at the way it framed the extraterrestrial question. Often as not, a head would poke inside my doorway with a wry comment such as, "There's a little green man downstairs who says he's looking for you," or, "Just checking to see if there's any intelligent life in this room."

You might say that the sign was my title on the door. Or maybe an orderly splash of graffiti. It made a manifesto of the fact that I had revealed my long-secret personal thoughts and dreams at last, taken action on them, and had won the freedom to espouse them. Certainly everyone at the observatory, and perhaps everyone in radio astronomy, knew me now as a researcher with a serious interest in alien life. And yet the sign I chose was whimsical, almost tentative. Whimsical and tentative, still, were other people's attitudes toward the subject. One could now broach the idea aloud, thanks to Project Ozma and the Cocconi-Morrison paper in *Nature*—but not without looking over one's shoulder to see who might be laughing.

More than a year passed by in this twilight zone of semirespectability, when I got a call one summer day in 1961 from a man I'd never met. His name was J. Peter Pearman, and he was a staff officer on the Space Science Board of the National Academy of Sciences. In his first few words, Pearman established himself as an urbane, well-spoken Englishman, with an enviable Oxford accent. This dash and polish somehow gave more credence to what Pearman was actually saying, which was that he'd followed Project Ozma throughout, and had since been trying to build support in the government for the possibility of discovering life on other worlds.

"I conclude it's crucial that a meeting be organized as soon as possible," Pearman said, "to investigate the research potential. I wonder if I might count on you for help?"

"Well, sure," I answered, not needing a moment to consider. "What can I do?"

Pearman wanted two things he thought I could help him get: approval to hold the meeting at Green Bank, since it was the site of Project Ozma, and the names of experts to be invited.

Right then, having only just met over the telephone, we immediately began planning the date and other details. We put our heads together to name every scientist we knew who was even thinking about searching for extraterrestrial life. That turned out to be all of ten people, including Pearman and me.

The guest list had practically assembled itself over the course of Project Ozma. The first two invitees had to be Giuseppe Cocconi and Philip Morrison, who were the authors of the seminal paper in *Nature*. They had both been teaching at Cornell when I was an undergraduate there, but I didn't know either one personally.

I suggested Dana Atchley, the radio ham and electronics entrepreneur who had donated his parametric amplifier to Project Ozma. And Barney Oliver, the inventor and research magnate from Hewlett-Packard, who had dropped out of the sky to watch Ozma in action. We decided not to invite theologian Theodore Hesburgh, though, as this was to be a strictly scientific discussion.

I don't remember which of us mentioned Carl Sagan's name first, but we both wanted him. Since the time the hot surface of Venus had brought us together two years previously, I had learned that Sagan's interest in other planets was fueled in part by his desire to know if life could thrive on them. He knew more about biology than any astronomer I'd ever met, and was fast making a never-before-heard name for himself as an "exobiologist"—a researcher who studies the life of other worlds. Pearman, himself a biologist by training, knew that Sagan was a member of the Space Science Board's Committee on Exobiology, as well as a separate Academy of Sciences group called the Panel on Extraterrestrial Life.

The fact that such a committee and panel even existed—and their existence was news to me—gave further indication that the idea of alien life was gaining a foothold in research circles as a subject for legitimate inquiry. Pearman told me that Joshua Lederberg, a distinguished professor of genetics at Stanford University who had been one of Sagan's mentors, served as chairman of the panel. Though Lederberg did not strongly support the idea of *intelligent* or *communicative* life on other planets, he believed extraterrestrial life of some kind was a foregone conclusion, and he encouraged Sagan in his exobiology pursuits. When Lederberg had established the exobiology committee in 1958, he of course asked Sagan to join it. (As Carl tells the story, "I sort of glided effortlessly from attending late-night bull sessions about exobiology at Lederberg's house to advising the government on the issue.")

At the moment, Sagan was in Berkeley, with a research fellowship in space sciences at the University of California. There he was conducting experiments to demonstrate how life might have begun on Earth, working with a renowned chemist named Melvin Calvin. It was Calvin who, in earlier work, had unraveled and explained the process of photosynthesis, whereby green plants use the Sun's light to make food from water and carbon dioxide. We put Calvin's name on the guest list, too.

"Let's see," I said. "We've got astrophysicists, astronomers, electronics inventors, and exobiology experts. All we need now is someone who's actually spoken to an extraterrestrial."

I was joking, naturally, but Pearman surprised me because he had already selected such a person.

"John C. Lilly," he replied without skipping a beat. Lilly was a neuroscientist—a medical doctor famous for his experimental interests in consciousness and communication. And while he hadn't exactly achieved extraterrestrial contact, he was actively engaged in attempts to communicate with dolphins—then thought to be a prime example of nonhuman intelligent creatures.

"And your director, Otto Struve," Pearman put in. "He should be our host and chairman."

"Yes, and I ought to go clear the whole plan with him right away," I said.

I ran to see Struve the moment I hung up the phone. Now that Pearman and I had pushed the idea forward this far—the meeting had already grown into a three-day conference in our minds—I hated to think that Struve might object. What if he denied his permission to hold the sessions at Green Bank? But it was just my sense of having taken observatory matters into my own hands that made me so anxious. There was no real reason to think Struve would object to the meeting. In fact, he was delighted at the prospect of it, and immediately agreed to serve as the host, which was fitting and proper. Not only was Struve the director of the observatory, but also his observations and theories about the existence of planets outside our Solar System had given the concept of extraterrestrial life its first solid astronomical footing.

"There is someone else I would like you to invite," Struve said, jumping into the event by adding one more name to the guest list. It was his former student Su Shu Huang, a Chinese émigré who had just joined the new National Aeronautics and Space Administration. Huang and Struve had collaborated in studies about the kinds of stars that might support habitable planets.

Over the next several weeks, Pearman and I telephoned each other back and forth, plotting and planning. Stationed in Washington, D.C., as he was, and keyed into the affairs of the whole National Academy, he knew everything that went on in science even before it happened.

"I have it on a strong, reliable rumor that Melvin Calvin will get the Nobel prize in Chemistry," Pearman called to say. Calvin had already accepted our invitation to the Green Bank conference. The Nobel committee might or might not be aware of his current studies on the origins of life, but he'd surely been nominated for his explication of the process of photosynthesis.

"If he should win," Pearman told me excitedly, "he'll find out at Green Bank. The announcement date comes plunk in the middle of our conference. The committee will have to get word to him at the observatory."

"What do we do?"

"Just answer the telephone, dear boy," he said with a laugh. "Then break out the champagne."

A champagne toast would be no mean feat in the semidry state of West Virginia, and I told Pearman so. He promised to smuggle a few bottles in his luggage, just in case, and urged me to see what I could do.

West Virginia apportioned one state-operated liquor store to each county. The one closest to the observatory stood in a little lumber town called Cass, about ten miles away. The observatory's staff now included a driver—a West Virginian with the fairly common (for those parts) first name of French, and the improbable surname of Beverage. For a moment I considered sending him to buy the champagne, but it would have been too silly. Instead, I drove over to Cass myself that weekend. I had expected to spot the outlet easily, as the town was very small. After driving around and through the town a few times, however, I realized the liquor store must literally be hidden away on some back alley—evil influence that it was. I approached the only person out on the street, who happened to be an aged mountaineer sitting on the steps of a modest building.

"Pardon me," I said. "Do you know where the liquor store is?"

"Yup," he answered, eyeing me suspiciously. Then he paused for what seemed like a long time. "But I ain't gonna tell ya."

I stared at him in disbelief. All of a sudden I realized the basis for this strange response: The building behind the steps he occupied was the local Baptist church.

Finally I came upon a little door with the sign "State Liquor Outlet." There was champagne inside, much to my relief, so I bought a caseful, took it back, and hid it in the basement of our newly built residence hall, where we were planning to house the visitors and hold the meeting. We had just enough rooms to accommodate the group.

Immersed as I'd been in my technological approach to the question of extraterrestrial life, I'd had no idea how much work was progressing on related fronts. When Project Ozma undertook the first serious hunt for extraterrestrials with modern instruments, Calvin's experiments to duplicate the origins of life had already been under way for ten years.

In 1951, Calvin and his colleagues at Berkeley put a mixture of carbon dioxide, hydrogen, and water into a closed flask. They used the university's 60-inch cyclotron (an early atom smasher) as a source of intense energy to give the gas mixture a jolt. The cyclotron's spark approximated a burst of cosmic rays from outer space—the sort of bolt from the blue that could have given life on Earth a jump start. As a result, Calvin's group found that the molecules of carbon dioxide, hydrogen, and water were fused into several organic chemicals. Each of these products—formaldehyde, formic acid, and glycolic acid—contained carbon and was indeed associated with the production of the actual components of living things.

Later, at the University of Chicago, Harold Urey and Stanley Miller repeated Calvin's experiment, using gases that simulated the primitive atmosphere of Earth, according to the ideas of the 1950s. It was then thought that aeons before green plants filled the atmosphere with oxygen, "air" was a mixture of water vapor, hydrogen, methane, and ammonia. Miller and Urey combined these gases in a flask, then zapped it with an electric charge—the kind Nature might have provided in the form of a lightning streak. They wound up with organic molecules, too, but this time the results included an astounding variety of amino acids—the basic building blocks of proteins, which are prime components of all life on Earth.

The chemists had demonstrated that life could arise from inanimate matter. It was as easy as following a recipe: You take the ingredients in the Earth's primitive atmosphere, microwave on HIGH for a moment, and *voilà*—primordial soup. Life was so easy to make that it had apparently cooked itself up on Earth soon after the planet's own genesis four billion to five billion years ago. Indeed, we now know from fossil evidence that life appeared on Earth at the earliest time it could have: only a few million years after the formation and subsequent cooling of the planet. (Nowadays we think the primitive atmosphere had much less hydrogen and more carbon dioxide, and was thus a more oxidizing atmosphere, but such an atmosphere also works well to produce the materials of life.)

The Berkeley and Chicago experiments had universal significance: No extraordinary circumstances were needed to catalyze the diversity of life we see around us. And if Earth life is the product of ordinary processes, then it is more than likely that Earthlings are not alone in the universe. In 1958, unbeknownst to me and before

I'd even proposed Project Ozma, Calvin had written, "We can assert with some degree of scientific confidence that cellular life as we know it on the surface of the Earth does exist in some millions of other sites in the universe."

There was far more evidence for my ideas than even I had suspected. And now I was going to get the chance to discuss every aspect of the quest for extraterrestrial life, from every conceivable angle, with the handful of people in the world who viewed the subject as seriously as I did.

I took on the job of setting an agenda for the meeting. There was no one else to do it. So I sat down and thought, "What do we need to know about to discover life in space?" Then I began listing the relevant points as they occurred to me.

Surely we needed to know the number of new stars born each year—and not just any stars, but "good suns." These were not too big and not too small—medium-size stars that could be expected to have planets around them and that bathed at least some of those planets in life-supporting light.

If there were planets out beyond the Solar System that were suitable for life, how many would actually become homes to living things? In other words, given a place where life *could* develop, how likely was it that life *would* develop? That was another important point.

Even granting that other worlds swarmed with alien life-forms, how many of those might be *intelligent*? What form would their intelligence take? Would we be able to detect them and communicate with them across interstellar distances?

All the places we might look for life would be very far away indeed. And in the universe, distance is time. It seemed that our chances for finding our alien counterparts would be greatly enhanced if civilizations, once they established themselves and became detectable, lasted a good long while. Ideally, it would be nice if they remained detectable for as long as it might take us to find them. It would also be nice if we remained detectable, despite the fact that we humans had developed nuclear weapons along with our radio telescopes.

I looked at my list, thinking to arrange it somehow, perhaps in the order of the relative importance of the topics. But each one seemed to carry just as much weight as another in assessing the likelihood of success for any future Project Ozma. Then it hit me:

The topics were not only of equal importance, they were also utterly interdependent. Together they constituted a kind of formula for determining the number of advanced, communicative civilizations that existed in space.

I quickly gave each topic a symbol, mathematician style, and found I could reduce the whole agenda for the meeting to a single line:

$$N = R f_p \, n_e f_l f_i f_c \, L$$

Of course, I didn't have real values for most of the factors. But I did have a compelling equation that summarized the topics to be discussed: The number (N) of detectable civilizations in space equals the rate (R) of star formation, times the fraction (f_p) of stars that form planets, times the number (n_e) of planets hospitable to life, times the fraction (f_l) of those planets where life actually emerges, times the fraction (f_i) of planets where life evolves into intelligent beings, times the fraction (f_c) of planets with intelligent creatures capable of interstellar communication, times the length of time (L) that such a civilization remains detectable.

My agenda equation later became known as the Drake Equation. It amazes me to this day to see it displayed prominently in most textbooks on astronomy, often in a big, important-looking box. I've even seen it printed in *The New York Times*. It's currently being made the focal point of an interactive exhibit at the Smithsonian Institution's Air and Space Museum in Washington, D.C. I'm always surprised to find it viewed as one of the great icons of science, because it didn't take any deep intellectual effort or insight on my part. But then as now, it expressed a big idea in a form that a scientist, even a beginner, could assimilate. Sometimes people who are unfamiliar with the scientific picture of cosmic and biological evolution think the equation is highly speculative. In fact, it is just the opposite, since each phenomenon it assumes to take place in the universe is an event that has already taken place at least once.

On the big day, which fell on Halloween, the guests flew in from all over: Morrison from New York; Calvin, Sagan, Huang, and Oliver from California; Lilly from St. Thomas in the Virgin Islands, Atchley from Boston, and Pearman from Washington. Cocconi didn't come. He had wired his regrets from Geneva, where he was working in particle physics at the European Center for Nuclear Research, called CERN.*

French Beverage doubled back and forth over the fifty-five miles between Elkins and Green Bank, chauffeuring the guests from the airport to the observatory.

What an assortment of wonderful characters arrived at our door! What contrasts they cut with one another! Oliver strode in and took Struve's aristocratic hand in his two brawny ones, addressing him respectfully in his booming, gravelly voice. I recognized Pearman immediately, although I'd never seen him before, because he looked even more British than he sounded on the telephone, with a narrow face and aquiline nose reminiscent of Basil Rathbone. He immediately attached himself to Huang, whose English I found incomprehensible.

Lilly didn't look at all like the kind of man who had secluded himself in isolation tanks and pounded electrodes into his own head to find out what parts of the brain were centers for pleasure and for pain. He looked handsome enough to be a movie actor playing the role of John Lilly. Atchley, on the other hand, was the prototype for a Silicon Valley executive. He would have made a great nerd, but no one had invented that concept yet.

Morrison, small and stooped, had some difficulty getting out of the car. He walked with a cane, having been crippled by polio in childhood. I shook his hand eagerly. The last time I had seen him, I was one of hundreds of nameless faces he'd held spellbound in a lecture hall. You couldn't be a science student at Cornell and *not* go to Morrison's lectures, even if you were not enrolled in his courses. Once behind a lectern he became a majestic figure. I remembered how his words had come out in a rush of passion almost too fast for note-takers to follow. (His speech is still that way today.)

Calvin appeared incredibly calm for a person about to receive

* Cocconi, so soon after launching the science of searching for extraterrestrial life by coauthoring the paper with Morrison, dropped out of the field, never to return. In years since, he has declined every invitation to participate in meetings—even gatherings held near his home in Geneva, where he eventually became director of CERN. Always, he replies cordially that he has not kept up with recent developments and could make no valuable contribution to the debate. I met him only once, while visiting CERN long after the Green Bank meeting.

science's highest distinction. He was no doubt aware of the rumors linking him to the Nobel prize, but he was utterly focused on the matter at hand—he had been deep into it with Sagan all the way from Berkeley to Green Bank. Calvin gave an immediate impression of warmth and sincerity. I liked him from the very first.

Struve, born before the turn of the century, was the senior member of our group; Sagan, dark, brash, and brilliant at twenty-seven, was the youngest. I was an old man of thirty, Pearman was about forty, and the rest ranged in age from late forties to early fifties. By nature, we covered the whole range of research personality types from pure theorists, such as Morrison, to the most practical of applied scientists, such as Oliver and Atchley. What bound us all together was our strange, strong conviction that the universe was widely populated. Among this group of people—and nowhere else I knew of—one could abandon oneself to the vociferous discussion of extraterrestrial life, without any hesitation, or embarrassment, or fear of ridicule. In retrospect, it was certainly a landmark occasion in my life, as well as for some of the others, I'm sure. But no one thought the meeting to be of historical significance at the time, and so no one taped the proceedings. No one photographed us, either, although that doesn't seem like nearly so big a loss as the detailed content of those talks.

On Wednesday morning, November 1, we all gathered in the small conference room in the residence hall. Struve welcomed everyone officially, and then I got up and wrote my equation on the blackboard. I explained the factors as I went along. People started murmuring before I was halfway through it. Just as I had hoped, the formula gave immediate and pointed direction to our discussion. (Knowing what place that equation has taken in the world of science, I make a pilgrimage to the lounge where we met and reminisce about that moment every time I go to Green Bank. Where the blackboard stood there is now a commemorative plaque on the wall, bearing the equation with its description.)

The astrophysicists in the room were soon volunteering values for R, the rate of star formation in the Galaxy. To get the birth rate of solar-type stars, all we had to do was take the number of such stars in the Galaxy—roughly ten to the tenth power, or ten billion—and divide that number by the average lifetime of such a star, which is about ten to the tenth power, or ten billion years. Scientists always talk about very large numbers in powers of ten. But even a nonscientist unaccustomed to working with such big numbers could see that ten to the tenth power divided by ten to the tenth power was going to turn out to be one.*

The conservative answer, everyone agreed, was one—at least one new star was born each year in any given galaxy. Under the equation, I wrote "$R=1$."

All right, then. How many of those stars have planets?

"Solar-type stars are rarely born alone," opined Struve, explaining that stars of the Sun's size most often emerge from their nests of gas and dust as twins—double stars—or as solo suns with planets surrounding them.

"About half the F-, G-, and K-type stars exist in binary systems," he said, "so one could assume that the other half has planets."

"Or less than half," suggested Morrison. "The remnants of the stellar nebula could have some different fate. The leftovers might be served up as little asteroids, unsuitable as habitats. They might be blasted into space. We don't know. Maybe only one in five stars has planets." All right, we had a range of values there: Perhaps one fifth to one half the stars in the Milky Way might be expected to have a retinue of planets something like our Solar System. That was a degree of uncertainty we could work with.

Pearman said it was a shame we didn't have better figures because it seemed like the sort of question that could be answered with straightforward observations. He was right, too. Observing techniques had been developed that could identify the presence of stars' invisible companions, but astronomers had not yet adequately applied those techniques. If just one other solar system were found, what a tremendous positive contribution that would make to our considerations. (We are still groping observationally for those other planetary systems to this day. We think we have found several.)

On the question of the number of planets in each solar system that might be suitable for life, Huang said he thought the number was at least one. For our Sun, he said in his halting English, the habitable zone included three planets: Venus, Earth, and Mars.

---

* Scientific shorthand for writing out large numbers helps make the numerical description of the vast universe and the submicroscopic atom altogether manageable. In this system, one million is 10^6, which means a one with six zeroes after it; five million becomes 5×10^6. (One millionth is 10^{-6}.) The importance of the notation becomes obvious in discussions of numbers that are all but impossible to say in words, such as 10^{22}.

Life existed on one of them for sure, and possibly more than one. Venus seemed too hot, and Mars too cold, but perhaps some kind of creatures did live on those planets. The question wasn't settled yet.*

Huang and Struve thought our Solar System was probably typical in size and number of planets. Around other stars like our Sun, planets would distribute themselves in a wide range of orbits. Some of those orbits would necessarily fall within Huang's "habitable zone." He suggested that probably at least one planet in each solar system was potentially habitable, and perhaps as many as five planets had the right conditions to support some kind of life. Sagan entered what was now an exciting fray with an important observation: an atmospheric greenhouse effect could make a planet habitable, even if it were quite far from its star. This possibility would increase the number of planets capable of supporting life. The minimum value of n_e lay between one and five.

It was all very well to have lots of habitable planets, but how many of them were actually inhabited? Calvin and Sagan were convinced that if the conditions for life were favorable, life would eventually appear. Sagan argued forcefully that, given the cosmic abundance of the elements, planets with atmospheres like that of the early Earth should be widespread. Sources of energy such as lightning and ultraviolet light would likewise abound. He pointed out that life arose extremely quickly on Earth. Indeed, life arose just as soon as it possibly could, and that was a strong indication that the development of life was easy. Given enough time, it was reasonable to expect life to arise through the sheer force of the laws of physics and chemistry. Indeed, life was more likely than not. And what's more, the early stages of life on other planets would probably resemble the first one-celled organisms on Earth. The extraterrestrials we detected would be extraordinarily different from us, of course, having followed their own evolutionary path from single cells to highly complex, intelligent life-forms. But we probably started out the same way, from the same materials.

Where life could appear, it would appear: That was the logical

---

* It still isn't settled today. The 1976 *Viking* lander, which looked for life on Mars, did not provide a definitive "yes" or "no" as to whether anything lives on Mars now—or did live there in the past, before all the water froze and then evaporated.

conclusion. The rest of the group went along with this theory, giving f_l a value of one. It was time for lunch.

Discussion didn't stop at lunch, of course, or at any other time during those three days, except when the participants split up to go to sleep. It was a talk marathon, and when we weren't talking formally in the conference room, we were talking over the table in the cafeteria, or talking while walking around the observatory and surrounding hills in small groups. We started talking early in the mornings, and we talked late into the night.

When we formally reconvened after lunch, we turned our attention to the number of life-supporting planets where the life-forms could reasonably be called intelligent.

The one among us who did the most talking about other forms of intelligent life was John Lilly. Much of that first day, he regaled us with tales of his bottlenosed dolphins, whose brains, he said, were larger than ours and just as densely packed with neurons. Some parts of the dolphin brain looked even more complex than their human counterparts, he averred. Clearly, more than one intelligent species had evolved on Earth.

There was a popular television series at the time called *Flipper*. It was a *Lassie* spin-off about a pet dolphin who did wonderful things, and routinely held himself upright in the water to squeak and click at his human friends. Lilly told us that dolphins could indeed utter numerous noises that sounded like nothing so much as rusty hinges, creaking doors, and rasps on metal. These sounds were part of their sonar vocabulary, and helped them identify and find food, for example, or each other. They communicated among themselves with whistling sounds, emitted through their blowholes in a range of frequencies that rose far out of human earshot. He had recorded all varieties of dolphin-speak at his Communication Research Institute, and he brought the tapes to play for us.

Lilly was convinced the sounds constituted a complex language that he was only beginning to understand. For example, a dolphin distress call, he said, sounded like two whistles in a crescendo-decrescendo pair. If one dolphin whistled twice, another would rush to his side. He saw a heartwarming demonstration of the call's effectiveness the day one of his dolphins got chilled to the point of shivering during an experiment. On being returned to the main tank where two other dolphins were swimming, the chilled animal found himself too cold to swim. If he didn't swim to the surface periodically to breathe, of course, he would die of suffocation. The dolphin whistled twice. His two tankmates actually lifted the frozen-stiff one between them until his blowhole was out of the water. Then the three of them whistled and chattered at length as they submerged again. They were apparently hatching a disaster plan, because the two helpers started swimming purposefully and repeatedly near the lame one's hindquarters. Each time they swam under him, their dorsal fins would brush against his private parts, and he'd contract his powerful fluke muscles by reflex. The motion was enough to buoy him to the surface. And the other two obligingly kept up their strange lifesaving technique for several hours until their companion warmed up enough to swim freely again.

Lilly had many other anecdotes of dolphins coming to the aid of ailing dolphins. He even told a few in which dolphins helped waterbound humans. He described their behavior in human terms because it looked humanlike to him. And he fully expected to be able to communicate with them someday. In fact, if he slowed down the playback speed of the tape recorder enough, the squeaks and clicks sounded like human language.

We were all totally enthralled by these reports. We felt some of the excitement in store for us when we encounter nonhuman intelligence of extraterrestrial origin. In retrospect, however, I now think that Lilly's work was poor science. He had probably distilled endless hours of recordings to select those little bits that sounded humanlike. You know how that goes: If you give enough typewriters to enough monkeys, one of them will type a Shakespearean sonnet. It wasn't long after the Green Bank meeting that some of Lilly's dolphins apparently committed suicide as a reaction to experiments in captivity. He set the survivors free and moved on to his introspective experimentation with LSD.

"Dolphins," Lilly told us at Green Bank, "could be trained to rescue pilots whose planes go down over open ocean. They could scout out enemy submarines or even serve as detection-proof delivery systems for bombs to be detonated in foreign harbors."

But before the conversation wandered too far in this direction, Morrison brought us back to the point by observing that dolphins, intelligent as they were, probably weren't too interested in astronomy, given the fact that they couldn't see the stars except in the odd moments when they surfaced to breathe at night. And even if they were interested, they couldn't build telescopes with flippers.

Seriously, Morrison said, the facts of life probably favored the evolution of intelligence, as evidenced at least by humans and dolphins on Earth. Intelligence would no doubt have so much survival value that many kinds of intelligent creatures could evolve on a single planet. The rest of the group concurred that there was great survival value in intelligence. This made it likely that intelligence would prosper, according to the principles of natural selection, on any planet where life took hold. In the language of the equation, $f_i = 1$.

It was during the first night of the Green Bank meeting, when everyone had retired to the farmhouses and rooms of the residence hall, that a committee at the Karolinska Institute in Stockholm voted to award the prestigious 1961 Nobel prize in Chemistry to Melvin Calvin. The call came in from Sweden, six time zones away, shortly after 4:00 A.M. There were no phones in the residence hall where Calvin was sleeping, so the night watchman learned the news first in the administration building. Having been forewarned and instructed what to do in such an event, he dashed across the grounds to summon Calvin.

Everyone else got up, too. The whole observatory was in an uproar. We hauled the champagne out of the basement and hailed our hero. This may sound crazy, but sharing that moment with Calvin was almost like sharing the prize itself. I felt somehow that our group and the topic we were discussing had suddenly been raised to a higher credibility level by Calvin's new standing in the public eye, for the Nobel prize is such a coveted honor that it rubs off on everything the recipient touches.

Phone calls from reporters and telegrams from well-wishers began pouring in, but by midmorning Calvin felt it at least good manners to talk about extraterrestrial life again. He seemed a bit apologetic that all the hubbub was disrupting our agenda.

We spent the rest of that day, between interruptions, trying to assess the fraction of extant intelligent life-forms that might have the desire and the wherewithal for interstellar communication. On the agenda equation, this was topic f_c. It was perhaps the most open question of all the ones we had considered so far.

Morrison took heart in observing that sophisticated civilizations had developed separately in three isolated areas on Earth: China, the Middle East, and the Americas. He assumed the same sort of scenario had played itself out across space, on a more technologically advanced level, so that there might be many civilizations that had developed with no knowledge of each other, isolated by the great distances between the stars. There might even be a wide community of advanced civilizations that were in contact with one another, and always on the lookout for newcomers to divert and amuse them.

Lilly claimed to be more or less communicating with dolphins in the Virgin Islands, which was a major achievement, to say the least. But what if he had to reach them from the opposite end of the Galaxy? It seemed more than likely that an intelligent species would need radiophysics and electromagnetic communication to send a message to another star system.

"Let's imagine what these creatures are," said Calvin. "We have no idea what they look like, of course, but I think we can safely assume that they'll have organs for sight and sound, because the universe in which they live is a universe of light and sound. Maybe they don't see what we call visible light. Maybe they see in the ultraviolet or the infrared, but they must see and hear something. They probably have sensing organs for touch, so they don't bump into each other, and they must have some way to process the information from their sensors—something like a brain, though what shape it might take, I can't tell."

Calvin said he couldn't picture any evolution occurring in the absence of electromagnetic radiation. He was talking about sunlight and heat, which, from his biochemical viewpoint, were the two forms of electromagnetic radiation crucial to life. Electromagnetic radiation not only made life possible, he was saying, but also shaped that life to some degree.

Electromagnetic radiation had shaped the lives of the astronomers and physicists in our group in another way: We devoted our own intelligent lives to analyzing the electromagnetic spectrum, from gamma rays to radio waves. We were probing our "universe of light and sound," as Calvin had called it, with ever more sensitive instruments that extended the reach of the organs we were born with. It seemed reasonable to us that other intelligences would go the same route. Some of them, such as dolphins and whales, would plumb the full possibilities of sound in an intelligent but nontechnical way. Others, who lived on dry land, would eventually build transmitting towers and telescopes that let them reach across space.

Even if they weren't thinking of communicating with galactic neighbors, their capacity for communication might give them away.

The people of Earth, to cite the only example we knew, had just recently become a detectable civilization with the advent of television in 1947. Our television programs were already leaking into space as electromagnetic signals that could be picked up at enormous distances by instruments not much bigger than our own radio telescopes. *I Love Lucy* or *Gunsmoke* would stand as proof of intelligent life on Earth. Whatever impression such missives might make on alien minds, they were already wending their way among the stars. The evidence of us was out there. What evidence might we find of them if we continued our search? Intentional messages beamed our way full of useful information about the universe? Or alien sitcoms?

"Why not?" Oliver asked with a laugh. The possibility was infinitely more plausible than the arrival of an alien spacecraft. There was absolute consensus on this point—that space was too vast to permit easy physical visitations between civilizations. Achieving speeds high enough to complete interstellar voyages in reasonable times would make energy demands that were too great, even for very advanced civilizations. "Contact" would be in the form of electromagnetic signals passing between worlds at the speed of light. (No matter how far into the realm of the fantastic our ruminations took us, we didn't even discuss the notion of interstellar travel at Green Bank, on the grounds that it was irrelevant. I will, however, look into this widespread and admittedly intriguing idea in a later chapter.)

With barely a sketch of extraterrestrial anatomy and no inkling of alien sociology, we could not begin to assess whether they would want to communicate with us, or what reasons they might have for keeping their existence a secret. Given all the possibilities we could think of, we assumed that 10 to 20 percent of the intelligent civilizations would try to locate and communicate with alien civilizations; the value of f_c, then, was probably one fifth to one tenth.

The last value to be determined had the most to do with our own destiny. This was L, the longevity of a civilization capable of interstellar communication.

L posed a pointed question: Once a civilization has the technology to reveal its existence across space, how long does it remain a civilization? We Earthlings already had the means to annihilate ourselves in one fell swoop. We achieved this ability almost at the same time as we became visible to the cosmos. Indeed, one of our

Green Bank discussants, Phil Morrison, had worked on the Manhattan Project—had actually armed the second atomic bomb, dropped on Nagasaki on August 9, 1945, though he became an activist for arms control almost immediately afterward. If the capability for total planetary destruction lay within the reach of every technologically advanced civilization, how likely were we to find anybody out there?

Maybe countless civilizations came of age in the universe but came to an end before making contact with those on other planets. Or maybe we would find worlds where the inhabitants had learned to live in peace. Indeed, it seemed likely that any civilizations we found would have worked their way through the era of threatened nuclear destruction and could prove to be good role models for us. The issue fairly rang with social relevance. Whatever we might discover one day about the actual existence of alien civilizations, above all, the act of searching cast our own civilization in a new light.

Even if some other worlds achieved a global society before they developed weapons for mass destruction, as Sagan suggested, there were other catastrophes that could blow a planet away. Collisions with asteroids, for example, might limit the number of civilizations that survived. (Recent research has shown this to be a much greater threat than we then imagined.) Or perhaps the extraterrestrials squandered the resources of their planet, and grew so numerous that they could no longer feed themselves.

In the end, it seemed that the lifetimes of civilizations would either be very short—less than a thousand years—or extremely long—in excess of perhaps hundreds of millions of years.

The numbers we'd plugged in by now were all either equal to one, or canceled each other out. For example, multiplying five, which was a possible value for the number of planets in a solar system that could support life, times one fifth, one of the suggestions for the number of stars that might have planets, yields a product of one. The value of N thus hinged solely on the value of L. There was a new, streamlined form of the equation: $N=L$.

"We've reached a conclusion," I said. "Our best estimate is that there are somewhere between one thousand and one hundred million advanced extraterrestrial civilizations in the Milky Way." (The values for the various factors in the equation have changed over the years, but this answer remains the most probable range.)

"Perhaps we can find the others," Morrison chimed in. "I think we all agree that is what we ought to do."

We would be satisfied to find just one other, and we spent the last part of our time together figuring out how best to do that. We discussed the kinds of signals to look for and the "magic frequencies," such as the waterhole, where we might detect their signals. We talked of the wisdom of dedicating whole telescopes to the endeavor, or whether it would be better to buy a little time at a whole bunch of observatories. The latter was my personal preference, because such a plan would involve a great number of scientists, and no one of them would be limited to searching, but would have the time to pursue other stimulating research during the long wait for success.

"Just imagine," added Morrison. "One scientist spends a whole lifetime doing nothing but searching for this needle in the haystack, then retires. The very next day, a young scientist walks in and finds the needle immediately. What a personal disaster that would create!"

"This is work for society, not for individuals," Oliver concluded. "The distances we're talking about mean that communication will proceed over decades, maybe even centuries. It isn't going to be one human talking to one alien. The search itself must be a group effort."

Morrison talked of making the search a "living science," with plans that would keep changing every few years as new techniques and strategies were developed.

We didn't fool ourselves by thinking there would be much money available to fund our giant dreams. Pearman said the current talk at NASA centered on an altogether different project: The United States would send a man to the Moon by the end of the decade. The populated worlds of other galaxies would have to wait in line far behind that priority.

But our day would come, we believed, if we kept the idea alive and made sure that the scientific arguments were sound and unbiased.

The ten of us had been through so much together in the course of the meeting that when the time came to say good-bye, we didn't want to let the newfound spirit of community die. We expressed that feeling by dubbing our group "the Order of the Dolphin," as though we were lodge members with regular gatherings to look forward to.

We split the one remaining bottle of champagne, and as we raised our glasses, Struve offered the toast:

"To the value of L. May it prove to be a very large number." And we parted on that hopeful note.

A few weeks later, I received a small package in the mail from Melvin Calvin. There was an identical package addressed to Struve, and I later learned that each conference participant had received one. Inside the box was a silver pin—a museum replica made from an ancient Greek coin in the shape of a leaping dolphin.

CHAPTER 4

▲
▲
▲

To Build
a Better Mousetrap

Innumerable suns exist; innumerable earths revolve about these suns in a manner similar to the way the seven planets revolve around our sun. Living beings inhabit these worlds.

—GIORDANO BRUNO,
Italian monk of
the sixteenth century

Had I not undertaken Project Ozma myself in 1960, then I feel certain someone else would have done it. Maybe not the exact same search with the identical equipment, but something quite similar, and quite soon. I say this because the idea of searching had occurred simultaneously—independently of any input from me—to several people I could name, including Giuseppe Cocconi, Phil Morrison, Barney Oliver, and Carl Sagan. The necessary calculations were not difficult. It was almost as though the existence of radio telescopes forced the issue of interstellar communication, because such instruments so conspicuously put the means to search in your hands.

I know I've talked a lot about how hard it was for me to keep my ideas to myself, and how long I waited for opportunities such as Ozma and the Order of the Dolphin to breathe life into my secret dreams. But the truth was that I had fared extremely well, especially when compared to earlier thinkers who looked to the stars for signs of life. For espousing the multiplicity of inhabited worlds, Giordano Bruno was burned at the stake in the year 1600, in the Field of Flowers, which is now a parking lot in central Rome. I, on the other hand, by the simple good fortune of expressing the same basic idea in the right century, had been rewarded with research funds, telescope time, public acknowledgment, and a coterie of like-minded peers who had rallied round my flag. I gained another true friend—and the search endeavor a strong supporter—early in 1962, when a German radio astronomer named Sebastian von Hoerner joined the staff at Green Bank.

Von Hoerner is one of the great unsung heroes in astronomy, as well as in the search for extraterrestrial intelligence. Although he arrived in America too late to be part of Project Ozma or the Order of the Dolphin meeting, he studied both at length, and then immersed himself in our deliberations with his typical curiosity, insight, and zeal.

Like Joseph Pawsey, von Hoerner did groundbreaking original work but never promoted himself. This kept him perpetually out of the limelight. He had studied under Werner Heisenberg, and was brilliant enough to tackle the really hard questions in relativity theory and cosmology. In his research at Green Bank, he was using radio sources to establish the structure and history of the universe.*

Von Hoerner was one of very few astronomers I've known who seemed equally at home with theoretical questions and practical, nuts-and-bolts applications. He was always an optimist, and pleasant, too, with a great love of music and zest for the outdoors. It was von Hoerner who turned the occasional cave explorations I'd carried out with Dave Heeschen into a shared passion. The three of us got so good at it, through constant practice, that we became a cave rescue team, volunteering our services to the state police. They would call on us from time to time to go after college students

---

* Years later, von Hoerner developed the concept of homology, which is a way of ensuring that the reflecting surfaces of radio telescopes remain the proper parabolic shape even though the steerable dishes sag under their own weight. His ideas have been incorporated into the design of every steerable dish built in the past twenty years, beginning with the 300-foot telescope at the Max-Planck-Institut für Radioastronomie (MPIFR) near Bonn, which is the largest of its kind in the world.

who'd gotten injured and stranded in the caves while spelunking during semester breaks. I will never forget one frigid winter day and night spent rescuing a Princeton University student from the bottom of a 125-foot cave waterfall. As we emerged, soaked and exhausted, we found a West Virginia forest ranger waiting for us, ax at the ready, prepared to—what? We couldn't imagine how he might have aided the rescue effort by holding an ax at the mouth of the cave. As for the student, neither he nor his friends, who'd spent an anxious ten hours waiting for us to drag him out, ever uttered a word of thanks.

Von Hoerner's first official act in the search for extraterrestrial intelligence was to take the quintessential quantity L from my equation—the longevity of detectable civilizations—and show mathematically that it was probably a very large number.

He conceded from the outset of his calculations that alien civilizations faced a variety of destinies that might lead to their disappearance. At that time, nuclear war seemed perhaps the most plausible of all the possible routes to annihilation. A cosmic accident, such as a collision with an asteroid, was another. And even if a civilization were not destroyed outright by a natural or artificial catastrophe, it might fade into oblivion through stagnation and overpopulation, or a loss of interest in science and technology. In such a world, von Hoerner imagined, the quality of life would diminish drastically. Stagnant civilizations just struggling to hang on would spend no money on space exploration or colonization. They might not undertake new projects of any kind—certainly no attempts to search for other intelligent civilizations, and no activities that would make their own civilization detectable to others.

As he ticked off the various doomsday scenarios, von Hoerner allowed that many, perhaps *most*, civilizations in space might follow those courses. He assigned probabilities to each outcome. And he concluded that it was reasonable to assume that a small percentage were peace-loving, lucky, and smart, with a fair chance of finding each other and establishing communication. They might continue to use powerful radio transmitters for a long time in the course of their discourse, granting them high visibility over millennia. And it would be these select few, by virtue of their achievements and their staying power, who would dominate the value of L. The number he came up with was sixty-five hundred. I thought it was closer to ten thousand, but we were in the same ball park.

Then von Hoerner had another thought: The longer a detectable civilization lasts, the larger L becomes. What if a fraction of the few long-lived civilizations kept on an even keel for an extremely long time—a billion years, say? He figured out that if just 1 percent of alien civilizations had a lifetime of a billion years, then the value of L would make an enormous leap, from ten thousand to ten million.*

"That's truly amazing, Sebastian," I said when he showed me his numbers and I realized they were correct. "That's not at all what intuition would suggest."

"No, it's not," he agreed. "But it makes a compelling argument to continue the search." It meant that most civilizations we might detect would be very old and very advanced. And so he began thinking of what signals of theirs to search for, and how. He was convinced, as the rest of the Dolphins were, that the radio region provided a good, logical place to look. But it was by no means the only place. He welcomed the ideas of physicist Freeman Dyson, at the Institute for Advanced Study in Princeton, who thought that distant civilizations would leave inadvertent clues to their whereabouts in the infrared region of the electromagnetic spectrum.

Dyson didn't want to have to depend on the benevolence of extraterrestrials beaming messages our way. His strategy was to snare the uncooperative, uncommunicative civilizations and not wait for those seeking to make contact.

As early as June 1960, Dyson had published a paper in *Science* claiming that a truly advanced civilization might fully exploit its home star by constructing a giant sphere around it to trap and tap all its energy. While we on Earth were content to make do with the small percentage of the Sun's light and heat that happened to fall on us, our extraterrestrial counterparts were building "Dyson spheres" to power their worlds. These and other great feats of stellar engineering, Dyson thought, would leave a trail of waste heat that we could see: There would be infrared emissions from Dyson spheres, detectable across the Galaxy.

Like Dyson, von Hoerner thought it would make sense to search the infrared along with the radio, though infrared astronomy was

---

* At the same time, Carl Sagan was also arguing that only a small number of very long-lived civilizations need exist for the value of L to be high.

even more of an infant than radio astronomy.* Von Hoerner also considered the idea that extraterrestrials might communicate among themselves with laser systems that we could detect optically if we tried.

"We can't be sure that any of these approaches is the best method," he said in one of our many delightful talks. "We might be a thousand years away from the best technology for searching. And if we waited a thousand years to do it, one could still argue that we'd be better equipped in another thousand years. The point is, it's impossible to know what is the best method. We just have to try what is feasible and seems most promising. So we might as well start right now with the one method we know for sure, which is a radio search on the most likely frequency."

Despite von Hoerner's encouragement, I wasn't pushing to do any more searching just yet. I was not one to suggest waiting a thousand years, but I was convinced we had more technological hurdles to leap before we could make a search that would be significantly better than Ozma. Most of all, we needed multichannel receivers, which simply did not exist at the time, though I knew they were coming. The Ozma receiver had operated on a single channel, searching back and forth through a frequency band about 100 cycles per second (100 hertz) wide. But the full scope of the region where the universe is darkest and quietest extends far beyond the tiny "waterhole" that Ozma explored. It extends over some one hundred billion channels. A thorough search should monitor all one hundred billion, ideally, or at least several million. In theory, it was possible to search all one hundred billion channels with a single-channel receiver. The only catch was, it would take forever.

I had no idea how long the wait would be for multichannel receivers. (It turned out to be fifteen years.) But I thought it best to postpone searching until we had them, while keeping the dream alive.

---

* The first good device for doing ground-based infrared astronomy didn't come along until 1963, and no extensive infrared investigation of the universe was made until 1983, the year that the Infrared Astronomy Satellite, called IRAS, was launched. It turned up many objects that have the expected spectrum of Dyson spheres, but since we can't tell how distant these objects are, we can't judge their true brightness in the infrared. They could be Dyson spheres, or they could be new stars forming.

To be perfectly honest, I could not have proposed another extra-terrestrial search in 1962, even if the technology had been in place to do the job right. As a young scientist, I was free to undertake an Ozma once. Twice would likely have been professional suicide. I was supposed to be enhancing my reputation and pursuing opportunities for job advancement, especially since I now had a wife and three young sons to think about. So I threw all my energy into my work on the planets. And indeed I made a discovery in that field that was to have an enormous effect on the future course of my career as a scientist.

In the early 1960s, we were just beginning to make radio measurements of the planets successfully. These planetary radio emissions were extremely faint, compared to the far more powerful emissions from cosmic radio sources such as stars and galaxies. This was because the planetary emissions arose simply from the internal heat of the planets, while the cosmic emissions were generated by vast numbers of charged particles orbiting massive bodies in magnetic fields. We had just gotten used to these characteristic differences between planetary and stellar emissions when radio astronomers at the Naval Research Laboratory detected intense radio emissions from Venus. What could their strength imply? If our theory was correct, and the emissions depended solely on Venus's body heat, then the temperature on that planet had to be hellish—perhaps 500 degrees Kelvin (441 degrees Fahrenheit). All along we'd been expecting Venus, our sister planet, to have the same temperature as the Earth. Scientists began to wonder whether the readings from Venus might be incorrect, or if there were some other process at work causing the strong emissions.*

I used the new 85-foot telescope at Green Bank to measure the radiation from Venus at several frequencies, and showed that the

---

* Several years earlier, other astronomers at the naval lab had found anomalously high radio emissions coming from the planet Jupiter. My Green Bank friend Hein Hvatum and I examined Jupiter's radio emissions over a wide range of wavelengths, and found the source of the radiation was *not* the heat of the planet but highly energetic particles moving in Jupiter's magnetic field. This turned out to be the same phenomenon spacecraft had just detected in the outer atmosphere of the Earth, where particles orbited in what are now called the Van Allen radiation belts. Hvatum and I discovered the Van Allen belts of Jupiter, where the number of particles was at least one million times greater than in the Earth system.

emissions were indeed caused by the heat of the planet. The surprisingly high temperature values were real!

It was exciting to discover new and quite remarkable things about other planets. The work on Venus inspired me to look in more detail at the way planets radiate. At the time, we assumed that all the radiation created in the body of the planet by its heat would escape. We expected it all to be transmitted through the planet's surface and across space so we could measure it accurately with our radio telescopes on Earth. I realized that we had been quite naive in this assumption. *Some* of the radiation would escape and be detectable at Earth. But some of it might get reflected at the planet's surface and go back inside the planet. The true temperature of Venus, according to this line of reasoning, might be even hotter than we had recorded.

My ideas on this topic derived from the work of the great nineteenth-century French physicist Augustin-Jean Fresnel. Fresnel had shown that when light shines on the surface of water, some of the light's waves enter the water, while others are reflected off the surface and return to the air. I was sure that this same phenomenon, which Fresnel called "transmission and reflection at an interface," was governing planetary radio emissions.

It struck me that Fresnel's work implied that the radiation from a planet should become partially polarized as it passed through the surface—that is, the radio waves would vibrate preferentially in the same direction, instead of in random directions.

Fresnel had worked out elaborate formulas to describe what happened to light—or any electromagnetic radiation—as it moved from one medium to another. From these I could see that the nature of the planetary surface would determine the extent to which the radiation became polarized. The surface material—the type of rock or liquid—would affect the polarization. For example, radiation from a liquid water surface would be very highly polarized. The roughness or smoothness of the terrain would also govern the degree of polarization. In fact, an observer should be able to use the degree of polarization, measured from different viewing angles, as an indicator of the surface geography. This was a new idea. No one had looked for these effects before, so they had never been observed. If I could show that such effects existed, the results would enable astronomers to attain much more accurate measurements of planetary temperatures.

I applied this theory to the planetary problem. I was able to show that the actual planetary temperatures were about 25 percent greater than the values we'd assigned to them, which was a significant difference. I arrived at a new surface temperature of Venus, based on this work. I called it 750 degrees Kelvin (890 degrees Fahrenheit)—some 225 degrees Kelvin (400 degrees Fahrenheit) above the value declared by the Naval Research Lab. (Space probes later confirmed my calculation of the planet's temperature.)

The following summer, a young student named Carl Heiles helped me carry out detailed calculations of this phenomenon— calculations that define the whole process to this day. Heiles and I also confirmed the existence of the surface polarization phenomenon by successfully observing polarized radio emissions from the Moon that followed the theory perfectly. (Heiles went on to become a highly regarded and prize-winning astronomer at the University of California at Berkeley, where he is now a professor. And the technique of measuring the degree of polarization as observed from various viewing angles is used extensively today in activities such as the mapping of Venus by the *Magellan* spacecraft.)

I was invited to give a talk about this research at the Jet Propulsion Laboratory in Pasadena early in 1963. The conclusions so captivated the head of the Space Sciences Division there, Bob Meghreblian, that he offered me a job on the spot.

I was very happy at Green Bank, but my family and I had been isolated there for five years. Culturally and socially, Pasadena was a far better place to live. JPL itself was a ferment of exciting activities, from basic research to spacecraft and powerful computers. And the job waiting for me was as section chief of Lunar and Planetary Science. It was all so flattering and tempting that I accepted, only to find the move a disaster.

I had expected, having been hired on the basis of my research, to continue with it, or at least to be involved in the research activities of the other scientists. But all I did at JPL was draft budgets. Every other day a request would come from NASA headquarters for a "revised budget." Those were the magic words. Any time I thought the budget questions were settled and that I might actually get to think about Venus or Mars or the Moon, I would be asked for yet another budget revision. I was sharpening pencils and putting dollar signs on sheets of ledger paper. The contrast between this drudgery and the atmosphere of scientific excitement I'd left behind me at Green Bank was painful to contemplate. Within months I was looking for another position.

I knew that the College of Engineering at Cornell had been at work building an enormous radio telescope that was just nearing completion. I had loved Ithaca as an undergraduate, and thought how satisfying it might be to return there as a faculty member now that the university's interest and opportunities in radio astronomy were growing.

Aside from being an alumnus, I had an ally at Cornell's newly formed Center for Radiophysics and Space Research. Its director, the Vienna-born, Cambridge-educated Thomas Gold, had been an active radio astronomer at Harvard when I was a graduate student there. As soon as I approached Gold to describe my situation and see if Cornell had an opening, he offered me a tenured faculty position. Academic affairs were conducted differently in those days, without the arcane, lengthy, and democratic action of search committees, not to mention layer upon layer of university administration. And Tommy Gold was famous for acting impulsively. That was his signature in science as well as in personal relations. No one was surprised when Gold made outrageous speculations that went far beyond the data at hand.* Not surprisingly, his ideas often proved to be wrong, but they were so dazzling and so ingenious that most people readily forgave Gold his bad ideas.

Largely as a formality, Gold invited me to Cornell for an interview in December 1963, and arranged for me to visit the new telescope, which was located in Puerto Rico, the following month.

"You have to see it to believe it," Gold said. He described the telescope as an odd-looking, upside-down contraption, with its massive reflector dish, 1,000 feet wide, lying immobile in the ground, and all the receivers and transmitters hanging 50 stories above it in the air.

"Hanging from *what*?" I asked him. He explained the rest with pictures that had recently been taken. Sure enough, the wire mesh of the dish lay nestled in a huge hole shaped like a bowl. (Once there, I calculated that the bowl could hold 357 million boxes of

---

* Gold was one of the original proponents of the "steady-state universe"—the idea that the universe stays virtually the same over time, as opposed to having started off with a "big bang," as most cosmologists now believe, though the issue is far from clear.

cornflakes.) Three concrete towers stood around this hole. And slung from the towertops on thick cables was a massive triangle of steel girders, carrying the antenna and other receiving equipment.

"How much does this thing weigh?" I asked, pointing to the hovering white triangle of steel.

"It weighs 625 tons," he said. "I'm afraid I had something to do with making it so heavy." Gold explained that the original design had provided no steering capability at all, which would have grossly limited its use for radio astronomy.

"The telescope has been in the hands of ionospheric physicists in the Engineering College," he said with obvious displeasure. "They don't care about looking at anything in deep space. That's why they didn't care about steerability."

But Gold had seen that even if the reflector in the ground wasn't steerable, there might be a way to steer part of the suspended platform, so that stars and galaxies could be tracked across the sky. He had fought for that change, and won. The platform had been modified so that part of it could rotate a full 360 degrees. This part, which hung below the triangle and looked like an inverted railroad bridge, was called the feed arm, because it held the feeds, or antennae, that picked up radio waves collected and reflected by the dish below. Along the underside of this feed arm, two carriage houses could ride on tracks, carrying feeds to the desired positions.

"We can't do much with the telescope at short wavelengths," Gold conceded, "but there's a lot of potential there. I want you to go and judge for yourself."

The details of my first visit to Arecibo, and the unexpected emotional impact of seeing the telescope up close, still stand out in my memory more clearly than most other events I can recall.

Not the least of my mental pictures is the sheer difficulty of getting to the site. In our quest for locations remote from man-made interference, astronomers are always setting telescopes on inaccessible mountaintops or in isolated valleys. (The optical instruments go on the mountaintops, where the air is thinnest; radio telescopes prefer the valleys, where the surrounding hills shield the telescope from radio interference.) The Arecibo Observatory was in the limestone karst country of northern Puerto Rico, nearly a day's drive from San Juan over an unpaved road. A young ionospheric physicist named George Thome met me at the airport and drove me to the observatory. The traffic was bumper-to-bumper until we got well past the city, and, since the road had only two lanes, all cars moved at the rate of the slowest truck. I had plenty of time to appreciate the beauty of the *flamboyan* trees lining the roadside, which Thome said would turn the highway into a tunnel of red flowers come June, and the African tulip trees already in blossom.

Between the town of Arecibo and the observatory, the road wound around the hills, changing altitude and direction every few feet. Thome told me there were ninety-one blind curves along that stretch alone. (Later I would have plenty of opportunities to count them myself, and confirm his claim.) The landscape was alive with banana trees, with pigs and chickens and children flying into and out of one-room hovels, dogs asleep in the middle of the road, and cows and donkeys wandering about outside pastel-colored stucco houses. The road had narrowed to one lane now, so whenever we encountered another vehicle coming in the opposite direction, one driver needed to back off the road to let the other pass, amid much horn-honking and gesticulating.

I had just gotten used to the slow pace and sleepy setting when I found myself suddenly catapulted far into the future. Rounding the next turn, one of the telescope's support towers loomed into sight, standing stark white, high above the lush, blue-green vegetation. The one tower, which looked to be the size and shape of the Washington Monument, and about one third of the suspended steel triangle were all I could see among the hills. Yet these fragments were immense beyond what I had imagined, and futuristically geometrical. The observatory looked so much like the scenery for an elaborate science fiction film that I almost fancied I heard music. Then it was gone. The road had reversed again. Now you see it, now you don't. For the next ten minutes I kept getting glimpses of the site from different angles as the road twisted toward the gateway. And when I was finally standing at the edge of the bowl, staring across the wire mesh surface to the tower on the opposite side, I marveled at the fact that it was impossible to see the whole telescope at once from any vantage point on the site. It was too big. The pictures Gold had shown me were all aerial views.

While I stood there gawking, two men having an animated discussion walked by me and got into what looked like a cable car. It really *was* a cable car, I realized, just like the ones you ride at a ski slope, and it ferried them up to the platform in about four and a half minutes by my watch.

"Could I go up there?" I wondered aloud.

"Well, sure," answered Thome, who hadn't left my side. "We

should probably wait for them to bring the cable car down, but if you're really eager, we can walk up from over there." He was pointing to a catwalk about fifty yards from us that led up to the platform at a steep angle.

"I think I'll wait, thanks," I said.

In the control room, Thome introduced me to the director, William E. Gordon, an ionospheric physicist from Cornell's College of Engineering who had conceived and helped construct the observatory.

"I'm sure the telescope is wonderful," I said as I shook Gordon's hand, "but what I want to know is, how did you haul all the concrete and steel girders over that road?"

Gordon laughed. "That was the real feat of engineering," he said.

It was Gordon who had envisioned a dish so large and so sensitive that it would be too big to steer, and who had turned standard telescope plans upside down to achieve his goal.

He needed a site that lay near the equator, where the Moon and planets would hover almost directly overhead, since the telescope was destined to make radar studies of these objects. The site had to be in American-controlled territory, thus narrowing the choices to Hawaii, Puerto Rico, or Samoa. The hills of northern Puerto Rico offered unusual terrain, pockmarked by sinkholes where limestone had dissolved and collapsed. Gordon and several experts had combed this region for a natural depression in the ground about the right shape for the reflector bowl, as they knew this would save millions of dollars in excavation costs. This particular hole in Barrio Esperanza, Gordon told me, was the most nearly perfect in shape, precisely the right size, and the most isolated, too.

"How did you find it?"

"We had aerial photographs and topographical maps of a scale on which a thousand-foot hole was about the size of a quarter. We just moved an actual quarter around until we found a good fit."*

All of Gordon's rational explanations for the location of the

---

* The enormous diameter of the reflector dish, I later learned, was the result of a big theoretical mistake. The original designers determined that one *thousand* feet was the telescope size needed to get a detectable radar echo from the ionosphere. As it turned out, a one-*hundred*-foot dish would have sufficed. Fortunately for the history of astronomy, no one discovered the error until construction was well under way and it was too late to change the size.

telescope skipped over one striking point: The place was exotic and exciting, especially to a northerner like me. The wet air smelled like a jungle. And as I walked around the site after sunset, I was serenaded by the sound of the tiny tree frogs, the *coquí*, calling to each other in the dark. I would have loved to have spent the night in the visiting scientists' quarters, but every bed was occupied, so I took a room in a crummy hotel on the main square in Arecibo. I remember that vividly, too. The room was hot and dirty, with a metal shower in one corner and enough traffic noise to wake the dead.

The gigantic telescope, perched like an alien visitation in that steamy landscape, was everything Gold had hinted. I could see its potential to become the most sensitive instrument ever applied to radio astronomy research. All you had to do was figure out a way to stabilize the platform so it didn't sway in the wind or rise and fall with the temperature changes, and then you could have access to all wavelengths. Granted, that was a tall order—an engineering brainteaser that would cost millions—but I suspected it could be done. And if and when that happened, the instrument would be uniquely suited to search for life in space.*

I had picked up enough innuendo in Gold's tone and Gordon's words to realize that the two of them were engaged in a bitter battle for the Arecibo turf. Gold, as director of Cornell's Center for Radiophysics and Space Research, wanted the Arecibo telescope freed to do more research in radio astronomy. He was lobbying the university administration to put it under his jurisdiction. Gordon, on the other hand, who fairly burst with proprietary pride when he discussed the observatory, could not bear to relinquish control of it. He couldn't even bear to leave the place, and had been living in Puerto Rico for four years, ever since the telescope construction had begun. As an electrical engineer, Gordon wanted to keep the

---

* At the moment, it wasn't searching for anything. A heavy price, indeed, had been paid for the telescope's steerability, since the shape of the reflector had to be spherical instead of the usual parabolic. The giant sphere could not focus collected radiation to a point, as a parabolic reflector did, but only to a line that was as much as ninety-six feet long. Whole new sophisticated antennae had to be developed to meet this configuration. The first one, built by some of the best-known designers, hardly worked at all. The telescope was a miserable failure, although this news was successfully suppressed for the three years it took to perfect the line feed, and then the telescope dwarfed those of the rest of the world.

telescope for the College of Engineering, and keep it focused on the electrical properties of the atmosphere. I had to sympathize with both their desires. I knew that if I joined the university faculty, I would be caught in their struggle, but I knew I could cope with that. The telescope had stolen my heart, too.

I moved back to Ithaca just a few months later, in June 1964, as soon as I settled my affairs in California and found a place to live. I felt no qualms about leaving JPL to become a professor of astronomy at Cornell.

I loved teaching. I liked organizing my thoughts into lectures, I enjoyed reading the students' papers, and I delighted in taking classes on nighttime field trips to the university's optical telescope, where I pointed out the moons of Jupiter and literally opened up new worlds for them.

Equally satisfying was the fact that the university expected me to continue my own research. I did this by taking routine trips to Green Bank, where I created a new, improved map of the galactic center using the 140-foot telescope, which had finally been completed. My frequent traveling, though somewhat frenetic for me, was not the least bit unusual. Indeed, radio astronomers came from all over to make observations at Green Bank. It was part of the NRAO charter, as a national center, to open its doors to visiting scientists from around the country and around the world. When I had worked there as director of telescope operations, one of my responsibilities had been to schedule the telescope time, some 70 percent of which went to visitors. I was well acquainted with the procedures. Now I was seeing them from the other side.

I also started traveling to Arecibo to conduct studies there. My work on the galactic center required access to short wavelengths, which I could have at Green Bank. Arecibo was more sensitive, being larger, but operated only at the longer wavelengths. This was because of the instability of the platform, which I mentioned earlier, as well as the crude reflector surface. With the platform assumed to be unsteady, the builders had installed a cheap wire mesh for the reflector. It had inaccuracies on the order of a couple of inches, so it couldn't pick up any but the longest wavelength signals.

I went to Arecibo to look for "interplanetary scintillations"—an ideal project for long wavelengths. My goal was to examine distant radio sources to see whether they scintillated, or twinkled, in the charged particles of the solar wind. I would observe each source along a line of sight near the Sun. Those sources that did twinkle when viewed through the charged particles around the Sun could be assumed to be very far away and very compact. These would be "point sources" that might turn out to be quasars or other interesting phenomena. Sources that did *not* scintillate could be assumed to be relatively large or close by.

You can observe a similar effect with your naked eye when you watch the sky at night. The stars, which are very far away, look like twinkling points of light. Turbulence in the atmosphere above you causes the air particles to be a little thicker here, a little thinner there. These pockets of dense or sparse air act as lenses. For a fraction of a second, such an air lens may focus a star's light on you, making it appear brighter, or bend that light away from you, apparently dimming the star. The planets, on the other hand, being closer and looming larger in the sky, don't twinkle. They are not single-point sources of light, but clusters of many such points. And so, while each individual point actually does twinkle, due to that same phenomenon, the randomly twinkling bits of planet tend to average each other out, making the planets appear to shine with an overall steady brightness.

The interplanetary scintillation work was interesting and necessary to establish the location and nature of new radio sources, but the real challenge of those months was negotiating a safe path between Tommy Gold and Bill Gordon.

By 1965, the Arecibo Ionospheric Observatory was officially an arm of Gold's radiophysics center. But Gordon remained the on-site director, and as unwilling as ever to give much ground to the astronomers. Gordon had allies in the federal agency that provided funds to the observatory—the Department of Defense's Advanced Research Projects Agency. He continued to make independent decisions and take action without getting Gold's permission, which aggravated his adversary no end. Gold retaliated by pointing out to the university administration that Gordon had been off-campus far longer than the bylaws allowed. It was a fact people might have been willing to overlook, but once Gold seized on it, Gordon was forced to make a choice: If he intended to remain in Cornell's employ, he had to resume his teaching duties. He could come home, or quit, but he could no longer serve as observatory director. Beaten, Gordon flew back to Ithaca, then left soon afterward to become an outstanding dean of engineering and science—and later provost—at Rice University in Houston.

Gold celebrated his victory by installing John Findlay, my colleague from the early days at Green Bank, as the new director at Arecibo. Findlay was perfect for the position, since he'd entered science as an ionospheric physicist, but then converted to radio astronomy—exactly what Gold wanted to do to the observatory.

Unfortunately, the directorship didn't work out personally for Findlay. After ten months at Arecibo, his wife and family were still living in Green Bank, and he resigned to return to the NRAO and be reunited with them.

I had been at Cornell for two years by that point, and worked well with Gold, so he offered the directorship to me. How quickly did I jump at the chance? I'm exaggerating only slightly when I say I just about hopped the next plane to Puerto Rico. I soon found my family a lovely house surrounded by guava and tamarind trees, near the Arecibo neighborhood called Radioville.

The schools in Arecibo weren't as good as the ones in Ithaca, and the prospects for family amusement were few, but in my day-to-day experience as director of the observatory, I led a charmed life. The scientific atmosphere was even more stimulating than at Green Bank. I went to work each morning with a sense of great anticipation, and came home feeling that I had really accomplished something. I was involved, at least marginally, in all the observations, and sometimes worked as a "friend of the telescope," which meant I showed the ropes to a visiting scientist and helped him or her in any way I was asked to. On the rare occasions when I didn't have my hands in a project, I could listen at lunch to excited talk about discoveries made that very morning.

I was there when the rotation of Mercury was tracked accurately for the first time. Astronomers had long believed that Mercury's rotation period was the same as its orbital period, so that the planet always kept the same face toward the Sun. This had been considered a Great Truth of the Solar System. But the Arecibo telescope showed that Mercury rotated more slowly than it circled the Sun, presenting alternate faces each time it passed close by. Over time, all parts of the planet took a turn facing the Sun.

I watched as the telescope's radar discerned the first features on the surface of Venus, which had long been shrouded in secrecy by the planet's thick covering of acid clouds. I witnessed the unveiling of Maxwell Mountain, Venus's highest summit, which stands a good deal taller than Mount Everest.*

The telescope was scheduled every minute of the day and night throughout the year. Maintenance work, too, had to be fitted in to the crammed observing schedule, and done when time allowed. Often that meant that a technician would have to show up in the middle of the night to change some esoteric gizmo on the feed arm.

By the end of my first summer in Arecibo, I was convinced that the platform simply was not moving as much as people thought. In the course of day-to-day activities, I spent a fair amount of time walking around up there—impressed at how solid the footing was. I took this as evidence that the platform was stable, despite what I had been told about it. If I was right, then improving the reflector surface might allow us to make successful observations at short wavelengths. I got the perfect opportunity to test my hunch in late August, when Hurricane Inez threatened to wreak such chaos that I closed the observatory and sent almost everybody home. I stayed at the site with two graduate students, John Comella and Linda DeNoyer. We were going to watch what happened to that platform in a hurricane-force wind.

We taped an ordinary ruler on the side of the platform as a target, and set up an engineer's theodolite in the control room, with the cross hairs trained on the ruler. We had an anemometer to measure wind speed, so we collected good data all through the storm on platform motion vs. wind speed. The storm cooperated by passing directly over us. We felt so strange to find ourselves alone in a place that was normally full of people, while the wild tumult raged around us. I hadn't experienced such a storm since taking Navy ships through hurricanes. The winds were clocked at two hundred miles an hour, but the rugged terrain around the

---

* The actual image we saw was a very blurry digital radar return with one conspicuous white spot, announcing a single feature on Venus that gave an extremely strong radar reflection. We couldn't tell at first that it was a mountain, but that's what it turned out to be. The discoverers named it after James Clerk Maxwell, who worked out the theory of electromagnetic radiation. Soon afterward, the International Astronomical Union decided that all features on Venus would be named for women. Today, Maxwell stands alone, the only male name on the whole planet.

telescope must have slowed the wind at the platform's height. The maximum we recorded was sixty-two miles per hour.

The results were even better than I had expected, because the hurricane's peak winds barely budged the platform half an inch. It was extremely stable. We plotted a graph, which showed that the ordinary trade winds blowing over the site could not possibly make the platform move more than a few millimeters. We had evidence to justify the expense of installing a more accurate reflector.

That inspired me to think up a way to fix the problem of the "thermals," or temperature changes that made the platform rise and fall as the cables expanded and contracted. We already had stabilizing cables, much thinner than the support cables, which went from the three corners of the platform to the ground. If we tied these tightly, with turnbuckles, they would actually pull the platform down a bit. But then, when heat made the big cables stretch out and drop the platform an inch or two, these cables would also expand, and *loosen* their hold, allowing the platform to rise. If we achieved the right relationship between the angles and the cross sections of the two kinds of cables (and I developed an equation to do that), then the changes in the supports and the tie-downs would cancel each other out. The platform would not move up or down.

I showed these results to the engineers and scientists, who saw the implications immediately: The cheap wire mesh of the reflector surface, which had been picked to match the supposedly bouncy platform, was all that was standing between us and extremely accurate observations at even the shortest wavelengths.*

When I say that I started each day at Arecibo certain that something unpredictable and potentially wonderful would happen, I am including nonscientific events, too. For example, we had a vampire scare early in my tenure as director. One of the night guards, a young Puerto Rican, claimed he saw a man in a black cloak walking the narrow trail around the perimeter of the bowl. He told us in all seriousness that he believed the man to be a

---

* That realization was the beginning of a major, long-term upgrading project to put a shiny new aluminum surface in the bowl. The resurfacing and related modifications were finished in 1974 at a cost of roughly nine million dollars. Most of the important results from the telescope since, such as the understanding of the distribution of galaxies in the universe, were possible only because of this change.

vampire. I accepted his report courteously, saying I would look into the situation. Two days later I really was forced to look into it, despite my skepticism, because a cow was found dead on a nearby farm, with all the blood drained from its body. The vampire rumor had already spread through the observatory staff, and now the cow incident whipped the fears of many people into a frenzy. The night guards began reporting more figures in black cloaks, and demanding that some action be taken to cleanse the observatory of the vampire presence.

I telephoned Donald Griffin at Cornell; he was an expert on real vampire bats. Just as I'd hoped, he was fully knowledgeable about vampire folklore as well as bat natural history, and told me that humanoid vampires hated the smell of garlic. Legend had it that their aversion was so great that victims could successfully drive vampires away simply by eating lots of garlic.

"Thank you, Dr. Griffin. I know what I have to do."

I met with the kitchen staff, instructing them to increase the amount of garlic used and to make special efforts to prepare dishes that called for garlic. Then I circulated the news that this strategy was in place. Every one of the staff who feared vampires had also heard at one time or another of the garlic connection. They felt satisfied that the director was pursuing the proper course to protect them. And lo, the vampires summarily deserted the observatory.

Soon we faced a more palpable threat from a group of radical political activists who called themselves *independentistas.* They liked to attract publicity by attacking "ugly" and visible American interests in Puerto Rico. They had set fires in American stores and bombed a few American-owned businesses. I had been following their exploits in the newspapers, half wondering if they would target the observatory, so I can honestly say I was not surprised, though certainly not pleased, when I received a call from an FBI agent warning me of an impending *independentista* attack.

"We have their telephones tapped," he said matter-of-factly, "and they're talking about blowing up your transformer."

"Thanks for the tip," I said. "But we don't have a transformer at the observatory." What we had was a trans*mitter.* I supposed that was what the terrorists meant, though I couldn't be sure. I had no good idea what they would try to blow up.

"I can't help you there," the agent said. "But I do know they're serious. They've flown in an explosives expert from New York City. They've set him up in a farmhouse about half a mile away from you. He passes most of the day holding pistol practice in the backyard. We're watching him, waiting for him to do something illegal."

The FBI agent dropped off pictures of this man for us to post at the observatory. He looked evil and ugly, with lots of scars on his face, as though he'd been sent by central casting. The agent called me every day with updates, and although I knew our suspect was under constant surveillance, I was nervous. I spoke to our personnel manager, Victor Olazabal, about beefing up observatory security.

Olazabal had fought as a major in Fidel Castro's Cuban army, but then became disillusioned when Castro turned Communist. Olazabal made a dramatic escape from Cuba by feigning illness and submitting to a real operation in a Havana hospital, where his confederates intentionally infected him. That was an indication of how badly he wanted to get out of Cuba, and his near fatal infection won him an emergency medical transfer to the United States for treatment. He still hated Castro, and he hated the *independentistas* by association, because they were known to be Castro sympathizers.

"I'll take charge of this," Olazabal assured me. And I let him. He set up a security command post at the north tower, closest to the administration building. He put all the security guards on overtime and had them patrolling with walkie-talkies twenty-four hours a day. Olazabal himself took to carrying a .45 pistol with him all the time.

At night he sat up with the guards at the north tower, where he said he could see the road and know in advance of any car's approach. Just as a person driving to the observatory gets the first dramatic glimpse of this concrete tower from afar, so a guard at the tower can spot the car at the same moment, even in darkness, because that particular stretch of road passes in front of a chalk-white wall where the hillside was cut away to build the road.

None of us slept much during those weeks. One night, instead of pacing around my house, I got into my car and drove to the observatory with my headlights out. I knew the road well enough to do that, I thought, and I felt the need to test Olazabal's security measures. I had a Triumph TR-4, a very small sports car that I thought might escape surveillance—though I was hoping I was wrong.

When I roared up to the gate at about 3:00 A.M., my heart in my mouth, what did I find? All the floodlights lit up, with me in their focus. Six helmeted guards with clubs came out of nowhere and surrounded my car. Olazabal stood in the guard booth, his .45 pointed right at me. I felt strangely reassured.

A few nights later, another car with no headlights on arrived at the gate at midnight, to the same menacing welcome. Olazabal said he saw four men inside, but no one got out and he could not make out their faces. The car stood in the circle of floodlights for a moment, then turned and sped away. The very next day, having heard of our experience, FBI agents visited the bomber on his farm and tried a direct approach.

"We know who you are and we know why you're here," they told him. "Now, why don't you leave?" And to everyone's great relief, he did just that.

These are the kinds of everyday experiences I had at the observatory, which was the stage for a constant interplay of dramas on both the human and galactic scales. Soon after we banished the *independentistas* from Arecibo, the bombshell of the decade—the most startling discovery in all of astronomy—struck in February 1968. I was sitting in my office, catching up on some correspondence, when a young Australian astronomer named John Sutton came running in with the latest issue of *Nature*, just out of its mailing wrapper.

"Look at this!" He had sprinted all the way from the library, and was shouting to me as he burst through the doorway. "Look at this! LOOK at this!" He had the journal open to an article by a group of Cambridge radio astronomers describing what they called "rapidly pulsating radio sources." They had detected three radio sources emitting regularly spaced pulses, or bursts of radiation. It was an unprecedented finding. No one had ever seen any radio source pulsate—blink its radio waves on and off—as these astronomers claimed. What's more, they reported, one source was pulsating continuously every 1.3 seconds, and had been doing so for months!

Every 1.3 seconds, a burst of radiation for 0.01 second, more regular than any clockwork. What in the universe would account for that? How could anything as massive as a star blink its radio emissions on and off as though by the flick of a switch? The paper alluded to several possible explanations, and the authors allowed that, early on, they had thought the pulses might be signals from an intelligent civilization elsewhere in the Galaxy.

We had to see this for ourselves. The article gave the position of the source the group had observed for the longest time. We hurriedly checked the position against our observing schedule and found we could look for it that very day. But when we tried, we were terribly disappointed to see nothing. The problem was that we were searching the frequency of 430 megahertz, where the object was weak. We hadn't had time to set up equipment at the Cambridge frequency before the source came in view. The Cambridge group, with a far less sensitive receiver, had been observing at the even lower frequencies near 100 megahertz. And so, before the next observing opportunity came around the following day, we went up to the platform to hook up a lower-frequency feed. We were well rewarded for the effort, too, because as soon as we pointed the telescope in the right position, we saw it and we saw it big. The source really was pulsating, banging the chart recorder pen off-scale every 1.3 seconds.

These pulses were certainly not sporadic terrestrial interference. They were extraterrestrial, extraordinary, and extravagant in their energy.

I dropped everything to study these strange new pulsating radio sources. It was all so ironic. Here we'd been so dismayed that our telescope was limited to long-wavelength, low-frequency observations, and now the hottest objects in the universe were broadcasting on frequencies even *lower* than our feeds could handle.*

We needed new feeds right away. There was no time to write proposals and wait for funding from the National Science Foundation (NSF) or NASA. I walked into the Sears, Roebuck store in

---

* A further irony was the fact that the pulsars had been discovered accidentally by a graduate student at Cambridge, Jocelyn Bell, while doing interplanetary scintillations for her doctoral thesis. The pulsed signals showed up on her chart recorders because the Cambridge telescope was not steerable, and observed whatever passed through its beam. If Arecibo had been built according to the original plan, without any steering capability, pulsars probably would have been detected many years earlier in Puerto Rico instead of England. Later, in 1974, Bell's professor, Anthony Hewish, who had supervised her project and helped her interpret and announce her findings to the scientific community, was awarded the Nobel prize in Physics for the pulsar discovery. Bell, who now uses her married name, Burnell, has become an X-ray astronomer. She doesn't think it amiss that she didn't share in the prize, since she was just a student at the time, but I and most others disagree. She deserved it.

Arecibo and bought the biggest TV antenna they had with my charge card for about thirty dollars. It was actually a very sophisticated device, and the television frequencies were precisely the ones we wanted. John Sutton carried it up to the platform in the cable car, hooked it on the feed arm, and then we were really in business. Arecibo could observe these objects far better than any other telescope and soon became the prime source of detailed information about them.

Cambridge then released the positions of three other pulsating radio sources they had found, and about ten more were quickly identified by other researchers. One of the sources was out of our range, however, and this drove me to distraction. It was well beyond the swath of sky we could track anywhere along the length of the feed arm. But, this being a time of high excitement and crazy experimentation, I saw that we could watch that source if we somehow managed to stick another feed on one of the support cables leading to the platform. We tried that, and it worked. We couldn't steer that feed, of course, but once a day the Earth's rotation carried it into observing range, and that was good enough. We felt such team enthusiasm in those days that if I had asked people to climb to the tops of the towers and hold feeds in their bare hands, any member of the scientific or technical staff would have volunteered.

My first thought was to observe the shapes of the pulses, to see if they gave any hint of the objects' nature. If the sources were truly pulsating stars, as many people assumed, then each pulse should have the same characteristic shape. Another possibility—that the pulses were caused by a series of periodic explosions—would generate pulses that had abrupt beginnings and gentle ends. But neither of these ideas panned out. Each pulse shape was different from the one before. Each pulsar had a different characteristic pulse shape, too, as only Arecibo could show. And although pulsar pulses were abrupt, they surely didn't indicate explosions.

I did not rule out the possibility that the pulses were intelligent signals. The Cambridge group had already discounted that idea, however, on the grounds that the signals were so strong and spread out over such a broad band of frequencies that no civilization could have squandered the energy to power such a transmission. And there were just too many pulsating sources for all of them to be the work of "little green men."

These negative arguments didn't hold much water for me. I

thought the signals could well be natural, broad-band sources that were somehow turned on and off thanks to intelligent intervention. Indeed, there were numerous references to the "Morse code" nature of the signals, and several astronomers called the pulsating radio sources "Morse code stars" or "LGMs" (for Little Green Men).

I made long recordings of the pulse intensities, on tape and on chart paper, and then sat scrutinizing the charts, trying to discern signal patterns in them. I stared at them for hours at a time, but even in my eagerness to find an alien message, I never saw any evidence to make me think these tracings were of intelligent origin. Had I known then what I know now, I would have been much more excited about the possibility that the pulses were intelligent signals, for they turned out to be highly polarized, just like the radio waves broadcast from a terrestrial transmitter. At the time, however, the polarization went unrecognized. Nor did we have the sophisticated computer programs needed to analyze the pulses for patterns, possibly of intelligent origin, that might elude a human observer. The pulses seemed to be a purely natural phenomenon, though the astronomical community was hard-pressed to account for them with a solid theory or model.

Meanwhile, I'd gotten tired of trying to get my mouth around the term "rapidly pulsating radio sources." In a paper I wrote for *Science* with two of my graduate students, Hal Craft and John Comella, I coined a shorthand term—"pulsars"—and the name stuck. We could now talk about them with ease, even as we struggled to determine what they were.

Speculation heaped on speculation as flurries of hastily called scientific meetings brought astronomers together to discuss the pulsars. At one such meeting, Tom Gold proposed a shocking partial explanation that eventually turned out to be true. He said the pulsar was a rapidly spinning star with all of its radiation coming out in a single beam, like a lighthouse beacon. Thus the star didn't really pulsate, but whipped its powerful beam around and around every second or so, which accounted for the pulses of signals we'd been observing.

The rest of the explanation came from an earlier theory outlined at Cornell by Franco Pacini, a visiting Italian astronomer from the Frascati Observatory near Rome. Fully a year before the pulsars were discovered, Pacini had thought about what happens when a massive star explodes as a supernova: the outside shell of the star is blown into space, but the explosion compresses the stellar core to an incredibly dense ball of matter called a neutron star.* These neutron stars spin very rapidly and possess strong magnetic fields because of the compression they have undergone. Pacini recognized that these powerful spinning magnets would emit copious amounts of electromagnetic radiation. The only thing Pacini hadn't predicted was that the radiation would come out in sharp pulses. That was the surprising part, and that, perhaps, was why nobody jumped on Pacini's work right away as the explanation for the pulsars. But when Gold suggested that the pulses were the rotating beacons of neutron stars, things started falling into place.

All right, then. If these were neutron stars, then they were the remnants of supernovas, and we could find new pulsars by hunting among known supernova remnants, such as the Crab Nebula. Several investigators started searching there, but with no immediate success. Months went by before observers at Green Bank reported pulses from the Crab Nebula, but these came widely spaced—every five minutes or so—not at all like the rest of the pulsars, which had periods of about one second.

Astronomers were in roughly two camps now—those who believed the pulsars to be spinning stars, and those who clung to the idea that they were pulsating objects. But there was a way to determine who was right.

If these were pulsating objects, they would get denser over time as they lost energy, and that would make them pulse even *more* rapidly. If they were spinning objects, they would slow down eventually, the way a spinning top does when it loses energy, and then they would pulsate *less* rapidly. With the two prime theories predicting opposite effects, all we had to do was observe a change in one pulsar's period and we would have our answer.

The problem was, pulsars didn't seem to be changing their periods one way or the other. They were so regular that you could observe one, then predict when its pulses would arrive three or four months later. Amazingly, such predictions were accurate to within thousandths of a second.

We needed a rapidly changing pulsar. And we finally found one.

---

* Neutron stars were first suggested by Walter Baade and Fritz Zwicky of Caltech in the 1930s. The quantitative theory that made them credible objects was carried out in 1939 by J. Robert Oppenheimer of Manhattan Project fame, and by Lev Landau in the Soviet Union.

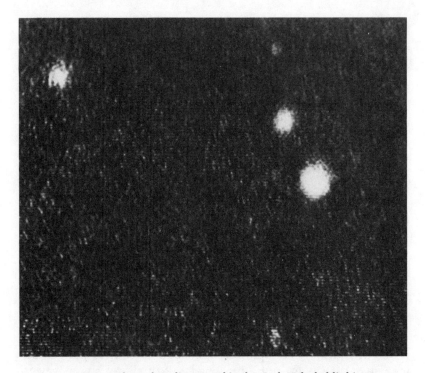

FIGURE 4.1. The pulsar discovered in the Crab Nebula blinking on and off thirty times per second. Now you see it.

David Richards, a graduate student at Arecibo, chose to observe the Crab Nebula pulsar because of the way it had frustrated the people at Green Bank. They couldn't make any sense of its long, irregular pulse period. With the greater sensitivity of the Arecibo telescope for such work, Richards found that there was a regular, rapid rate of pulsation, but that every five minutes, the expected pulse would come with an enormous added burst of energy. The Green Bank group had been picking up only these giant bursts, and missing the many smaller ones in between. And there were many indeed. The neutron star in the Crab Nebula turned out to be not the slowest but the fastest pulsar yet on record. It pulsed *thirty times every second*. The speed was apparently due to the youth of the neutron star. The supernova in the Crab Nebula is known from Chinese celestial observations to have exploded in the year 1054. It was spinning fast because it had just started spinning scarcely a thousand years previously.

Now you don't. (Lick Observatory Photographs)

In February 1969, a full year after the first pulsar announcement appeared, Richards discovered the first change in a pulsar's pulse period. By closely observing the source in the Crab Nebula, he showed that the pulse rate was slowing down by thirty-six billionths of a second a day. That was an infinitesimal change, but enough to establish the fact that the pulses were coming more slowly all the time and thus that a pulsar was a spinning neutron star.

The youth of the pulsar in the Crab Nebula accounted for its great speed, and also for the speed at which its rotation rate was changing. As a top spins, it slows relatively quickly, but then, the slower it spins, the more slowly it slows down. Pulsars behave in the same way.

The Crab Nebula pulsar remains to this day the only one that alternates its ordinary pulses with giant pulses that are about one thousand times more powerful. In fact, those giant pulses are among the brightest radio signals we have found in the universe. They are so strong that you can see them on your television set with an ordinary household antenna. Just turn to a channel that has no program and stare at the screen. Every five minutes you'll get a lot of snow that covers about one third of the screen. That's coming from the pulsar in the Crab Nebula, about six thousand light-years away.

Some six months into the pulsar excitement, my two-year term as director at Arecibo came to an end. I suppose I could have asked to stay longer, given the situation, but my family, longing for home, had already gone back to Ithaca. That was the deciding factor in my leaving Arecibo in 1968. I continued to supervise graduate students writing their dissertations on pulsars, however, and to find myself called back to Puerto Rico to do everything from making observations to settling labor disputes among the employees. This caused my Spanish to improve markedly, instead of fading with disuse, as I had expected. I also got many chances to sleep in the visiting scientists' quarters; in fact, I made enough trips to the observatory to sleep in every room of both the old and the new quarters at least twice, maybe three times. And one night, awakened by a terrible earthquake, I sat up in my bouncing bed, thinking, "Am I about to hear the sound of a six-hundred-ton steel platform crashing to the ground? I wonder what that sounds like!" But I never found out, and I hope I never do.

In 1969, the NSF took over the support of the observatory, making it a national center, though it continued to be operated by Cornell. And in 1971, when its name was changed from the Arecibo Ionospheric Observatory to the National Astronomy and Ionosphere Center, I became director of the center as a whole. There were many more administrative headaches: running a facility from afar, heading a staff that stretched from Ithaca to Puerto Rico, and traveling regularly to Washington for meetings. But I was in a stronger position than ever to press for the continued upgrading of the telescope itself. And I could introduce the concept of searching for extraterrestrial intelligence to scientists and government officials who made funding decisions.

My three sons were especially pleased with the move, as they needed to experience the much richer educational and cultural environment in the college towns and nearby big cities. From Ithaca, Paul went on to become a very successful photographer in

Boston, Stephen joined the Nashville Symphony as a cellist, and Richard pursued his musical career in San Francisco.

As a coda to my time in Puerto Rico, I learned that the Hamilton Watch Company had taken the name Pulsar for the first digital wristwatch. This was a very expensive clock without hands, costing about a thousand dollars, with glowing red numbers that appeared at the push of a button. You needed two hands to tell time on it, however—one to wear the watch and another to push the button. Still, it surely would have been nice to have a Pulsar, particularly because it was my namesake.

Not having a thousand dollars to spare, I wrote to the Hamilton Watch Company, explaining that the name Pulsar was copyrighted in my *Science* paper, and I therefore felt I was owed some kind of royalty or recompense. I would gladly have settled for a watch. But the next week's mail brought a not-so-cordial reply from the company's attorney, on letterhead stationery that listed the names of sixty-five lawyers. The attorney pointed out that as many as six products already existed bearing the name Pulsar, including a chain saw and a device for cleaning teeth. Copyrights didn't apply to trade names, he said. I should go buy a watch if I wanted one.

▲
▲
▲

CHAPTER 5

Counterintelligence

The Earth is the cradle of mankind, but one does not
live in the cradle forever.

—KONSTANTIN TSIOLKOVSKY

Being an optimist, I support a persistent search for
beacon signals of extraterrestrial civilizations.

—ANDREI D. SAKHAROV

All through the Cold War years of the 1960s, when the idea of *glasnost* was far more improbable than the prospect of interstellar communication, scientists in the Soviet Union took up the search for extraterrestrial life. They drew inspiration from English and American scientific literature, especially the Cocconi-Morrison paper in *Nature*, Freeman Dyson's report in *Science*, and my accounts of Project Ozma in *Physics Today* and *Sky and Telescope*. But unlike us, Soviet scientists at big institutions had money to spend on search efforts, and met no opposition when they opted to build special equipment or staff projects devoted to detecting alien civilizations.

The early Soviet radio telescopes consisted of wire antennas on posts, called dipole antennas, like those built at Cambridge, England. They were far less sensitive than the steerable-dish antenna Grote Reber set up in his backyard and that typified the early instruments at Harvard, Cornell, and Green Bank. Yet even a primitive radio telescope confers on astronomers an ability to call out to the stars, and listen to them from afar for signals of intelligent life.

In the Soviet Union, the idea of such searching was actually embraced more readily and enthusiastically than in the United States. And while I wish we American astronomers had enjoyed a warmer reception on this account, I believe that the Soviet acceptance was not entirely benign. Indeed, it had little to do, in my opinion, with wide regard for the search enterprise itself, but was more a reflection of the state of Soviet science in general, particularly the lack of peer review. There was also a political motive behind the governmental support for these activities: The authorities correctly perceived the search enterprise as an area where Soviets could compete with and possibly excel over American efforts.

In the United States, scientists have traditionally and routinely solicited the skeptical criticism of other knowledgeable researchers—peers in their field. Soviet scientists were insulated from other opinions, however, and did not compete for research funds. Every institution more or less went its own way. Each year, it received the same funding as the year before, and the senior people within the institution decided how to allocate those funds. No one questioned these judgments, nor did one institution criticize another. And so, if a highly placed scientist decided, for example, to mount a search for intelligent signals from elsewhere in the Galaxy, he could do so—even if no one at his institution was really capable of building the kind of equipment required. Later in the course of the work, if that scientist should want to discuss his methodology or his findings with another person working toward the same goal, he might need to take certain risks, and even leave the country periodically to make contact with a wider circle of colleagues.

The inherent failings in Soviet science, coupled with the devoted persistence of a few extremely talented Soviet individuals, forged close ties between scientists from the United States and the Soviet Union in the search for extraterrestrial intelligence—ties that persist to this day and project into the future.

Iosif Shklovsky, a brilliant astrophysicist from the Ukraine, spearheaded the Soviet interest in life in space. Not only did Shklovsky brim over with important insights in radio astronomy, he also possessed the kind of humanity and humor that attracted and held devoted students. He himself had dropped out of high school in poverty to spend his teen years as a railroad construction worker in Siberia. But then, by chance, he read a magazine article about the discovery of the neutron. The idea that much of the natural world lay still unexplored—that unexpected entities could emerge to surprise us—took hold of his imagination. He vowed to study physics, educated himself to enter a university, and proceeded all the way up to an advanced degree from the Shternberg Astronomical Institute in Moscow.

Shklovsky first distinguished himself in the 1940s by predicting the existence of the hydrogen 21-centimeter line—the line that was later to play such a central role in the design of extraterrestrial searches. It is the bright line that shows up in the radio region of the electromagnetic spectrum as the natural emission of neutral hydrogen atoms. Shklovsky also correctly predicted the 18-centimeter line of the hydroxyl (OH) radical, which forms the other boundary of the "waterhole," in the frequency range where astronomers have since been searching for extraterrestrial life.

At the time of these predictions, however, Shklovsky was not yet thinking of aliens. He looked to the hydrogen line for its fundamental significance in astronomy, since hydrogen is the chief component of stars and, for that matter, the universe as a whole. But Shklovsky lacked the equipment to test his ideas. The telescopes he used simply weren't good enough. It was left to a wild young American I knew at Harvard, Harold "Doc" Ewen, to make the first observation of the 21-centimeter line, in 1952. Ewen wrote his doctoral dissertation on the discovery, and took great pride in the fact that his thesis was the shortest one—only twelve pages—in the history of the Harvard physics department.*

By 1956, the Soviets had their first dish-type radio telescope, in the Crimea, where Shklovsky undertook his own detailed observations of the 21-centimeter line in the Milky Way and other galaxies.

---

* A Dutch astronomer named Hendrik Van de Hulst independently predicted the hydrogen line at the same time Shklovsky did, during World War II, but neither one knew of the other's work because of the wartime barriers to communication. Soon after the war, Van de Hulst and his colleagues began building a radio receiver in the Netherlands that surely would have detected the line—beating Ewen to the discovery—but the equipment caught fire and burned while still under construction.

The *Nature* paper by Cocconi and Morrison, which proposed searching the 21-centimeter line for signs of intelligent life in the universe, arrived late in the Soviet Union—months after the September 1959 publication date. Reading it at last, Shklovsky leaped at the portentous new significance in the hydrogen line. Not only would it reveal basic truths about the stars, but also it could be the channel of communication for interstellar cultural exchange. Suddenly the chance that an unusual record taken at the observatory might turn out to be an intelligent signal cast new excitement over all findings in the hydrogen-line region. At leisure on the Crimean beach with his students, Shklovsky started endless discussions about the possible nature of extraterrestrial life.

I first met Shklovsky in 1960 at a meeting of the International Astronomical Union (IAU) in Moscow. I took an instant liking to him. It was impossible not to like him—impossible not to be won over by his warmth and optimism. I thought he'd make a great maître d'. He was already a major figure in radio astronomy, not only for his prediction of the 21-centimeter line but also for having deduced the true nature of cosmic radio emissions. Astronomers at first thought such emissions were simply part of the normal radiation emitted by hot objects in space. But Shklovsky suggested that certain cosmic radio emissions were results of so-called synchrotron radiation.* In space, Shklovsky hypothesized, powerful magnetic fields and other processes in the vicinity of celestial objects would boost charged particles to tremendous energies, making them generate bursts of synchrotron radiation in a broad band of radio and optical frequencies.

On the matter of synchrotron radiation, too, just as with the 21-centimeter line, Shklovsky was thwarted by inadequate telescopes in his attempts to test his own theory. He knew precisely which observation would serve as a good test, however, and that was to measure the polarization of the emissions from the supernova remnant in the Crab Nebula. If supernova radiation was indeed synchrotron radiation, then the emissions would be highly polarized linearly, just like the radiation observed at synchrotrons.

---

* A synchrotron is a machine that makes charged particles circulate in a magnetic field inside an evacuated, doughnut-shaped chamber. As the particles attain higher and higher energies, their mass begins to increase, in accordance with Einstein's theory of relativity, and they may give off a blue-white light, which is called synchrotron radiation.

Shklovsky tried to measure the polarization at an optical observatory in the Caucasus, but the telescope was too small and of too poor a quality to produce a dramatic result. Other observers outside the Soviet Union, particularly at the famous 200-inch telescope on Mount Palomar, then took up his investigation and showed that he was right. Today we recognize that quasars, radio galaxies, and supernova remnants—the brightest sources radio astronomers observe—are all strong emitters of synchrotron radiation. Star-forming regions, on the other hand, are thermal emitters that generate radio waves almost always by heat alone.

I remember talking to Shklovsky about his heroic predictions during a social hour at the IAU meeting. He spoke English fairly well, and I had studied Russian in college, so between us we had the necessary vocabulary for informal discussion. We said not a word about extraterrestrial intelligence, not because of a language problem, but because each was ignorant of the other's interest. Neither of us had yet come out publicly as a believer. Even though my head was full of Project Ozma plans at that time, I didn't mention them. Nor did Shklovsky tell me that he had seen the Morrison-Cocconi paper, and was so fired up by it that he was already planning to write a popular book on the subject.

Shklovsky's chance came along very soon. The Soviet Academy of Sciences invited him to help commemorate *Sputnik I*'s fifth birthday in 1962 by writing on some scientific subject of general interest. Shklovsky's book—called *Universe, Life, Intelligence*—explored his new hope for finding life in space and explained how the science of radio astronomy made such a search possible. Shklovsky pointed out that other civilizations might already know about life on Earth, because we were signaling our presence in the universe with our television broadcasts. These passed freely to the stars, he said. Earth, as the source of these television beacons, would shine as brightly as the Sun on certain radio frequencies, and Earth's radiance would call alien attention to our civilization. This extraordinary idea, which would have been labeled science fiction in the United States, gained instantaneous acceptance in the Soviet Union because of Shklovsky's brilliant reputation as a scientist. If he said it, it must be so.

Very few people outside the Soviet Union were even aware of the book, but Carl Sagan had heard of it even before publication, as he had been in correspondence with Shklovsky on the question of interstellar spaceflight. Carl was determined to get an English translation published in the United States. This took several years of transatlantic collaboration in a strained political climate. Indeed, as Shklovsky once wrote to Sagan: "The probability of our meeting is likely to be smaller than the probability of a visit to the Earth by an extraterrestrial cosmonaut." Nevertheless, they did complete their joint project, *Intelligent Life in the Universe*, which was published in 1966, containing as much new material by Carl as original text by Shklovsky. Their book was widely circulated and well known in the States.

Shklovsky was wrong, by the way, about the low probability of his ever being allowed to travel outside the Soviet Union. I remember a jolly walk with him on the first day of a meeting in Brighton, England. As though he had lived there all his life, he somehow knew how to lead us directly to his prime goal: a shoe store. He stood in front of the window and exulted at the shoes he saw; he knew they would be of a quality commensurate with their appearance, that he could buy them, and to him all was right with the world. On a subsequent trip to Berkeley, his major purchases were a package of playing cards with dirty pictures on them and a campaign button that said "Pray For Sex." Of the cards, he explained matter-of-factly, "I can give one card as a gift to each of the scientists at my Institute." He took a kind of fiendish pleasure in the button: "In your country, this slogan is offensive for one reason. In my country, two reasons."

During one U.S. visit, Shklovsky's colleagues were astounded when he showed up at a restaurant without enough money to pay for his own lunch. They were sure he was wealthy as a result of his American publishing success. Shklovsky told them, however, that since the Soviet Union had not signed the international copyright agreement, the American publishers owed him nothing and had in fact paid him nothing. He was a published pauper. While it's true that the Soviet Union had failed to sign the copyright agreement, Carl would not hear of Shklovsky's being cheated out of his share of the royalties. He appealed to the publisher, insisting on payment for Shklovsky, and won the argument. Shklovsky received a handsome check as a result, but never cashed it, apparently fearing trouble with the secret police force known as the KGB.

Shklovsky never did any searching for extraterrestrial life himself, but he put other people up to it. He was the driver of the movement. He kept it alive, popularly and scientifically, while he turned his own research efforts to other problems in radio astronomy, from solar physics to the variable flux of radio emissions from distant celestial objects.

It was Shklovsky's star pupil at the Shternberg Astronomical Institute, Nikolai Kardashev, who mounted the first Soviet search for extraterrestrial intelligence, in 1963. Kardashev also called the first all-union meeting of scientists interested in extraterrestrial civilizations—a sort of Soviet Order of the Dolphin—at the Byurakan Astrophysical Observatory in Armenia in 1964.

Kardashev is a disturbingly youthful-looking man of about my age, who got interested in astronomy when he was five years old because his mother took him to the Moscow Planetarium. There, not only were the stars and planets simulated, but also actors dramatized moments in the lives of Galileo, Copernicus, and other heroes, making the planetarium show a theatrical event. This may have been the feature that attracted Mme. Kardashev to the planetarium in the first place, since her grasp of astronomy wasn't all that great: When young Nikolai asked her how many points were on the stars in the sky, compared with the five-pointed stars of the Soviet flag, she answered, "Five also." Despite this red herring, Kardashev went on to discover the truth for himself, and now serves as director of the Astro Space Center of the P. N. Lebedev Physical Institute of the Academy of Sciences in Moscow, Russia's most prestigious physics research establishment.

In 1964, Kardashev greatly stimulated us with his published predictions of supercivilizations billions of years ahead of us in their technology. One thing they might be able to do, he proposed, would be to harness *all* the energy radiated by their sun. We, at our comparatively primitive stage of evolution, take only what shines on our planet—and we don't make efficient use of even a tiny fraction of that.

Truly advanced civilizations, Kardashev imagined, wouldn't stop at their sun; they'd figure out ways to harness the energy output of their entire home galaxy—perhaps by engineering a gigantic structure to surround the galactic core and tap its power. Kardashev classified extraterrestrial civilizations into three types according to their wealth in energy. The Type I aliens, more or less our technological equals, would be just sophisticated enough to capture and utilize the energy resources of their home planet. The more advanced Type II civilizations could control and utilize the entire power output of their home star, while a Type III civilization would be using all the stars in its galaxy as a powerhouse.

If supercivilizations had the technology to wield the energy of a whole galaxy, Kardashev reasoned, we could find them fairly easily. We wouldn't even have to search for intelligent radio signals, but simply hunt for signs of their handiwork. We might detect the heat radiating from their enormous energy contraptions, for example, by searching in the infrared region of the electromagnetic spectrum. Here Kardashev agreed with Dyson about the wisdom of tracking aliens along the trail made by their waste heat. In fact, Kardashev went beyond Dyson in his enthusiasm for the infrared, because he felt that intentional signals might also be broadcast and detected in this region. In his first search, however, he directed his efforts at the low-frequency radio wavelengths of the electromagnetic spectrum.

As I mentioned earlier, the antennas Kardashev used in this initial search were of poor quality, but he created a network of them clear across the Soviet Union. He placed five antennas at widely spaced locations, all the way from Vladivostok, on the Sea of Japan, to Murmansk, near the Finnish border. By listening simultaneously over an area spanning some five thousand miles, Kardashev had a ready means for ruling out Earth interference: Any signal received at just one or two of the ground-based stations was probably local interference; anything received by all five at once had to be of extraterrestrial origin. This was a very important part of Kardashev's design, because his antennas listened at such low frequencies that they picked up lots of interference and set off a fair number of false alarms. Good, strong extraterrestrial signals came in, too, though most of these turned out to be natural radio emissions from the Sun. Nothing in Kardashev's search data remotely resembled an intelligent signal.

Then, in 1965, while Kardashev was investigating cosmic radio sources at the Crimea Deep Space Station with his colleague Evgeny Sholomitsky, a suspicious signal did arrive.

Decidedly extraterrestrial in origin, the signal proved to be changing its intensity with time. Over a period of months, as Kardashev and Sholomitsky watched, it slowly increased and decreased the strength of its radio emissions. The signal had no other earmarks of intelligence. In fact, it was broad-band instead of narrow-band, but its slowly changing nature was unprecedented in radio astronomy, and made the signal look as though it were trying to call attention to itself. What's more, it was powerful enough to make the astronomers think that it might be the broadcast of a Type III civilization dwelling near the radio source known as CTA-102.*

The Shternberg Institute readily convened a press conference, and Sholomitsky announced with happy excitement to the world at large that he and Kardashev had detected signals from an alien civilization in space. I later learned from Shklovsky that the entire courtyard of the institute was crammed with more than one hundred luxurious foreign cars driven by the leading correspondents in Moscow. Although Shklovsky himself had been reticent to publicize the finding without rigorous verification, the others had prevailed on him, and the news went out with great fanfare. Then Shklovsky joined in the hoopla—an uncharacteristic move that embarrassed him ever after.

Among the immediate reactions the Soviet astronomers received were one telegram from me, congratulating them and requesting more information, and another from scientists at Caltech, containing this sobering detail: The varying radio signal touted at the press conference was definitely not a beacon from extraterrestrials. Similar optical variations had recently been observed with the big Palomar telescope. The source was undeniably a strange galaxy known as a quasar, and its "signal" the result of changes in the radio-emitting material at its core.

Quasars, or quasi-stellar objects, are mysterious entities that appear to telescopes as stars but are in fact turbulent galaxies from whose cores fantastic amounts of energy are released. Quasars also appear to be receding from us at great speed, with their spectra Doppler-shifted far into the red by the motion.†

---

* Like most celestial objects, CTA-102 has a catalog number for a name. The CTA stands for Caltech Catalog A—a compilation of small but bright cosmic radio sources, called near-point sources, published by the California Institute of Technology; the 102 marks it as the 102nd such object observed by Caltech astronomers.

† We think the quasar's prodigious energy is a consequence of whole stars being gobbled up by a giant black hole at the heart of the galaxy. A black hole is a collapsed massive star so incredibly dense that nothing, not even light, can escape its gravitational pull. New material being sucked into a black hole, however, is accelerated to high speeds in a vortex of infalling debris, where it collides with all the other matter being swallowed. These accelerations and collisions on the way to annihilation are the sources of the heat and energy around the black hole. As soon as objects enter the black hole, of course, all traces of them disappear.

Thus the signal that looked intelligent turned out to have a natural explanation after all: the erratic behavior of a strange, distant radio source.

There was tremendous embarrassment in Moscow. I sympathized with my colleagues there, and I learned a lesson I will never forget about the folly of rushing to release news of such a discovery. Still, in Sholomitsky's defense, he made an important and surprising contribution with his discovery that the radio emissions of quasars could vary. Such variable emissions from quasars have since become a big area of study in astronomy, but they were unknown at that time.

The hasty reporting of the "aliens" and the rapid rejection of the Soviet claim by Caltech did not, I'm pleased to say, dampen Kardashev's enthusiasm for search activities. The fanfare even attracted some new supporters, at least on this side of the world. A popular American rock group called the Byrds recorded a song about the quasar that became a semihit. Roger McGuinn, who was the Byrds' lead guitarist and something of an astronomy buff, worked on the music and lyrics:

> CTA-102, we are here, receiving you.
> Signals tell us that you're there.
> We can hear you loud and clear
> With our radio telescopes.
> Science tells us that there's hope
> Life on other planets may exist.

There was some gibberish in the middle, as though the recording were being played backward. That was supposed to be the extraterrestrials, or at least that's how it sounded to me. I met McGuinn not long after the CTA-102 affair. He showed up at a talk I gave about pulsars at the Aerospace Corporation, a federal think tank in Los Angeles. (To the best of my knowledge he never wrote a song about pulsars.) I remember remarking to myself how McGuinn, with his long hair and original clothing style, stood out in that roomful of conservative engineers. Later that night, though, he took me to a Hollywood party, where I saw Jane Fonda wearing a fishnet nondress, and so many other movie stars in wild garb that my business suit and tie looked nothing short of weird. It was the first and only time in my life that I felt like an extraterrestrial.

My next encounter with Soviet search activities came in Sydney,

Australia, in 1973, at another meeting of the IAU. Yury Pariisky, who was then director of radio telescope operations at the Pulkova Observatory in Leningrad, approached Carl Sagan and me quietly between sessions to introduce himself and suggest we take a walk together. Pariisky looked like Bob Newhart, but bald, and spoke English very well. As the three of us headed down the street together, past a park and a movie theater playing *Last Tango in Paris*, Pariisky said he'd detected extraterrestrial signals that seemed to be of intelligent origin.

"They are very broad-band, like noise," he said. "They come in for a few hours, then they disappear. Next day, same thing. *Next* day, same thing again. We are watching this now for several months." Pariisky didn't have an insensitive wire antenna like the ones in Kardashev's network. He was using the big 60-foot radio telescope in the Crimea. Pariisky, a former student of Shklovsky, was searching American-style, with a big dish. I gave him credit for that, although I doubted he'd found the real thing.

Pariisky himself was cautious about the signals and puzzled by their behavior. They were encoded in a peculiar and provocative way: 1, 2, 7, and 9 pulses. Pariisky was not about to go public with the news and set himself up for another fiasco like CTA-102. He hadn't dared write to Carl Sagan or me for consultation, because it was dangerous in those days for a Soviet scientist to divulge research data to an American through the mail, as censors read all the letters. But Pariisky sensed, as we did, that our common goal transcended questions of national identity, and he seized the Sydney opportunity to share his findings.

"The daily pattern of repetition troubles me," I said after some minutes' thought. "You wouldn't expect that kind of attention from aliens." The signals were more likely to be coming from one of the artificial satellites that were taking up residence in near-Earth orbit. Pariisky told us he had already asked Soviet military authorities whether he might be picking up a Soviet or American satellite. They had said, "No." Then Carl told Pariisky he was crazy to believe anything Soviet military authorities said about classified Soviet satellites, much less classified American satellites.

Over the next several weeks, Carl was able to confirm the existence of a gigantic American reconnaissance satellite called *Big Bird*. Its orbital period exactly matched the pattern of signal appearance and disappearance Pariisky was describing. *Big Bird* did not represent extraterrestrial intelligence, but it was in the business of intelligence-*gathering* from an extraterrestrial vantage point. It transmitted its information over a tremendous range of frequencies at once, so as to guard against attempts to jam its signal. This was why Pariisky's recordings of *Big Bird* transmissions sounded like broad-band noise. He had suspected, correctly, that buried in the noise was a cleverly encoded message. But Pariisky, Carl, and I were at an equal disadvantage in deciphering this message, which was the brainchild of American cryptographers.

Having helped solve Pariisky's immediate puzzle, Carl and I began to worry about its implications. *Big Bird*'s transmissions appeared noiselike because they covered many frequencies. Maybe there were other situations or conditions that would make an intelligent signal masquerade as noise. Suppose, for example, that information could be very densely packed for efficient transmitting. Maximum-efficiency encoding might also look like noise, and then how would we recognize the signal as intelligent? If extraterrestrials were really trying to attract our attention, they might well design their signals for easy detection and decoding by giving the signals all the earmarks of intelligence—very narrow bandwidth, with slow modulation, high polarization, and regular repetition. Those are the features that would readily distinguish an intelligent signal from one that was naturally generated. A signaling society should make its call clearly artificial. We continue to hope that they will help us in this way, particularly with any special signals designed to attract newcomers.

The true hope of all search efforts, however, hinges on being able to detect *unintentional* signals from extraterrestrials, and not just waiting for them to send us a message. Surely there must be more signals of this kind than signals intended for the benefit of other worlds. We would hope to eavesdrop on escaped television broadcasts, for example, satellite communications, operating instructions beamed to spacecraft, and high-level communiqués between space stations and their home planets. We might even tune in to radio information exchanges between two or more very advanced civilizations already in contact with each other. These signals, too, should look intelligent—that is, they should be regular in some regard, and thereby distinguish themselves from the background noise of the universe. But if even intelligent signals came to resemble noise when their sophisticated information content was highly compressed, how would we single them out? How would we keep them from passing right by us without our recognizing them? We had to prepare for the fact that intelligent signals might not stand out in stark contrast to random noise, but admit only the subtlest distinctions.

Serious searching, I concluded, was going to require technological advances on several fronts. In addition to the multichannel signal processors, we would one day rely on sophisticated computers that could ferret out noiselike signals that really were of intelligent design.

Meanwhile, the Soviets opted to continue the search with existing equipment. In 1968 Vasevolod Troitsky used the 45-foot telescope at the Radio Physics Institute in Gorky (now Nizhni Novgorod) to search for intelligent signals from the twelve nearest stars. It was a short-lived attempt, spanning just a few nights' observing, but it boasted twenty-five channels, compared to Ozma's one.

Troitsky is a forbidding-looking but extremely affable man whose wife and children are also radio astronomers. The institute where he and his wife work is one of the major research centers in Russia. Gorky itself had been, under the Soviet regime, a forbidden city—completely classified. No Westerners had ever been there. The radio science institute was said to have a staff of four thousand and to play a key role in the development of military radar and communications systems. An installation of comparable size in the United States would be the Jet Propulsion Laboratory in Pasadena, or the NASA Ames Research Center at Moffett Field, California.

Troitsky set up his own network of stations for detecting extraterrestrial intelligence in 1969. It was even bigger than Kardashev's, though independent of it, and just as insensitive, with no energy-collecting area to speak of, because it used dipole antennas made out of wires. Troitsky found no alien civilizations with this equipment, although he did detect sporadic radio emissions from particles in the Earth's magnetic field.

In these searches the Soviets were using an entirely different strategy from ours. They did not make any educated guesses about which frequencies might make the most sense as alien broadcast bands. Instead they concluded that the extraterrestrials would realize the inherent difficulty in selecting a particular frequency, and transmit a signal that could be picked up on *any* frequency. A very short burst or pulse-type signal would fill this bill, because the transmission of such a short pulse causes radio power to appear over a very broad range of frequencies. Following this hypothesis about the thinking of extraterrestrials, the Soviets traditionally searched for pulses with very broad-band receivers; Americans, meanwhile, have hunted continuous-wave signals with narrow-band receivers. These are almost institutionalized national differences in search strategy. Both make sense, and both are comparably challenging in equipment design and dedication.*

Although Kardashev conducted several searches for pulsed signals, he later came up with his own "magic" frequency, the positronium line, at a wavelength of 1.5 millimeters and a very high frequency of 203,385 megahertz. (The hydrogen line, in comparison, is 1420 megahertz.) Kardashev deemed the positronium line important as a cosmic signpost because at this frequency we detect the peak radiation from the remnants of the big bang. Kardashev's magic frequency, however, cannot penetrate the Earth's atmosphere.

Other Soviet scientists ventured out of the range of radio wavelengths altogether, opting to look for pulses of visible light. One of the project scientists still pursuing this optical search is Gregory Beskin, who devotes his spare time to directing and acting in Russian productions of Shakespearean plays. Beskin claims that the Bard himself inspired the optical search with this classic line from *Romeo and Juliet:* "But, soft! What light through yonder window breaks? It is the east, and Juliet is the sun!" Americans have never favored optical searches, however, because it takes one million times as much energy to communicate at optical wavelengths as compared to radio wavelengths.

In the midst of all this Soviet search activity, Kardashev and Carl Sagan cooked up the first international meeting on extraterrestrial communication, which was held at the Byurakan Astrophysical Observatory in Soviet Armenia, in September 1971. It picked up where the Green Bank meeting ten years earlier had left off, but lasted a whole week, with many more participants and some strong new blood. In addition to Carl, Phil Morrison, Barney

---

* There is a flaw in the Soviet hypothesis, pointed out long ago by Barney Oliver. When the aliens' short pulses encounter electrons in interstellar gas clouds in space, they will be slowed down. Electrons slow the speed of light (or any electromagnetic radiation), but not uniformly so. They slow the lower frequencies more than the high ones. As a result, a radio pulse will arrive at different times on different frequencies, making it much harder to detect.

Oliver, and myself, we had Francis Crick, who had worked with James Watson to decode the DNA molecule; David Hubel, who in 1981 would win the Nobel prize in Physiology or Medicine for understanding how the process of vision works; Marvin Minsky, the artificial-intelligence genius from MIT; Leslie Orgel, the biochemist known for his experiments to trace the origins of the genetic code; and Charles Townes, who had shared the 1964 Nobel prize in Physics with two Soviets for the invention of lasers and masers. Minsky brought along toy rockets and Frisbees, which were a revelation to the Soviets. Minsky himself was a revelation to me, because he was in constant motion—a human perpetual-motion machine. No one at the conference ever saw him sleep.

The Soviet contingent included Shklovsky, Kardashev, and Troitsky, of course, with some thirty of their colleagues. (A full list of the participants appears in Appendix A.) Carl co-chaired the meeting with Viktor Ambartsumyan, president of the Armenian Academy of Sciences, director of the Byurakan Observatory, and a real political climber who had achieved membership in the Supreme Soviet. He was also Armenia's most eminent citizen— a super-Armenian chauvinist who really looked down on many of the other astronomers at the meeting as "dumb Russians." He didn't say so out loud in their presence, of course, because he certainly knew how to comport himself diplomatically, but he couldn't avoid insinuating as much by his attitude. Our American contingent immediately dubbed Ambartsumyan "Smokey the Bear" because of his uncanny resemblance to that character, although, naturally, we didn't say so out loud in his presence. (I have since learned that Shklovsky once poked fun at Ambartsumyan by calling him "Ursa Major," which is the Latin name for the constellation known as the Great Bear, and which contains the Big Dipper. As Shklovsky explained, "There's no logical reason why some constellations are more famous than others.")

George Marx of Hungary and Rudolf Pesek of Czechoslovakia, two more radio astronomers interested in extraterrestrial life, also participated in this truly international forum. Marx was already considered one of the most eminent scientists in Hungary. Pesek was equally prominent in his country, and later became a leader in the International Astronautical Federation (IAF). (After Pesek died in 1988 another space society, the International Academy of Astronautics (IAA), endowed a lectureship in his name, and it was my honor to give the first Rudolf Pesek Memorial Lecture at the 1990 joint IAF and IAA congress in Dresden.)

Unlike the Green Bank meeting, the Byurakan conference included social scientists, too. This was Carl's doing, and it was a great idea. For example, he invited Richard Lee, an anthropologist from the University of Toronto who had lived among the Bushmen of the Kalahari Desert and learned to speak the !Kung language, clicks and all. Lee contributed an informed perspective on contacts between advanced and primitive societies. He also contrived to spend one night sleeping outdoors in the grass beside the observatory dome, so as to awaken to the sight of Mount Ararat in the morning light. During that week in early September, the weather was still warm enough to permit such escapades. The rest of us Americans dutifully boarded the buses and headed for the "luxury" hotel in Erevan, where our hosts put us up. The Soviets stayed in scientists' quarters on the observatory grounds, filling all the available beds.

The attempt to integrate the social with the physical scientists backfired only with regard to historian William McNeill, from the University of Chicago, who became extremely upset by the discussions. He had an impressive reputation as a philosopher and interpreter of history, but he could not seem to comprehend the time scale of the universe. To him, it was as if everything that had ever happened had taken place since the third dynasty of the pharaohs. He would not venture back in time to the billions of prehistoric years available for life and intelligence to evolve, both here and elsewhere, and so could not envision an enormous diversity of civilizations throughout the universe.

Many of the Soviet scientists chose to speak English as a point of honor; they felt that it was better to give a talk in terrible English than to rely on an interpreter and appear to be unschooled in the language of science. Nevertheless, we had an able interpreter, Boris Belitsky, who had been a friend of Shklovsky's from their university days. Belitsky was not only skilled at simultaneous translation but also was a colorful participant who freely interrupted the proceedings to correct speakers' grammar—in either language—and occasionally to make scientific comments as well.

Carl had arranged through the National Academy of Sciences for an American stenotypist, Floy Swanson, to record the entire conference so the proceedings could be published in book form. The result, *Communication with Extraterrestrial Intelligence*, contains not only the delivered papers but also all the discussion they generated, captured by Ms. Swanson. The stenotype machine itself, as I recall, created something of a furor at Moscow customs, and was almost confiscated on the mistaken belief that it could somehow be used in a Xerox machine mode to make copies of documents. This possibility generated near panic among the Soviet authorities.

The meeting excited us because the Soviets were so heavily invested in searching, while we had no such activity going on anywhere in the West at that time. In truth, I must admit our professional jealousies were aroused by the tales of efforts across the Soviet Union and at the big radio telescope in Nançay, France, where several of the Soviet scientists had visiting privileges.

My presentation outlined a new search strategy that I'd been thinking about for a few months. I addressed the question "Where is the most logical place to search the universe for signs of intelligent life?" In Project Ozma, I had searched the nearest Sun-like stars, because such stars were the most likely to have planets, and also because those particular stars, Tau Ceti and Epsilon Eridani, were at the limit of my instrument's range. But radio telescopes had increased significantly in power over the decade of the 1960s, and it was time to reconsider the best targets in light of our new capabilities. I was starting to plan the strategies I would employ in a future search, so that as soon as multichannel signal analyzers came along (and I was sure they would, though I couldn't say when), I would be ready to go ahead.

When I put my question to the group at Byurakan—*Where is the best place to look?*—most people stuck with the already obvious answer, namely, the nearest stars like the Sun. It makes intuitive sense to search there, because nearby civilizations *should* be the easiest to find. The universe, however, is inherently diabolical, and what appears to make sense often turns out to be otherwise.

I pointed out that hardly any of the brightest stars that showed themselves in the night sky were near us. This is because the processes of star formation have produced a huge range in the intrinsic brightness of stars, so that some shine one hundred million times more brightly than others, just by their nature. A very bright object will appear bright even if it's far away, while a faint star is hard to see no matter how near it is.

Of the twenty stars nearest the Earth, only three are bright: Sirius, Procyon, and Alpha Centauri. Most of the others are so faint as to be invisible to the naked eye. For example, our close neighbor, Proxima Centauri, has only one one-hundredth the brightness of the faintest star the naked eye can see. On the other hand, many bright stars that we can recognize without a telescope are in fact very far away. Two examples are Betelgeuse and Rigel, which form the right shoulder and left foot, respectively, in the constellation Orion.

In general in the universe, faint stars are plentiful and bright stars are rare. Indeed, the incidence, or density, of the faintest stars is roughly a million times greater than the density of the brightest stars in any given galaxy.*

Cosmic radio sources follow the same rules. Only a small percentage are bright, and most of the brightest ones are far removed from us in space and time. For example, the brightest radio source of all is Cassiopeia A, a supernova remnant far across the Milky Way. The second-brightest is Cygnus A, which is a radio galaxy near the edge of the known universe.

I wondered if extraterrestrial civilizations followed this pattern, too. It seemed logical to me that there might well be a large number of them to be discovered, but only a few that shone brightly, compared to the nearby typical ones. I felt confident that we could detect alien civilizations even at fantastic distances, provided they had the technology to make themselves appear very bright.

Given this line of reasoning, I told the conference group, we shouldn't design our searches to examine only the *nearest* stars. We should aim for regions of the sky that had the *most* stars, to give us the best chance of detecting the distant—but *bright*—civilizations. An ideal place to point our radio telescopes might be the central plane of the Milky Way, or toward the center of the Galaxy in

---

* Early astronomers classified the stars according to their relative brightness, putting the brightest ones in the "first magnitude" and the faintest that were visible in the "sixth magnitude." This scale is still used today, though greatly expanded. It is a logarithmic scale, on which every five jumps in number corresponds to a hundredfold change in brightness. The lower the magnitude number, the brighter the star, so that a first-magnitude star is one hundred times more brilliant than a star of the sixth magnitude. We must now give *minus* numbers to extremely bright objects in the sky, such as the planet Venus, which is magnitude minus four during its brightest phase. Big telescopes have extended our ability to see stars as faint as the twenty-third magnitude, and the Hubble Space Telescope can discern even twenty-fifth-magnitude stars.

Sagittarius, or beyond the Milky Way to other galaxies, because even at those distances the signals might still be detectable.

"I think Dr. Kardashev's civilization types provide important insights concerning wise search strategies," I concluded, bowing in Kardashev's direction. "Because the right strategy depends on the maximum amount of energy that a civilization can manipulate, and the fraction of civilizations that are radiating truly large amounts of power."

If, as Kardashev's scheme indicated, civilizations represented an enormous range of exotic technologies, then we should indeed look for the rare but intrinsically bright civilizations. But if, as Troitsky suspected, all civilizations tended to be about our age and operate at about our energy level, then we would be better served by looking at the nearest stars and hoping to find neighbors there.

The Soviets, in effect, were already pursuing the "brightest are the most detectable" idea in their search efforts, because Kardashev and Troitsky had used antenna networks that scanned the whole sky, with antennas that could detect only the brightest beacons. Although their antennas were not very good, they were looking far and wide enough to pick up distant objects such as CTA-102. The only extant American search effort, Project Ozma, had been a targeted search, aimed at two stars, as opposed to the all-sky survey technique. Unfortunately, we couldn't know which approach made more sense until we actually found some other civilizations, so we resolved to continue both approaches. (Four years later, Carl and I attempted a search of other galaxies, using the Arecibo telescope to look for distant bright civilizations—but more about this later.)

For the closing dinner of the conference, our hosts bused the whole assemblage to an elegant, beautiful old castle an hour's drive away, on the shore of Lake Sevan. There we were treated like royalty, with fabulous food and entertainment. Shklovsky recalled the event fondly in a book he was writing all those years but never dared to publish. It came out posthumously in 1991, under the title *Five Billion Vodka Bottles to the Moon*:

> Ambartsumyan was unanimously elected *tamada*, or toastmaster, but everybody realized that he was too grand and stiff to fill the post in anything but ceremonial fashion. A vice toastmaster was needed, and I was chosen. I think that was the highest office to which I have ever been elected. Those

were my stellar hours—Ambartsumyan, sitting to my left, occasionally nodded his head slightly, and I did the rest.

Though full of humorous anecdotes, as Shklovsky himself always was, his book makes the fundamental tragedy of his life abundantly clear. Not only did he lack the sophisticated instruments he needed to shepherd his own predictions into the world of observed fact, but also he spent about two thirds of his time battling the system—struggling for freedom in scientific inquiry and every other sphere of his existence. He was alternately angered and bemused by the anti-Semitism he encountered. He marched through life to a steady drumbeat of slights and digs, unfair treatment or unequal opportunity, even the loss of a job in 1951, all openly a result of his Jewish origins. Election to the Academy of Sciences or directorships of observatories? Those rewards were reserved for the *apparatchiks* and members of the "correct" ethnic group.

Even so, Shklovsky's heart was deep in Russia. Although he knew he could have any number of glorious jobs in the West, and could escape all the ill treatment he received in his own country, as far as I know he never even considered the numerous opportunities he had to leave Russia. In fact, whenever the subject was raised, he would not consent to talk about it. This was to the great benefit of the Soviet Union. He was an amazingly creative scientist. And he made a great toastmaster, too, as recounted in his memoir:

> Following local Caucasian customs, I called for a toast from Professor Lee, demanding that he respond in the Bushman language. The magnificent landscape around us resounded with weird clicks and sibilants. The anthropologist explained that he was chanting a primeval hymn which accompanied the ritual of sharing a collective delicacy, some rare bird or other. The toast made a strong impression.

From the Byurakan meeting came the impetus for a number of new searches by both American and Soviet radio observatories. We laid the groundwork for a Soviet master plan for later searches, the construction of a giant antenna system on the Earth, and even the use of orbital radio telescopes for the pursuit of the elusive signals. We did all this, mind you, under the shadow of the Bay of Pigs, the Cuban missile crisis, and intense surveillance of Soviet scientists and their visitors by the KGB. Our unanimity of purpose gave us the courage to plot together for the future of all humankind. We were even considering the construction of a radio telescope that spanned the Israeli-Egyptian border, to search for extraterrestrial intelligence while promoting peace in the Middle East. The Negev Desert is actually a pretty good site for an observatory because there's little interference there, except, of course, from passing airplanes.

The meeting spawned new theoretical work, too, such as Crick and Orgel's theory of directed panspermia—the idea that numerous planets in the Galaxy may have been intentionally seeded with microorganisms by ancient aliens.

When it was time to return home, we Americans found ourselves with an unfamiliar terrestrial problem: It was midnight and our Soviet jetliner, already four hours late in leaving Armenia (presumably to allow time for our luggage to be searched—the plane had been conspicuously standing ready the whole time), was diverted by a tremendous rainstorm to Moscow International Airport, sixty miles from the domestic airport where we'd expected to land. Other Soviet scientists were waiting to meet us, but at the wrong airport.

We were an inconsequential group in the huge mass of travelers stranded by the storm, and now we were facing an interminable wait to pass through understaffed customs, even though our flight had been a domestic one. Rules were rules in the Soviet Union, and anyone who landed at this airport had to pass through customs, no matter if their plane had come only ten miles. Fortunately, and contrary to well-founded popular belief, Soviet officials could sometimes be influenced through the not-so-subtle application of bombast and anger. Bribes worked even better! After I harangued a customs officer in my college Russian for nearly half an hour, we were allowed to bypass customs, but on one condition: We had to retrieve our luggage and follow the aforementioned official, crawling backward on our hands and knees across the luggage delivery racks, dragging our bags behind us. Everything had to be done within the next five minutes, before anyone noticed this remarkable departure from established procedures.

Quiet pandemonium erupted as we scrambled to seize our

opportunity. And then several Soviets, ever alert for loopholes in the system, saw *their* golden opportunity. For a few minutes they pretended to be Americans, as best they could, to join the squirming conga line and escape this temporary gulag.

Our group happily disappeared into the night, having gotten a hint of what life on another world was like.

▲
▲
▲

CHAPTER 6

Interstellar Quarantine, or Visions Hatched on the Back of a Cereal Box

Looking at the stars always makes me dream, as simply as I dream over the black dots representing towns and villages on a map. Why, I ask myself, shouldn't the shining dots of the sky be as accessible as the black dots on the map of France?

—VINCENT VAN GOGH

From the outside, California's maximum-security facility for the criminally insane looks appropriately ominous. Its tan facade is only a couple of stories high, but the complex sprawls over a wide, bleak area completely surrounded by monstrous fences topped with barbed wire. As we drove along the entry road, signs warned us not to approach the gate in our car but to park first and walk up, in full sight of the guards.

"Please state your name and business," the gatekeeper barked through a microphone in the bulletproof glass.

"This is Carl Sagan, and I'm Frank Drake. We've made advance arrangements to visit one of the inmates."

"Which one?"

"Timothy Leary."

The guard had us walk through a metal detector—the kind that are commonplace in airports nowadays, but a rarity anywhere back in 1970. He searched the two of us the old-fashioned way, too, by slapping his hands down the lengths of our bodies, before instructing us to walk single file through the narrow iron doorway in the gate.

Leary, famed for his experiments with hallucinogens at Harvard in the early 1960s, had been apprehended on a drug-possession charge, and incarcerated here in Vacaville, near Sacramento, in a prison euphemistically named the California Medical Facility. After many months he'd written to Carl and me, inviting us to meet with him about a special project he was contemplating. Between Leary's notoriety and our curiosity we had found time to make this special trip to see him while we were both in California on other business.

Once inside the prison, we were taken to the visitors' waiting area, where we looked through a gift shop stocked with arts and crafts produced by the inmates. Maybe it was Leary's influence, maybe just coincidence, but most of the items for sale that day were ceramics shaped to look like psychedelic mushrooms of all shapes, sizes, colors, and degrees of artistic ability.

At last we were led into a small room, perhaps ten feet by twenty, with a table and half a dozen chairs—and a window through which a guard just outside kept constant watch. Other guards soon arrived, bringing Leary, dressed in jeans and sneakers. He looked extremely lean and fit. We shook hands and introduced ourselves as the guards retreated, leaving us more or less alone. Then Leary, without a word of explanation, began to jog around the table in the middle of the room. Throughout the hour we spent with him, he kept up his run *and* his half of the conversation.

Leary let us know right away that he had been framed. While flying to California to announce his candidacy for the governorship, he said, he had had drugs planted on him by a political enemy who set him up for arrest.

"The leaders of the major parties knew that if I tossed my hat in the ring, I'd win."

"How could they be so sure?" Carl asked, expressing the skepticism we both felt, but Leary ran on, unruffled.

"Oh, it's simple if you study the demographics and consider the various populations," he explained. "I would get the hippie vote, the freak vote, and the drug vote, and in California, that's enough to put me in the governor's mansion. Oh, they had to stop me, all right. This arrest ruined my chance to run for office."

Leary said that he had amassed considerable personal wealth beforehand, however, and that he also had rich friends who were going to help him mount the space project he'd invited us to discuss.

In brief, Leary and his group believed the world situation was heading toward a nuclear shoot-out that would totally destroy the Earth. Against that eventuality, he wanted to finance the construction of a starship to save humanity. He would build it big enough to hold the three hundred most important people in the world, whom he would select by his own criteria. Then he would ferry them, like a latter-day Noah with a spacefaring ark, to establish a new civilization on an Earth-like planet of some nearby star.

"What I would like from you gentlemen," he continued, not the least bit out of breath, "is some technical advice. Which of the stars is my best bet?"

Carl and I looked at each other. We knew Leary wasn't going to like what we had to say. The television success of *Star Trek*, not to mention the real-life TV adventure of the *Apollo 11* Moon landing, had convinced millions of people that interstellar travel was now feasible.

Carl gestured at me as if to say, "Your move."

"Dr. Leary," I began as politely as I could, "even if we could help you select a new-Earth destination in space, there is simply no way for you—or anyone else—to travel to the vicinity of another star. Every star in our Galaxy is terribly far away from us. Our rockets and spacecraft can't negotiate those enormous distances. We can't even determine, with our best telescopes, which of the stars actually have planets. We've never observed one directly. We only surmise that they're there, from what we understand about astrophysics and the way the universe evolves. Even if I could tell you for sure that there was an Earth-like planet circling the Sun's near neighbor, Alpha Centauri, it would take you an eternity to get to it.

"The light from that nearby star," I continued, "takes four years to reach us. And that's traveling at the fastest possible speed—the speed of light, 186,000 miles per second. Any real object—even an atom or a molecule—travels more slowly. Something as big as an interstellar transport carrying hundreds of people is going to go at a snail's pace, relatively speaking. You and your passengers would all die of old age before you reached your destination."

Leary ran a couple of laps in silence before he responded: "All right, not today. In ten years, then?"

"No, not in ten years," I assured him. "Not in this lifetime. Not with all the money in the world, and the best engineers to build your spacecraft. The fuel needed for interstellar travel does not exist. And even if it did, it would usurp so much energy that we can't even consider it."

"How can you say that?" Leary asked. "How can you know such a thing when you just told me yourself that neither the craft nor the fuel to power it exists?"

Leary must have thought me terribly smug, but I'd been thinking and collecting experts' opinions about this problem for years. Every time I spoke to lay groups about any aspect of astronomy, someone in the audience would inevitably ask about voyages to the stars. Often the question came up optimistically, as in "When will we be able to venture beyond the Solar System and establish ourselves as a presence in the Galaxy?" At other times it arose out of fear: "What if an alien civilization arrived at Earth to exploit and enslave us?"

My answer to both questions is pretty much the same—that the distances between the stars create an interstellar quarantine. Captain Kirk and Mr. Spock lied to us. You can't call up Scotty and order warp seven to zip anywhere in the Galaxy in two minutes. It's too energy-expensive. The energy required to visit another star prohibits even the most advanced civilizations from making such a journey. It would be an incredibly expensive folly for any aliens to attempt to attack us.

Leary paid close attention to the lecture that Carl and I delivered for his ears only in the Vacaville prison. And although the substance of it systematically destroyed his dream, he showed considerable intellectual appreciation for the fundamental problems involved. By the end of our talk, his look was veiled, preoccupied, crestfallen. Perhaps he was already devising another strategy. For our part, we were glad to take leave of the place.

The first person to convince me that high-speed space travel wasted terrible amounts of energy was Edward Purcell, whom I had met when I was a graduate student at Harvard. Purcell was the codiscoverer, with Doc Ewen, of the 21-centimeter line, and had been awarded a Nobel prize in Physics in 1952. Despite these achievements, Purcell was so unassuming and so young-looking that I took him at first to be a fellow graduate student. Indeed, I always saw him in attendance at our astronomy department's colloquia, where he asked excellent questions. After one such gathering, and having no idea who Purcell was, I got into a theoretical argument with him and a brilliant postdoctoral fellow named George Field. We were debating the physics of the interstellar medium, and I more than implied that Purcell didn't know what he was talking about. Even so, he very pleasantly continued the discussion without trying to pull rank on me. Later, when George told me, "That fellow you just raked over the coals is *the* Edward Purcell," I wanted to sink into the floor. But we have since become good friends.

In 1961, in a special report he wrote for the Atomic Energy Commission, Purcell worked out the physics of relativistic rockets, showing what energy it would take to accelerate to a respectable fraction of the speed of light. The answer boggled even Purcell's mind, and he ruled out such travel for any civilization, no matter how advanced. His conclusion was, and I quote, "All this stuff about traveling around the universe in space suits . . . belongs back where it came from, on the cereal box."

Sebastian von Hoerner did an even more thorough denunciation of the rocket-travel idea in 1962, in a paper he published in *Science*. Later, Barney Oliver pursued the implications of both Purcell's and von Hoerner's work in great depth. Barney showed me how to gauge the energy cost of interstellar colonization in graphic detail. I used his approach to reach some of my own conclusions, as follows:

You *can* estimate an energy-cost figure even in the absence of any knowledge of the spacecraft or its propulsion system. You simply assume at the outset that the civilization is smart: They will colonize space only if it makes sense to do so. If the energy used to put one colonist on a new planet is far greater than the energy required to give that colonist a good life back on the home planet, they won't bother.

Let's take our American energy consumption as an example. We know about how much energy each of us uses in a year to drive to work, fly somewhere nice for a vacation, have food and clothes, heat and air-condition our homes, and the like. Now suppose we took that amount of energy—per person, per year—and used it to power a spaceship to send one hundred would-be colonists ten light-years away, which is probably the minimum distance to a suitable star. What spacecraft velocity does this amount of energy yield?

If we allow a spacecraft mass of ten tons per colonist—about ten times the per-passenger mass of a typical airliner, just enough to provide meager rations and some shielding from cosmic rays—our cruising velocity turns out to be close to sixty miles per second. That's fast. It's roughly ten times faster, in fact, than our fastest spacecraft go. And yet, the time it takes to travel ten light-years at that pace is *forty thousand years*. Try to picture yourself sitting in a DC-9 for forty thousand years, eating airline food and watching the same movies over and over again.

If we abandon this unacceptable approach and step up the velocity to get to the star in a hundred years, we would need as much energy, *per person*, as it takes to provide a good life on Earth for *two hundred thousand people*. No government or private individual can afford to squander energy expenditures of that order. What makes this approach even more unrealistic is that, besides not allowing for inefficiencies in the production of fuel and in the propulsion system, the colonists would arrive at the distant star at a very high speed and have no energy remaining with which to stop. They'd just go whistling through that planetary system and out the other side. Slowing and stopping their craft would take at least as much energy as required to reach their destination—one hundred times what two hundred thousand Americans use up over the course of a lifetime.

If we get technical about rocket-mass ratios and other specifics, the actual energy required to send a group of one hundred colonists to another star is about equal to the energy needs of the entire population of the United States—every man, woman, and child, for as long as they live. Most of us will agree that is a ridiculous scenario.

The same limits on space travel that scotched Leary's grand escape plan also hold true, I believe, for alien civilizations. Without any knowledge of their propulsion systems or their psychology, I maintain that they, too, would be wise enough to refuse to make the energy sacrifices that interstellar travel demands.

I don't go unchallenged on this point. My colleague Robert Rood, who teaches astronomy at the University of Virginia, loves to point out that energy availability and cost change dramatically with the times. If you could go back two hundred years, Rood argues, you would find the people of that era unable to conceive of the energy luxury the developed countries take for granted today. Rood even found statistics for the number of water mills in England in the late eighteenth century, and calculated their total power production so as to compare it with that of England today. The jump in energy consumption from then to now, he claims, is the same jump needed to take us from an Earthbound civilization to a Galactic one. The leap of faith may be the same, too: The average Englishman of the 1790s would surely have viewed a transoceanic flight in a 747 as a profligate waste of energy— assuming, of course, that he could have conceived of such a thing.

Rood makes a compelling argument that is not easily dismissed. But even if civilizations have access to vast stores of energy, I don't think they will spend it all on interstellar flight. My second (and admittedly weaker) rebuttal is that no matter how cheap and available energy becomes, it will always be expensive to store and transport it. The more fuel you have to carry with you, the harder it is to launch your heavy vehicle and boost it out of the planetary system.

But why shouldn't modern astronauts, who stand so much closer to interstellar flight than our frontier pioneers stood to superhighways or supersonic aircraft, keep dreaming toward their goal? And what's to stop an individual or civilization, whether human or alien, from the acts of sheer energy extravagance that built the Taj Mahal, the Pyramids of Egypt, or the Great Wall of China? What if we just decided to go for broke to drive to another star? Could we do it?

One starship design that seems, at first blush, to make the dream possible is the vessel with a forward scoop that picks up fuel, in the form of hydrogen atoms, as it makes its way through space. The fuel is free for the finding, and since it is utilized immediately, it doesn't have to be stored or transported. The only problem, once you start seriously trying to design such a spacecraft, is that the scoop part has to be some two hundred fifty miles wide to gather sufficient fuel in the near vacuum of space. There's only about one atom in every cubic centimeter of the interstellar medium, as opposed to several million billion atoms in the same amount of ordinary air. It's a real challenge to collect meaningful quantities of material in that high a vacuum. What's more, the atoms you encounter in space hit your scoop with such force, due to your great speed, that they are more likely to bounce off it than fold into it. No one I know of has conceived of a scoop design sophisticated enough to gather interstellar atoms. A big bucket just won't do.

Assuming we figure out how to make this scoop someday, we still have to direct the atoms to the on-board fusion reactor. Oh, yes. I neglected to mention that we'd also have to master the technology of hydrogen fusion, and outfit our spacecraft with a reliable fusion reactor that would work safely over a period of years. What's more, unless we build this transport out in space, we still have to launch it in the conventional way. The only real advantage we've gained is that we don't have to send along the fuel to power its deceleration. The craft should be able to stop itself with the fuel and reaction mass it picks up en route.

Another way to cut down on fuel for deceleration might be to select a destination that definitely had an atmosphere. Simply by entering the planet's environs, you would encounter enough friction to slow your craft to a halt—just as the space shuttle brakes itself aerodynamically high in the Earth's atmosphere, by flying in at just the right angle. The success of this technique hinges on knowledge of the atmospheric density, not to mention pilot skill, because if you come in too steeply and slow down too quickly, your ship overheats and melts. If, on the other hand, your approach is too shallow, you don't slow down enough, and then you skip off the surface of the atmosphere like a stone skipped across the water. With no other way to brake yourself, you'd have to coast through space until you encountered the next suitable moon or planet, which could conceivably take another hundred years.

I often hear the argument that in the future our civilization—or an alien civilization—may discover new aspects of the physical world that could help us transcend these seeming barriers. For all we know, there may even be as yet undiscovered conduits through space that make interstellar travel quick and easy. Astrophysicist Kip Thorne of Caltech has postulated the existence of "wormholes" in space that might let you disappear in one place and reappear somewhere else without violating the mathematics of general relativity.

I don't rule out the possibility of discovering bizarre phenomena in the universe. No one can. But I suspect that for every potential facilitator to long-distance manned spaceflight, we will find an equal number of unknown hazards lurking in the cosmos that might work against us. For example, many regions of space could contain little, near-invisible meteoroids. These "iron basketballs" might be common by-products from supernova explosions of old, iron-rich stars, or the deep-space debris from impacts in alien planetary systems. Whatever their origin, hitting an iron basketball at interstellar speeds would be like running into a hydrogen bomb: It doesn't make a little hole; it vaporizes you. A stray comet or cometary fragment, flung out of its solar system by a gravity boost from a giant planet, would create the same kind of roadblock. You'd never know what hit you.

Cosmic rays already pose a clear and present threat of radiation sickness and leukemia—and not just to speculative future missions, but also to astronauts establishing permanent settlements on the Moon or Mars, as outlined in our current Space Exploration Initiative. I've been a member of this program's Science Working Group since 1989, and I can testify that cosmic rays have dominated the planning of spacecraft bound for Mars. To protect the astronauts from deadly bursts of cosmic rays during the three- to four-year trip to the red planet, we will need to launch them with the equivalent of a bomb shelter. Ideally, we should give the spacecraft walls of concrete three feet thick, but it would never get off the ground. The next best thing, which we're seriously contemplating, is to build inside the craft a "storm shelter" where the crew can dive for cover every time a solar flare looses a stream of cosmic rays. Designers will have to make it as small as possible, even though the crew may have to huddle in it for hours or days at a time. As things stand, the ten-square-foot storm shelter accounts for much of the payload mass. Nor can we go to a lighter substance, because it's the density of materials such as concrete and lead that offer the only true protection from cosmic rays.

These pessimistic estimates of the unlikelihood of interstellar flight have a direct bearing on my opinion about so-called unidentified flying objects. I do *not* believe that UFOs are alien spacecraft. I am adamant on this point, although I know it puts me at odds with some 60 percent of American adults. Many individuals, knowing my dedication to the search for extraterrestrial life, expect me to be receptive to the UFO idea. They seek me out to tell me they think they have spotted one, or that they have actually been abducted by aliens.

I hear them out, of course, and I've given such reports a lot of study. In fact, I've been involved several times in investigating UFO reports, including some objects that were conclusively identified as huge meteorites falling in flames through the atmosphere. In these

particular cases, my colleagues and I were hoping to locate meteorite fragments on the ground, so we interviewed people who had
witnessed the fall. We knew exactly what they had seen, which
was the fireball of a very bright meteorite. And I was amazed to
discover how many average, sane people had "seen" a spacecraft
with visitors from another planet in it and strange-looking creatures jumping out of it. But this vision was something concocted by
their own expectations, and in all innocence. Most UFO sightings
are just that—misinterpretations of natural phenomena, or of terrestrial aircraft, spacecraft, or weather balloons. Many reports,
however, turn out to be frauds or hoaxes. Their number is legion,
and some hoaxers will go to extraordinary ends to construct an
exciting, elaborate deception.

No tangible evidence exists to suggest that we have ever been
visited by an alien spacecraft. As strongly as I believe that intelligent life exists elsewhere in the universe, I maintain that UFOs are
not extraterrestrial visitors. They are the products of intelligent life
on this planet.

When I talk to contactees who claim they've been given information by occupants of UFOs, the material turns out to be totally
uninteresting. It is never anything that we didn't already know,
and usually consists of blandishments of friendship and goodwill.
This is what makes every story ultimately unbelievable, because if
a civilization could master interstellar travel—something that is
beyond even my wildest dreams right now—wouldn't they have
the most striking news to report? Wouldn't they have a handle on
the ultimate mysteries of the universe? I know they would, and
any part of it they shared would be a revelation. Not once has any
reported contact produced some new, previously unknown fact—
even a simple one—that we could verify.

Some contactees counter that the aliens really do fathom mysteries we haven't solved, and have already revealed their secrets. It's
just that they've also given every contactee a case of selective
amnesia, so that the information won't be revealed at large until
the time is right. This explanation, however, stretches my credulity
beyond the breaking point.

Still other individuals I meet view extraterrestrial life as a terrifying possibility, à la *The War of the Worlds.* They fear we will be
subsumed, like the primitive civilizations of Earth that were overpowered by more advanced technological societies. But everything
we know about physics and astronomy convinces me that the

extraterrestrials are not going to come and attack us or eat us. It would cost far too much in resources to attack us, compared to any possible gain. They are going to talk to us, long distance, by radio. I think they will agree that it doesn't pay to transport *things* through space as long as they can transport *information*. And the way to transport information at the speed of light is in the form of electromagnetic radiation—radio waves being the most economical to transmit or receive. I've heard Barney Oliver surmise, "The reason they don't travel to us is that radio works so well."

A plausible solution to Leary's space colony problem actually surfaced in 1974, just a few years after Carl and I met with him. That was the year Princeton University physicist Gerard O'Neill released his plan for building large-scale space colonies. With scrupulous obedience to the laws of science, O'Neill demonstrated that it was possible to travel to a beautiful new world in space without usurping all the energy of the world we know or risking unknown dangers. The answer was to build the colonies from scratch in near-Earth orbit, using materials mined from the Moon and passing asteroids, and bypass altogether the staggering obstacles posed by interstellar flight.

   O'Neill envisioned his outposts as truly delightful artificial environments, with landscapes, lakes, rivers, and a force resembling the Earth's gravity, due to the slow rotation (one revolution every minute or two) of the colony in space. A typical colony might be twenty miles long and several miles in diameter, with its long axis pointing toward the Sun. Huge mirrors, inclined to reflect sunlight through windows, would create daylight inside. Such new habitats would be expensive, yes, but not unreasonably so.

   Initially you might think that a space colony would be a horrible place to live, but in fact it could be ideal, complete with bug-free backyards and made-to-order weather: Open the mirrors a lot to have Hawaii week, or close the mirrors most of the way to have an Aspen skiing week.

   In this scenario, civilizations eventually leave their home planets and colonize space, where literally tens or thousands of millions could live and work in specially engineered environments fueled by solar power and sustained by bold new techniques for food production. The only people left on the Earth are park rangers, because the planet has been relegated to the status of a national preserve. People take their kids down on the Gray Line space shuttle to show them how terrible it was for their grandmommy and granddaddy, who had to endure tornadoes and mosquitoes and other horrible things.

I attended one of O'Neill's early lectures at Princeton about the space colonies, just about the time he wrote his popular book *The High Frontier*. I found him to be a first-rate physicist—a very ingenious, intelligent person with a good grasp of engineering. He is not the least bit flaky, though he attracts flakes like flies, and his name gets bandied about in lots of flaky places.

O'Neill's idea makes sense because so much less energy is needed to build space colonies in one's own planetary system—about one ten-millionth the amount required to travel to another star. Although some might argue that very advanced civilizations, such as a Kardashev Type III, will have access to much greater energy resources than we have, a factor of ten million is very hard to overcome.

Lord Kelvin once said that you don't know anything in science until you put numbers to it. When I put numbers to the idea of interstellar travel or colonization, it becomes clear that the cost of going to another star is too high. Civilizations can't venture far from home. Nor do they need to. There is enough energy from our Sun to support, believe it or not, more than a hundred billion billion human beings—an incredibly greater number than are living now—right in our Solar System.

O'Neill and I eventually parted company, however, when he predicted that in the future his colonies would expand into space until they literally infiltrated the Galaxy in a period of less than a million years. He expects them to reach such distances using rockets driven by a system that Edward Purcell considered years ago in theory—the combining of matter with antimatter.* Hypothesized fuel-injection systems far beyond our present capabilities would allow these oppositely charged particles to come in contact with each other as needed to accelerate or decelerate the space-

---

* For each particle of ordinary matter, such as an electron or proton, there is a corresponding particle of antimatter, which is equal in mass but opposite in electrical charge. A proton, for example, is a positively charged particle of matter, and its antimatter equivalent is the negatively charged antiproton. On Earth, antimatter does not exist, except briefly in the products of the nuclear disintegrations created by physicists in particle accelerators, or "atom smashers."

craft. The particles, which attract each other more readily than magnets of opposite poles, would combine instantaneously on contact to annihilate each other, converting all mass to energy in the most efficient process possible. Out comes a veritable burst of energy, primarily in the form of gamma rays.

If alien civilizations possessed such incredibly dangerous rockets, which I doubt, we could detect them by their blasts of gamma rays. Every time they sped up or slowed down, they would leave gamma-ray "skidmarks" in space, just as drag racers lay rubber on the road surface when making jackrabbit starts or sudden stops.

A British spaceship devotee named Anthony Martin first predicted these marks. Martin calculated that a matter-antimatter rocket would have to fire for a month to work up to cruising speed—accelerating at a rate that a living astronaut could tolerate. This long period of rocket-firing would produce a bright streak of gamma rays that appeared suddenly and persisted for weeks, tracing a telltale path through the interstellar medium. Investigators have looked for such skidmarks, using gamma-ray detectors on satellites high above the Earth's atmosphere. But no such signs of interstellar travel have been sighted. Observed gamma-ray sources are either very steady and long-lived, or transient in the extreme, emitting blasts that last only a second or so.*

One obvious problem with a matter-antimatter rocket is that you have to keep the matter and the antimatter separate until it's time for them to collide and propel you somewhere. It's easy enough to store matter in a container made of matter, but where do you put the antimatter? The antimatter tank has to be fashioned from antimatter, for if it were made of ordinary matter, it would explode as soon as you put your antimatter inside it. As far as I know, any realistic design for the construction of such antimatter storage tanks is still a matter of conjecture. Robert Forward, an ingenious physicist, is giving his attention to the problem, and is

---

* Martin also spearheaded the British Interplanetary Society's Project Orion, a spacecraft design study of twenty years ago that relied on hydrogen bombs for propulsion. The idea was to reach the stars and achieve nuclear disarmament all at the same time by launching an interstellar spaceship carrying approximately one thousand hydrogen bombs. From time to time the astronauts would throw a bomb out the rear of the craft and explode it to push them forward. Anyone want to volunteer to be a passenger?

exploring in particular the use of magnetic fields to create the equivalent of tanks to contain the antimatter. Until the bugs are worked out, O'Neill's colonies will stay inside the Solar System, which is where I think they belong.

The question of whether civilizations spread out through their galaxies is a crucial one in the search for extraterrestrial intelligence. A few scientists believe that colonization is an imperative for space-age civilizations. Since we see no signs of it, they suggest we are the first—or perhaps the only—advanced intelligent civilization in the Milky Way.

This thought apparently occurred first to Enrico Fermi, the Nobel prize–winning physicist who was a key member of the Manhattan Engineer District to develop the nuclear bomb. During World War II, while associate director at Los Alamos National Laboratory, Fermi started thinking about extraterrestrial life. He had made an analysis, which must have been similar to the one that led me to the Drake Equation, estimating how many civilizations might be out there. He concluded there were lots of them. But no conspicuous sign of their existence had been detected. This led to a paradox: "Where are they?"

Fermi delighted in confounding the other scientists at Los Alamos with this question. He would pop into people's offices and engage them in informal discussions about how common life must be across the universe. He would start off with the fact that new stars are continually being born throughout the Galaxy. He assumed planetary systems must be common because the Solar System was surely not unique. The origins of life were probably easy to duplicate on other planets, he said. (Miller and Urey had not done their famous experiments yet, so Fermi was grasping a bit here.) The fossil record seemed to show that intelligence arose early on Earth, and we should expect to find it wherever life evolved. In time, intelligent creatures would develop technology that would enable them to venture into space and fill every niche in the Galaxy. Given the age of the Milky Way, some extraterrestrial civilizations should be very old and very advanced. They should have arrived at Earth by now. But they haven't come. "Where are they?"

"They are among us," Leo Szilard, Fermi's Hungarian-born colleague on the Manhattan Project, supposedly replied, "but they call themselves Hungarians."

"Where are they?" The question, which has since become known as the Fermi Paradox, still fascinates us.

There are several solutions to this Fermi Paradox, for the fact that "they" are not here does not prove that "they" do not exist. Perhaps they are on their way here even now, but not radiating rapidly outward from their home planet like ripples in a pond, as Fermi imagined. Maybe they take a more roundabout route. Carl Sagan and William Newman have suggested that galactic population expansion might begin radially but then proceed more slowly, as a random walk through space. In that case, it would take about the age of the Galaxy to colonize it completely, so the extraterrestrials might show up tomorrow!

I don't expect them to, of course. I don't believe we will receive visitors from other planets of other stars—any more than I believe we have been visited in the past by ancient astronauts or UFOs that are alien spacecraft.

The argument I favor as a solution to the Fermi Paradox is simply that it makes better sense to colonize in your own planetary system than to endure the costs and hazards of going to other stars. This involves building the types of colonies O'Neill described, right in the home system, rather than settling new planets elsewhere or building colonies far from home.

"Where are they?" They are probably living quite comfortably, with a high quality of life, near the planets where their lives began. They are there in great numbers for us to find—via their radio transmissions. This is why I have pushed continuously over the years for the construction of larger, ever more sensitive receivers, the better to hear those signals.

If I believed the extraterrestrials would come out of the sky, I wouldn't bother. I would just sit out in a lawn chair and wait for them to show up. Or to send an envoy—perhaps a robot probe of the kind postulated by Ronald Bracewell, now at Stanford University. He thinks extraterrestrials might manufacture great numbers of scout spacecraft, which have come to be known as "Bracewell probes," and dispatch one to every candidate star they choose to search. Once arrived, the probe would orbit the star, watching and listening for signs of intelligent life on the surrounding planets. When it detected any, it would alert its home planet of the news, and might or might not beam a message to the emerging civilization.

Like interstellar travel, Bracewell probes are an enormously expensive and grandiose enterprise. To succeed, you have to send out millions of probes, each of which is a sophisticated spacecraft that can travel fast, enter a planetary system, and put itself in orbit there. Then the probes have to wait for millions of years, functioning perfectly, while the home planet monitors them for updates.

Because the universe probably permits only limited kinds of direct encounters among its residents, it makes the most sense to me to ply the radio course—to plumb the radio spectrum for magic frequencies and scan the stars for beacons sent by alien intelligence. Information-laden radio messages are the quarry we seek in the search for extraterrestrial life.

Most questions in physics and astronomy are answered from the farthest possible remove, via telescope observations, or sometimes from the vantage point of an armchair, as in thought experiments such as Einstein conducted. Occasionally, however, life experiences point the way to important conclusions.

On our return home from an International Astronomical Union Congress in Sydney, Australia, Carl and I stopped for a few days in Bora-Bora, near Tahiti. We went there intending to collaborate on a joint article about the search for extraterrestrial intelligence, which later appeared in *Scientific American*. The rest of the time we planned to enjoy ourselves snorkeling, which we had discovered was the one sport we both loved.

Bora-Bora is a beautiful place—a textbook South Sea island with a volcanic peak at its center and a wide lagoon around it. The lagoon's coral reef provided a home for much colorful aquatic life. After lunch one day, when Carl and I were standing on the pier of the Hotel Bora-Bora, watching the sharks swim by, we noticed a group of Polynesian outrigger canoes. These were replicas of ancient models, provided by the hotel for the use of the guests.

"You know," Carl mused aloud, "Polynesia was settled by voyagers crossing thousands of miles of open ocean in these canoes." He paused for a long time. When he opened his mouth again, his musing had turned to resolve. He wanted us to salute those intrepid explorers by making a token exploration of our own—to one of the barrier islands we could see across the lagoon. I had to admit that sounded to me like an unbeatable way to pass the afternoon. So we boarded the closest canoe and started paddling.

A little more than halfway across the lagoon, however, the canoe, which had been taking in water without our noticing the problem, suddenly sank. It didn't sink to the bottom, but submerged so that we were in water up to our chests. We must have looked like two inflatable beach toys, heads and shoulders bobbing above the surface. The outrigger, Carl pointed out, would probably discourage the sharks to starboard, but we had to get ourselves out of danger quickly. Our only hope was to paddle on, fighting the tremendous drag of the submerged canoe and the muscle-cramping work of wielding paddles above our shoulder level. In this fashion we brought our craft to a safe landing on the far beach at last.

Exploration showed the little island to contain nothing but coconut palms and rats. It was not a place where we wanted to spend the night. Yet it might be days before anyone at the hotel noticed our absence, let alone figured out where we were.

Just as the fear of sharks had propelled us from midlagoon to the island, so the rats inspired us to find our way back to Bora-Bora. We picked up several coconut shells, which promised to serve as excellent bailers, and convinced each other that if we were diligent, we could return the water to the lagoon as quickly as it seeped into the canoe. To our great delight, the plan worked. In the end, the lagoon claimed my camera as our only casualty. It was totally destroyed. Carl, on the other hand, had brought along an underwater camera, with which he got some wonderful shots of our predicament.

We reasoned afterward that the experience was a powerful allegory for interstellar travel. It confirmed our belief that radio communication is much easier and safer than direct contact.

▲
▲
▲

CHAPTER 7

Treasures of Deep Space

Why may not every one of these stars or suns have as great a retinue as our sun of planets, with their moons, to wait upon them? . . . They must have their plants and animals, nay and their rational creatures too, and those as great admirers, and as diligent observers of the heavens as ourselves. . . .

—CHRISTIAAN HUYGENS,
Dutch physicist and astronomer
of the seventeenth century

Oh, what a beautiful sight it would have been: fifteen hundred radio telescopes, packed cheek by jowl over a circular site in the Southwest, and all of them moving in unison, synchronized like a *corps de ballet.* Picture the great expanse of their white dishes shimmering in the heat of the desert sun, each one a full 300 feet wide, each reflecting a slightly different swatch of sky, like the compound eye of an insect.

I can see myself walking through that installation, dwarfed and lost in its cornfield rows of radio telescopes stretching miles to the horizon in every direction. What are they doing? They are listening. They are pointing together toward targets in deep space, hunting for signs of extraterrestrial intelligence.

This is Project Cyclops. It is an image conjured up in the summer of 1971 by a group of twenty engineers charged with the task of figuring out what it would take to detect extraterrestrial intelligent life, using existing technology.*

In operation, an enormous telescope array like Cyclops could detect extremely faint signals from distant civilizations. We could eavesdrop profitably with it, picking up even internal radio and television-frequency communications from civilizations several hundred light-years away. And we could employ it, in turn, as a powerful transmitter to *reply* to those alien signals, to offer evidence of intelligent life on Earth. Unfortunately, Project Cyclops remains just a pretty picture. Nothing of its size or scope exists anywhere on Earth.

A newcomer to the extraterrestrial-search fraternity, a former aerospace physician with the Royal Air Force named John Billingham, initiated the design of Project Cyclops. Though born in England, educated at Oxford, and trained at the RAF Institute of Aviation Medicine, Billingham found himself drawn to the States repeatedly in the late 1950s. His expertise and enthusiasm blended well with America's serious interest in rockets and astronauts. He landed a full-time job with NASA, first at the Manned Spacecraft Center (now called the Johnson Space Center) in Houston in 1963, and later at the NASA Ames Research Center at Moffett Field. One of Billingham's many contributions to the space program was his design of the water-cooled space suits worn by the *Apollo 11* astronauts who landed on the Moon.

From the moment he learned of our nascent attempts to detect other kinds of intelligent life in space, Billingham's interest shifted from flight medicine to interstellar communication. He likes to say that he became the obstetrician who fostered the birth of the search for extraterrestrial intelligence as a NASA-supported enterprise. Before Dr. Billingham came on the case, NASA's resident exobiologists were content to search for microbes on other planets of the Solar System. Billingham convinced the space agency that a wider field of life, including civilizations more advanced than our own, undoubtedly pervaded the Galaxy—and that NASA should search for them.

Working at the interface between human needs and space technology, Billingham ran annual summer studies of engineering

---

* This project was part of a series of summer Faculty Fellowship Programs run by NASA and the American Society of Engineering Education.

system designs in cooperation with Stanford University. He would invite, say, twenty faculty members from universities all over the country to meet at Ames during the summer semester break and map out a feasible way to build some interesting project—a manned Moon base, for example. Billingham would get all these strangers working together as a team, which is one of his great talents. He's a very hard worker himself, and relentless in his attention to detail—the sort of person who doesn't let anything fall through the cracks. At the same time, he has a ready sense of humor and the polished, charming manner of an English gentleman.

Billingham resolved to devote the 1971 summer engineering program to a study of intercepting interstellar signals. He wisely recruited my old friend Barney Oliver to codirect the effort with him.

Barney, a charter member of the Order of the Dolphin, was vice president for research and development at Hewlett-Packard, where he had helped introduce everything from the hand-held calculator to the atomic clock. In the course of patenting fifty of his own electronics inventions, Barney had continued to indulge his great love for the subject of extraterrestrial communication. He did this by writing scientific papers about the technical problems involved as well as by giving talks on the subject and attending conferences. Barney leapt at the chance to work with Billingham, and Hewlett-Packard graciously granted him a three-month leave of absence over the summer months.

Some very fine people joined the Ames effort at Oliver and Billingham's invitation. One was Charles Seeger, the folksinger's brother, who had established the Radio Astronomy Project at Cornell. Another was Robert Dixon of Ohio State University, who has since taken over the longest-running project in the United States to search for extraterrestrial intelligence. (More about him later in this chapter.)

Barney, himself a giant of industry and a giant of a man, christened the project "Cyclops" after the mythological giant who had a single eye, as round and wide as a wheel, right in the middle of its forehead. (His first choice had actually been "Argus" for the mythological watchman who had a hundred eyes, but rejected it because Argus was also the name of a cheap camera.)

Before the engineers tried to put a design on paper, they heard lectures from leading authorities on many subjects relating to their task: Philip Morrison on what Cyclops might detect, Ronald Bracewell on the design of the five-telescope array at Stanford, Sebastian von Hoerner on design principles for large radio telescopes, and many others. I did not speak to the original group, although I later became involved in publicizing what its members had done. And once I got to know Billingham, I made frequent visits to Ames, speaking at subsequent workshops and seminars.

The engineers of Project Cyclops saw another side of astronomy that summer—not astrophysics or planetary science, but exobiology. They took an idea some of them once viewed as sci-fi fodder and turned it into the blueprint for a doable science project with far-reaching humanitarian goals. Searching for extraterrestrial life, which had long been the highly speculative fantasy of a few people like me, suddenly gained new converts. The design that emerged at summer's end promised a search capability of unprecedented sensitivity.

Barney's report of the group's work filled a fat book rich in astronomical data, mathematical equations, graphs, and signal processing diagrams—and shot through with the human significance he saw in the "quest" he championed. Again and again throughout the text, Barney talked about the need to assume responsibility for the husbandry of the planet we dominate, lest we die a cultural failure, killing off our own kind. He showed that searching for extraterrestrial intelligence does not mean neglecting the terrestrial issues of human suffering and ecological crisis. Instead, it underscores their importance by looking at the Earth from space—from the perspective of others who have perhaps faced the same kinds of problems and survived:

"Underlying the quest for other intelligent life is the assumption that man is not at the peak of his evolutionary development, that in fact he may be very far from it, and that he can survive long enough to inherit a future as far beyond our comprehension as the present world would have been to Cro-Magnon man," he wrote. "To do this, man must, of course, solve the ecological problems that face him. These are of immediate and compelling importance and their solution must not be delayed, nor effort to solve them be diminished, by overexpenditures in other areas. But . . . the quest gives more significance to survival and therefore places more, not less, emphasis on ecology. The two are intimately related, for if we can survive (and evolve) for another aeon the chances are that many other races have also, and this reduces the problem of making contact."

The Cyclops report also recognized the potential existence of a galactic community of cultures, each maintaining its individuality but all benefiting from the accumulated wisdom of the group. "The pride of identification with this supersociety and of contributing to its long-term purposes," Barney pointed out, "would add new dimensions to our own lives on Earth that no man* can imagine."

For the first time, the potential benefits of interstellar contact were being spelled out in an official government document. The report rekindled interest in the search. Some twenty thousand individuals requested (and presumably read) the Cyclops report.

Had it been built, Project Cyclops would have dwarfed Arecibo, and rivaled the cost of the Apollo Project with its multibillion-dollar price tag. Indeed, Cyclops's high cost ($10 billion in 1971 dollars, or more than $50 billion today) alienated many people— even some of those already committed to the search endeavor. They complained that Cyclops implied you couldn't search unless you spent astronomical sums of money. In an even more negative interpretation, the report seemed to say that NASA should do nothing in the search vein until it could afford to do something on the order of Cyclops. And this misunderstanding hurt us. In retrospect, I would say it undermined NASA's involvement in searching for several years.

Barney and Billingham had hoped to get Cyclops off the drawing board one step at a time. In their minds, the great strength of the Cyclops design was that the number of antennas could be increased gradually until there were just enough of them to detect an alien signal. This plan would guarantee the minimum expenditure needed to achieve success. But few people ever understood this; all they could see were the glorious pictures of the fifteen hundred receiver dishes—the ultimate Cyclops. To some extent, Barney and Billingham were the victims of their own great skills. And the skill

---

* As much as I trumpet Barney's ideas and sentiments, I must apologize for his masculine idiom. He wrote the report in 1971–72, when "he or she" was just making its long-overdue replacement of the general "he." Also, when Barney went to school, in the 1920s, "man" and "mankind" were synonymous with "person" and "humanity," respectively.

of the artist Rick Guidice, whose three drawings of the fully expanded array were included in the published report. When Barney
and Billingham saw how Cyclops was misperceived, they got new
artists' views drawn up of the Cyclops site with just a single antenna on it, with ten antennas, and with a hundred. But it was too
late to make Cyclops look small-scale.

Nevertheless, Cyclops changed their lives, and it changed the
way NASA viewed life in space. By 1976, NASA had put Billingham in charge of the Exobiology Division at Ames and let him
introduce a few studies and fund small-scale projects in the search
for extraterrestrial intelligence. This made "JB," as he is affection-
ately known, the first person in the United States to head a civil
service unit giving official recognition to alien civilizations.

For my part, I must admit that I dearly wished to see Cyclops
built. I would have welcomed it out in the desert, or perhaps out in
space, as a later study suggested, where it would no doubt have
been even more expensive. I boosted Cyclops in every public
lecture I gave at that time, calling it the best direction for our space
program. Indeed, I still see it as probably the most rewarding use of
tax dollars in history.

Project Cyclops marked the first serious attention to the practical
question of searching for extraterrestrial life since Project Ozma
ended in 1960. Ozma and Cyclops represented the opposite ex-
tremes of the same idea: Ozma made minimal equipment expenditures and borrowed a couple of hundred hours from the busy
observing schedule of a single telescope; Cyclops hinted at huge
outlays of money to build many telescopes that would count the
continuous search for alien signals as the primary goal.

The two projects differed in another important respect: Ozma
had really happened; Cyclops was just a good idea. The next
attempt to listen for interstellar signals was necessarily a lot closer
to Ozma than to Cyclops in scope.

Ozpa, as radio astronomer Gerrit Verschuur humorously called
Ozma's successor, returned to the scene of the original search—the
National Radio Astronomy Observatory in Green Bank, West Virginia. Verschuur used both the 140-foot and the 300-foot telescopes to search nine stars in 1971. I had searched two stars with
one telescope, so this was definitely an improvement, although
Verschuur devoted only thirteen hours in all to his observation
effort. He examined the same frequency range—the waterhole

region—but he had 384 channels to my single channel. This enabled him to search 384 frequencies at once.*

Then came another search, which waxed and waned over a four-year period from 1972 to 1976, using the big 300-foot telescope at Green Bank. Ozma II was the brainchild of Patrick Palmer, of the University of Chicago, and Ben Zuckerman, from the University of Maryland. They spent five hundred hours looking at hundreds of stars (674 to be exact) on the 21-centimeter frequency, using the same 384-channel system employed by Verschuur.

At the same time, observers in Australia, France, and Canada, not to mention the Soviet Union, also mounted searches of their own. There was even a small-scale search from space, via the *Copernicus* satellite, which was pressed into service to look for ultraviolet laser emissions of intelligent origin from the vicinity of three stars. (A list of search activities appears in Appendix B.)

I haven't mentioned anything about results from these attempts, because there weren't any. All of these small-scale, isolated efforts were just beginning to test the waters, so to speak, of the cosmos. Astronomers were opening their minds to the possibility of discovering extraterrestrial life, and experimenting with equipment to gain experience. For my part, I was happy to see new people committing their energies and publicly declaring themselves in the "alien" camp. But none of us expected such tentative steps to yield results in the form of civilizations detected. We were not yet looking hard enough to be able to find anything. The tangible results of these trials came in the form of increasing support for the concept of searching, and in new blood—a growing contingent of interested individuals who would enrich future activities with their insights.

Robert Dixon typified this new generation of scientists. He combined the technical genius and the emotional excitement for the subject that could carry the search clear through to discovery

---

* Since that time, Verschuur has pursued many avenues related to aliens, including extensive interviews with contactees—and even someone who claimed to *be* an extraterrestrial. Verschuur, an astronomy instructor at the University of Maryland, opposes current search activities. He has denounced those of us actively searching today, saying that we are pursuing a quasi-religious goal. We, of course, don't see it that way.

someday. As a graduate student in electrical engineering at Ohio State in the late 1960s, Dixon had worked with radio astronomer John Kraus on detailed maps of the radio sky. They discovered and cataloged some twenty thousand new radio sources with the telescope Kraus built and christened "Big Ear." This instrument looks rather like a metal football field, with an Erector Set–style collecting area at each end, where the goalposts would be. In actual measurements, it is larger than three football fields, and utilizes a sensitive 21-centimeter receiver.

When funding for the stellar mapping project ran out in 1972, the big telescope lay idle, threatening to rust away. Dixon, by then a junior faculty member and a Cyclops veteran, suggested to Kraus that they initiate a search for extraterrestrial signals. Kraus, as director of the observatory, agreed and gave his full support. By 1973 their project was running full-time, making the Ohio State facility the world's first telescope dedicated to the search for extraterrestrial intelligence.

Other searches may have operated on small grants and shoestring budgets, but the Dixon-Kraus search ran on no money at all for the first few years. The two of them volunteered their time, and had a Tom Sawyer effect on various students, who were only too happy to work at odd hours of the night and on weekends. The researchers enjoyed a constant influx of new equipment, too. Several undergraduate engineering students became highly industrious when they learned they could get course credit from Dixon for designing and building new receiver components. Another two volunteers who had full-time jobs in nearby Columbus—an electrical engineer at Bell Telephone Labs and a radio astronomer from Franklin University—also joined the project staff, for love of the work alone.

It was the Franklin astronomy professor, Jerry Ehman, who went over the computer printouts one night in August 1977 and found a signal with numerous signs of intelligence. It rode in on the 21-centimeter frequency, which no terrestrial or satellite transmitters are allowed to use.* Then, too, it was very strong—some thirty

---

* The intelligent-looking signals I detected from the Pleiades, while working at Harvard, and from Epsilon Eridani, during Project Ozma, were also on the 21-centimeter frequency, but turned out to be terrestrial noise that had strayed into that protected radio bandwidth. So a frequency of 21-centimeter wavelength (1420 megahertz) is not sufficient proof of a signal's extraterrestrial origin.

times greater than the background noise. And it came through in just one of the receiver's fifty channels, making it an extremely narrow-band signal, with the look of artificiality. Its pattern of passage through the telescope's beam showed it to be moving with the stars, and therefore truly extraterrestrial, unlike the pattern of an intruding airplane or spacecraft. The ultimate hallmark of intelligence, however, was the way the signal turned itself on—or off—while it was in the telescope's beam.

The Ohio State telescope, with its strange shape, takes in two beams (two views of the sky, slightly offset from one another) simultaneously; then it automatically compares the views as a means of canceling out terrestrial interference. An object in the sky typically records itself twice at Ohio State, once per beam, but this particular signal appeared just once. It had turned itself off after showing up in the first beam. Or it turned itself on just before the second beam took in that stellar neighborhood. Either way, the signal was intermittent—like the ring of a telephone or the click-clack of Morse code—and not a steady drone. More and more, astronomers had been talking about the likelihood that extraterrestrial signals might be transient, as this one was, rather than continuous.

"Wow!" gasped Ehman. The signal's appearance in the data so stunned him that he wrote "Wow!" in the margin next to it, and it has been known ever since as the "Wow!" signal.

The "Wow!" remains remarkable to this day. It figures as one of our all-time best candidate signals—a candidate for true evidence of extraterrestrial intelligence. But, like all the other prime candidates we've amassed, the "Wow!" has never repeated. No one has heard precisely the same signal again at Ohio State or anywhere else. We have to conclude that the "Wow!" was either a very-hard-to-explain fluke, or the real thing.

Silence often speaks louder than words, and fleeting signals may be telling us something important about extraterrestrials that we did not anticipate. Space could be full of their signals, falling on our planet like raindrops, one after another, each one making a brief, barely detectable splash before it disappears. My own observing experience, when being especially attentive for any receiver output that might be of intelligent origin, is that there seem to be weak signals just popping up out of the noise all the time. Looking at the data, I often have the same feeling I get when I am deep in a forest and now and then sense brief, vague reminders of the civilized world around me—the drone of a jet plane far overhead, a distant auto horn, the faint shout of one person calling to another. Could it be that in our radio observations we are hearing, all the time, the murmurs of countless other civilizations blowing past the Earth as on the wind?

We would expect and hope to find their signals lasting—the longer the better—and repetitive, too. Our desire, as listeners, is for loud, steady signals that persist for weeks or even months. In that case, when we go back to verify what we've found in our data, we'll find the signal right where it was, and ready to submit to a host of confirmation checks and corroborating observations from astronomers at other telescopes.

We, however, are not regular broadcasters. We know nothing about the needs, desires, and strategies of those who may be sending these signals. I hate to try to psych out the extraterrestrials, because the practice can be so misleading, and we surely are amateurs at it. But suppose for a moment that you are a technically advanced civilization looking to communicate with others in space. You have a transmitter you can put to this purpose, and some amount of energy to expend on signal transmission. You could opt to broadcast continuously in all directions, so that you illuminate half the celestial sphere around you with a single antenna—and the whole celestial sphere if you put two antennas at opposite ends of your planet. That's a pretty good attention-getter because it's on all the time. Someone looking in your direction on the right frequency, with enough sensitivity, is sure to pick up your signals. The problem is, you're expending an enormous amount of energy—tying up two transmitters and two power-generating stations—to create a signal so diffuse and weak that it isn't detectable over very great distances.

Now suppose you took that same quantity of energy and focused it into a narrow beam. With all the concentrated power shooting in one direction, the signal might grow one million times stronger and remain detectable over vast distances. An alien Arecibo used in this way could pierce right to the heart, or reach the far edge, of the Galaxy. But the tiny beam would illuminate only one millionth of the celestial sphere at any given time. Thus the chances of others detecting it are still no better than one in a million—even if they know where to look for you!

Maybe your best option as a broadcaster is to send out a fan beam. This kind of transmission has its power concentrated into a

Looking excited at the prospect of building the world's largest hydrogen-line radio tele-scope, members of the Harvard University Radio Astronomy Group, pictured here in 1956, include, from left, front row, Harold I. ("Doc") Ewen, Mary Connelly, and Barton J. Bok; I'm at the far left in the second row, with William E. Howard III, A. Edward Lilley, T. K. ("Kochu") Menon, and David S. Heeschen, later to become the director of the National Radio Astronomy Observatory.

Set in the Allegheny Mountains of West Virginia, the observatory at Green Bank had more farm buildings than telescopes in the early 1960s. The eighty-five-foot Howard Tatel Tele-scope used for Project Ozma is the dark dot of a dish in the middle of the photo, to the right of center. *Courtesy of NRAO*

This close-up view of the eighty-five-foot telescope at Green Bank shows the metal canister, set on struts inside the dish, where I spent at least forty-five minutes each dawn during Project Ozma, tuning the parametric amplifier. *Courtesy of NRAO*

The staff of the NRAO in 1960 reported to the eminent, elegant Otto Struve, sitting at center and dressed, as always, in a suit and tie. John Findlay sits left of Struve, and Dave Heeschen right. Beverly Lynds is seated second from left, and her husband, Roger, is standing directly behind Struve, next to me. Hein Hvatum, my partner on the Jupiter study, stands behind and to the left of Roger. Margaret Hurley, who helped me with Project Ozma, is behind Beverly in a checkered dress. Ellen Gundermann, the second lady to the right, also helped, and standing next to Ellen is Sebastian von Hoerner. The tall fellow at the extreme left in that row is none other than French Beverage. *Courtesy of NRAO*

The three-hundred-foot telescope behind me was built on the cheap at Green Bank in 1963. It collapsed due to its faulty construction in 1989, fueling rumors that aliens had trashed it.

The "Big Ear" at Ohio State University Radio Observatory became the first dedicated (full-time) SETI facility in 1973. This is the instrument that detected the now-famous "Wow!" signal. *NASA Photo*

Flagship of the NASA SETI Microwave Observing Project, the Arecibo Observatory boasts a shiny aluminum reflector dish, one thousand feet wide, nestled in the hills of northern Puerto Rico. The total collecting area of this dish is twenty acres—larger than all the telescopes ever built since the 1600s. The bowl is big enough to hold 357 million boxes of corn flakes. Suspended five hundred feet above it is a six-hundred-ton steel platform carrying the receiving and transmitting equipment. *NASA Photo*

This view of the steel platform shows its triangular shape, 210 feet long on each side. One of the three support towers stands lower left, at the rim of the bowl. The long spars projecting from the carriage houses at the bottom of the platform are "line-feed" antennae for receiving radio signals focused by the dish. They can move along the curved bottom of the feed arm, which is longer than a football field and rotates through a full circle for maximum steerability. Extending from the top left of the photo to the platform is a covered walkway leading to the ground, and, if you look closely, you can see a person standing on it, to the right of the tower. The nearer carriage house holds a half-megawatt transmitter, whose power, when focused by the big dish, creates the strongest signal leaving Earth—one that outshines, by a million times or more, the radio emission of the sun. *NASA Photo*

In 1973, when this photo was taken, I was serving as director of the National Astronomy and Ionosphere Center at Cornell University, which operates the Arecibo Observatory for the National Science Foundation.

In this artist's conception of the large deployable reflector—a proposed space radio telescope—the space shuttle ferries a ninety-foot antenna into low-Earth orbit. *NASA Photo*

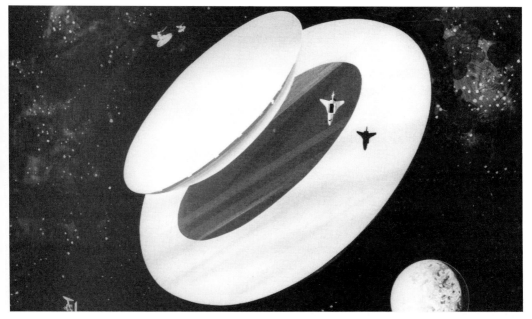

Space-based SETI systems would surpass most earthbound telescopes because they could receive radio frequencies that are blocked by Earth's atmosphere. Here is Arecibo in space—a one-thousand-foot antenna with a huge shield guarding it from Earth-generated radio interference. You can see the space shuttle nearby, its cargo bay open and its shadow falling on the shield. Two feeds, which are free-flying spacecraft, hover just above the dish, with a relay satellite at the lower left beaming the captured signals to Earth, bottom right. *NASA Photo*

This imaginative system utilizes a receiver dish nearly two *miles* wide and an even larger shield. Again we see the two feeds flying near the dish and the relay satellite in the near foreground, looking nearly as big as the dish, although it would be only a few yards in size. Earth is at lower right. *NASA Photo*

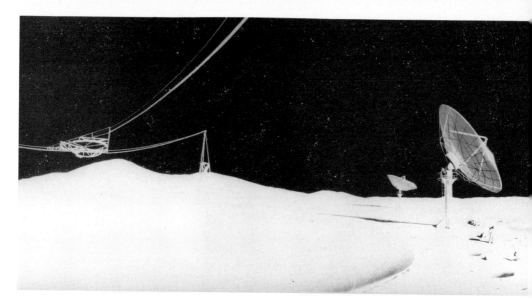

This is Arecibo on the moon, which could be up to thirty miles wide because of the lower gravity and the lack of atmosphere, wind, and weather. The far side of the moon is an ideal site because it is the only place in the solar system that is not frequently bombarded with radio signals from our civilization. *NASA Photo*

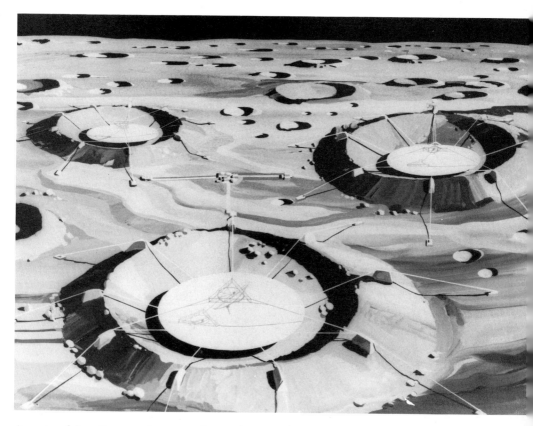

A spate of Arecibos on the moon is another good idea, exploiting lunar craters as ready-made foundations for the reflectors. *NASA Photo*

Bernard M. ("Barney") Oliver, SETI pioneer and former vice president for research and development at Hewlett-Packard, literally dropped out of the sky to view Project Ozma firsthand, and has produced a steady stream of key ideas for SETI ever since. *NASA Photo*

John ("JB") Billingham, chief of the SETI office at NASA Ames Research Center, is a former physician who is known as the SETI obstetrician, since he literally brought NASA SETI into the world. *NASA Photo*

Jill C. Tarter, project scientist (the senior scientific position) for the NASA SETI Microwave Observing Project, has conducted more SETI searches all over the world than any other person. *Photo courtesy of the SETI Institute*

Kent Cullers, who is chief signal detection scientist for NASA SETI, and blind since birth, joined the search effort after learning about Project Cyclops. *NASA Photo*

The sprawling campus of the NASA Ames Research Center in Moffet Field, California, is the headquarters of the Microwave Observing Project. *NASA Photo*

Assembled here for the first meeting of the Investigators' Working Group for the NASA SETI project in March 1991 are, from left, (first row) Barney Oliver, David Latham, Chris Neller, and John Billingham; (second row) Peter Boyce, Michael Klein, and Thomas Pierson; (third row) Samuel Gulkis, James Cordes, Peter Backus, and Kent Cullers; (fourth row) John Rummel, Jill C. Tarter, Kenneth Turner, and Paul G. Steffes; (top row) Dayton Jones, John Draher, Michael Davis, David R. Soderblom, and Woodruff T. Sullivan III. *NASA Photo*

In addition to our special commemorative T-shirts, some participants at the August 1991 U.S.-U.S.S.R. SETI Conference show off vanity plates promoting our cause. Mike Klein of JPL holds both his own (JPL SETI) and the one belonging to his wife, Barbara, a nurse (RN 4 SETI). Barney selected his plate (SETI), while the staff of the SETI Institute ordered one as a surprise for British-born John Billingham (SIR SETI). Mine is the abbreviated form of the Drake Equation (N EQLS L). Also pictured here is my wife, Amahl, in the front row between visiting Russian scientists Alexander Tutukov, left, and Nikolai Kardashev. The man in the wheelchair is David Brocker, program manager of the NASA SETI project. That's Carl Sagan next to JB at the far right of the front row of standees, and Paul Horowitz far left. In that same row, next to Paul, is Sue Robinson, the conference organizer, and Dava Sobel, my coauthor. At center is Vladimir Kotelnikov, with Barney Oliver, and Jill C. Tarter to my right.

Photo by Seth Shostak, courtesy of the SETI Institute

This 210-foot dish is part of NASA's Deep Space Network at Goldstone, California, which will be used in the targeted search part of the microwave observing project. *NASA Photo*

A near twin to the previous picture of one of the Goldstone telescopes, this instrument at Tidbinbilla, near Canberra, Australia, will help cover the Southern Hemisphere in the targeted search. *NASA Photo*

It pleases me greatly that the 140-foot equatorial telescope at Green Bank, which proved so difficult and so expensive to build, is scheduled to become a dedicated SETI instrument in 1995. *Photo courtesy of NRAO*

Housed in these unassuming-looking metal cabinets is the fifteen-million-channel receiver system for the NASA SETI all-sky survey. *Courtesy of the Jet Propulsion Laboratory*

What looks to be a star field is really a screen full of blips, or "hits," each one representing a radio channel containing signals or above-average noise. Look carefully and see if you can find the series of recurring hits that looks like an intelligent signal. (See next photo for the answer.) *NASA Photo*

With circles drawn around the right hits, the pattern becomes evident. It takes our computer system only the smallest fraction of a second to detect such a pulse train in a random jumble of radio signals or noise. *NASA Photo*

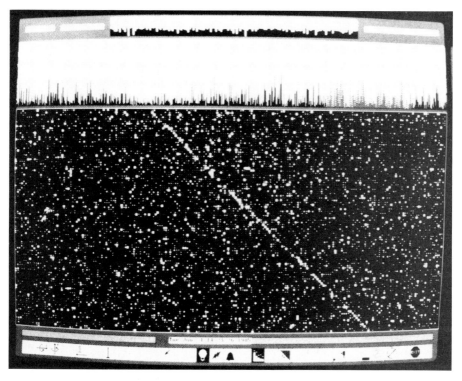

This diagonal trace on our SETI multichannel spectrum analyzer is a confirmed intelligent signal detected at a distance of 3.3 billion miles from Earth. It is not an alien communication, but the one-watt radio signal of the *Pioneer 10* spacecraft, heading out beyond the solar system, its message plaque on board. *NASA Photo*

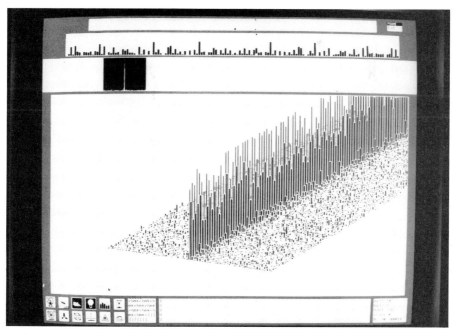

Here is an alternate way of displaying the detection of the signal in the previous photograph, using a three-dimensional-looking graph instead of a series of blips. *NASA Photo*

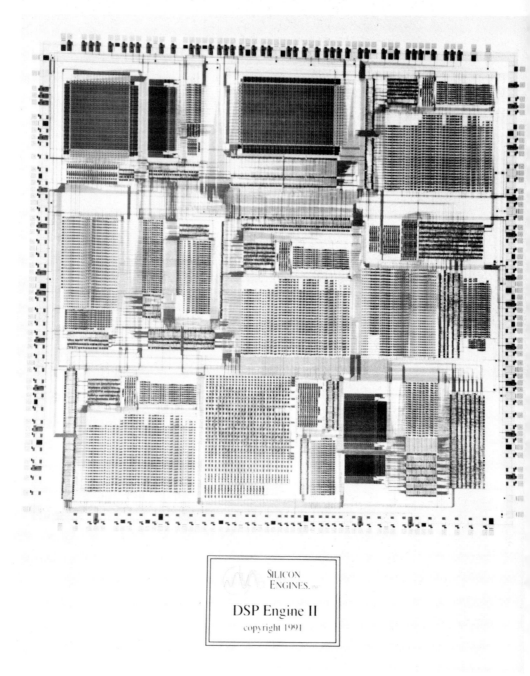

SILICON
ENGINES. ~

DSP Engine II
copyright 1991

This special-purpose computer chip, the size of a postage stamp, acts as a radio receiver in
the NASA SETI system. With its 276,000 transistors, the chip has the computational power
of a supercomputer programmed to perform the same task. *Photo courtesy of Silicon Engines*

narrow angle on the sky, just like the shape of a lighthouse beacon. As your planet rotates, this fan beam sweeps across the sky, illuminating much of the celestial sphere for some period of time every day. The power in the rotating fan beam is some fifty thousand times stronger—and therefore much more detectable at greater distances—than a widely dispersed signal. You can probably illuminate the whole universe with it, but, depending on the rotation of your planet, each entity may receive the signal for perhaps only ten minutes a year, or ten minutes a decade. It may have been just this form of signaling that created the "Wow!" and several other candidates we've detected. As you can see, this strategy buys the broadcaster the biggest bang for the buck, but it makes the listener's job quite difficult.

One thing the listener would have to do is keep a vigilant watch. By vigilant watch I mean an astronomer on duty who can immediately hop to and double-check a transient signal before it disappears. With quick reaction time, an on-the-spot observer could move the antenna to capture the signal a second and perhaps third time in the telescope's beam. Doing so would establish the fact that the signal comes from a great distance and moves with the stars. The "candidate" would be elected to office.

Then the observer would look for further evidence of intelligent artificial design in the signal itself. A narrow bandwidth in frequency would be one such sign. Polarization of 100 percent (all the radio waves in the signal oscillating or rotating in unison) is another clear indication of artificiality. The most definitive indicator of all, of course, is information coded in the signal—a stream of bits and binary numbers, for example, would do nicely, or unusual sounds, or television pictures.

This kind of instant replay and examination of the signal is simply not possible at most observatories. Funding is too scant to pay for someone to track the data in "real time" as signals are received. Typical observers discover signal candidates hours or days after the fact, while plodding through reams of computer printout, just as Jerry Ehman did. The discovery still stimulates a sense of "Eureka!"—still elicits a breathless "Wow!" in response—but it's too late to do anything about it. Ideally, a search program would boast enough staff members to require every radio astronomer to spend a small portion of each day watching the data come in, ready to jump if need be. But as Project Ozma showed, all these astronomers must have other research interests and duties to keep them vital. And they must serve short shifts, perhaps no more than four hours at a time, to keep boredom at bay.

Soon after the excitement of the "Wow!" signal, the Ohio State search program nearly ground to a halt. Lack of funding had failed to kill it all those years, but the future looked bleak when the university sold the land out from under the observatory to a developer who owned a neighboring golf course. The new owner set out to scrap the telescope to make room for yet another fairway, on this site. Negotiations and public outcry spared the telescope in the end, though it now pays an annual fee to the golf course. I salute John Kraus, who has since retired, and especially Bob Dixon, who keeps the search running, even today, in spite of everything.*

In 1973, when Kraus and Dixon were flying their observatory on a wing and a prayer, I found myself with an embarrassment of riches, spending roughly $9 million in federal grants to upgrade the Arecibo Observatory in Puerto Rico. Between 1970 and 1981 I was director of the National Astronomy and Ionosphere Center, a national research facility consisting of the Arecibo telescope with all its support staff, both in Puerto Rico and at Cornell University in Ithaca.

As a result of Arecibo's demonstrated stability in the teeth of Hurricane Inez, as described in Chapter 4, the NSF and NASA produced the money to stabilize the platform further, install new receiving and transmitting equipment, and completely resurface the reflector bowl. We could no longer be content with the lumpy, sagging wire mesh in the bowl. That mesh, after all, had been chosen to match a platform thought to bounce in the breeze. Our stable platform deserved a smooth, hard surface that would properly focus radiation at the short wavelengths needed for many studies in radio astronomy, including the search for extraterrestrial intelligence. We literally tore the observatory apart and rebuilt it to achieve higher accuracy, more wavelength coverage, and better resolution. It was a major undertaking that lasted several years, orchestrated to allow scientific observations to continue at some level for the duration.

First we stripped off the old wire mesh in the reflector bowl, a section at a time, the way a spider rebuilds its web. We rolled it up

* In recent years, John Billingham's group at NASA has provided some financial support to the Ohio State project.

and recycled it by offering it free to farmers in the area. They found it made good fencing for their chickens.

Then we replaced the mesh with about forty thousand panels of shiny, perforated aluminum attached to specially formed aluminum frames. Rather than risk transporting so many fragile panels over the corkscrew road leading into and out of Arecibo, we built an aluminum factory right on the observatory grounds and made them there. Our on-site factory processed some three hundred tons of aluminum, turning out the panel sheets as well as 277 miles of aluminum belt, which we fashioned into the gridwork frames. It occurred to me at one point that a 277-mile length of aluminum belt was almost enough to build a guardrail all the way around the island of Puerto Rico.

Compared to the old wire mesh, the smooth aluminum surface constitutes a precision instrument. The new surface is about ten times more precise than the old. We can adjust each panel individually, traveling under the surface on a special trolley system, and survey the entire surface of the dish to an accuracy of better than one millimeter in a single night.

The panels and their aluminum support frame rest on a network of steel cables traversing the bowl in east-west and north-south lines. These connect by tie-down cables to thousands of concrete blocks anchored in the ground around and under the dish. We laid roughly forty additional miles of cable during the upgrading, and another fifteen hundred concrete anchors to hold them. There was as much fresh concrete in these new anchors (4,100 cubic yards) as we had poured to build the tallest support tower at the observatory.

Soon after we started the reflector upgrading, some of the workers noticed that the ground around the southeast rim of the bowl was shifting. That was the part that had been constructed originally on dirt fill. With the added weight to hold, it needed a new foundation, anchored in the limestone fifty feet down. So we brought in an oil well drill rig by ship from Houston and bored eighty holes through the fill to the bedrock. We lodged a three-foot-diameter steel pipe filled with concrete in each hole. Then we lashed the pipes with steel cables to other, shorter pipes, driven into the rock of the mountain behind the bowl. We wound up with a structure resembling an enormous railroad trestle, but completely hidden underground.

You don't notice the greenery from above, but when you walk the winding path under the reflector surface, you thread your way through a dense growth of vegetation that keeps the soil from eroding. The whole bowl-filling expanse of concrete, steel, and aluminum ultimately depends on the delicate-looking ferns and orchids to keep the ground firm. The aluminum panels, each dotted with thousands of small holes, form a most unusual forest canopy. They let the rain pour through unimpeded, but admit only as much sunlight as shines on the surface of Mars. The ferns flourish nevertheless.

When the hard work of the upgrading was done, we threw a big party in November 1974 and celebrated the telescope's new power by flexing its muscles in the most flamboyant way we could imagine: We prepared a message for extraterrestrials, and beamed it deep into space during the dedication ceremony. (The following chapter offers a full discussion of this and other interstellar messages I helped devise.)

The telescope was now ready to search for signs of extraterrestrial intelligence. In the heat of the upgrading, I'd kept that goal in mind, but at the end I was almost too exhausted to take on the project. Carl Sagan began pushing me. He had been eager to search nearby galaxies with me at Arecibo ever since I had outlined the idea at the Byurakan conference in 1971.

"Let's do it," Carl would say over the telephone. We both had offices in Cornell's Space Sciences Building, and whenever I bumped into him there, or anywhere else on campus, he'd start up again with his "Let's do it." So we soon wrote a proposal requesting observing time for our project (which never had a name). Our idea was to look beyond the Milky Way, where we could examine whole galaxies at a time, hoping to ferret out the sages of very ancient civilizations.

Ron Bracewell of Stanford had just written a new book called *The Galactic Club,* in which he suggested that many advanced civilizations might already be in contact with each other. He thought the club members might send out strong beacons, such as fan beams, to attract newcomers like us. These narrow-band beacons would catch our attention and name the right frequency to tune to receive the broad-band channels carrying all the truly astonishing information gleaned from the club's collective experience. Arecibo was (and still is) the telescope most likely to detect and receive such transmissions.

The Project Cyclops report, too, had talked of an advanced supercommunity that might one day accept the Earth as a member. There might also be many civilizations in space that were less advanced. Nearly every consideration of the Drake Equation suggested that alien civilizations distributed themselves at various levels of development. We were unlikely, however, to find any civilizations less technically proficient than our own, for those that had not yet invented radios remained invisible to our telescopes. But all the ones more advanced than our own could be transmitting in our direction. Any civilization we detected would almost certainly be ahead of us—perhaps by thousands or millions of years.

Just as the visible stars and radio sources displayed a great natural range of brightness, we could well expect to see a wide diversity in the maximum powers transmitted by alien civilizations. If even a tiny percentage of extraterrestrials had reached superior heights of technological sophistication, their societies might shine brilliantly in the sky because of their radio and television transmissions, radio astronomy activities, and communication with other planets of other stars. Even if they were separated from us by enormous distances, they would still outshine more modest civilizations nearer to us—and by their brightness be the more readily detectable.

Carl and I planned to search for intelligent signals from four galaxies that lay just beyond the Milky Way. By scanning a chunk of a galaxy with each observation, we would be able to see huge numbers of stars simultaneously. It seemed like a very efficient approach: Instead of the two close stars I had examined in the first search at Green Bank, Carl and I would scan hundreds of billions of distant ones in practically no time at all. If there were but one supercivilization in a galaxy, we would find it. If one small outpost of ancient aliens could transmit signals a million times more powerful than our own, then we might well see this beacon from their home star shine a million times more brightly than normal on the wavelength of their beacon. That unnatural brilliance would be a sure sign that other intelligent beings were looking up into their night sky from very different worlds, asking the same kinds of questions we ask.

Even if they weren't broadcasting intentionally, we might still find them if their signals were strong enough. At Arecibo, the radar system used to study the planets emits a narrow-bandwidth signal that could be detected from the far side of the Milky Way by a telescope similar to that at Arecibo. On its particular radar frequency, Arecibo appears about ten million times brighter than the Sun.

The big multichannel receivers I had long been anticipating were in place now, so that Arecibo covered more than 1,000 channels at once, as opposed to the single channel I had used for Project Ozma in 1960. We would be able to monitor 1,008 frequencies simultaneously.

Carl and I stayed in a small hotel at the beach in the town of Guajataca, because there was no room for us in the visiting scientists' quarters at the observatory. What with the telescope time we had booked, the hour that our target galaxies rose in the sky, and the difficulty of driving to the observatory over the narrow, winding road, we asked the night attendant at the hotel to awaken us long before daybreak. The only other hotel guests up at that hour were the ones whose tropical sunburns wouldn't let them sleep.

I drove. Carl would sit propped up in the front seat, eyes closed, munching laboriously on scraps of dried-out garlic bread rescued from the previous night's dinner. It was all the breakfast we had during those days, but once inside the control room, our excitement sustained us. As the dawn sky turned pink, we steered the telescope antenna and scrutinized the instrument displays for patterns that could not have been made by chance alone—patterns that revealed intent and intelligence.

Every thirty seconds, one hundred thousand transistors would transmit the recorded emissions to the observatory's memory. Then the information captured in each of the thousand-plus channels would splash a wave of twinkling green points across the face of an oscilloscope. In 0.01 second, we covered more ground in space than I had done in two months in 1960.

We took M-33,* the Great Nebula in Triangulum, for our prime

------

* The M stands for Messier—Charles Messier, an eighteenth-century French astronomer and comet hunter who set out to catalog all the fuzzy objects in the sky that were *not* comets. Most of these later turned out to be galaxies and emission nebulas. Messier assigned his numbers almost haphazardly, with no regard for right ascension or declination—the latitude and longitude, respectively, of the heavens. His first catalog entry, M-1, is now better known as the Crab Nebula, which, by sheer coincidence, is the brightest and most important cosmic radio source of all.

target. It's a nearby spiral galaxy, much like Andromeda in appearance, but smaller. Its great beauty was that we could see all of it from Arecibo, whereas the telescope could take in only half of Andromeda. Our other targets were dwarf galaxies, small enough to capture in their entirety in one setting of the telescope's beam.

For this search, just as in Project Ozma fifteen years before, I was present in the control room. I was observing the spectra as they came in. Carl and I watched everything together, but it soon became apparent how differently we approached the task. Carl, who spent most of his time exploring other planets via flybys and remote landers, such as the Mariner and Viking missions to Mars, was used to the excitement of a discovery a minute. When he sat in the control room at JPL, phenomenal photographs from other worlds would stream in, another one every couple of minutes, and all the planetary scientists would have to hustle to interpret the strange new findings, with barely a moment to "Oooh" and "Aaah."

Our radio search, despite its exotic goal, was more like everyday astronomy—where nothing happens for hours on end. I think Carl's prior experience had led him to believe that we might discover an alien signal right away. Even the first half hour of our galaxy-combing strategy had let us look at ten billion stars. Perhaps that should have been enough. When a full hour passed and we still hadn't found anything, I could sense Carl's disappointment. After a few days he was even a little bored by the sight of the green dots appearing uneventfully on the screen. And who could blame him?

I was not immune to disappointment and boredom myself—just more used to a slower unraveling of the universe's mysteries. The search for extraterrestrial life is particularly slow going, as opposed to the hunt for pulsars, say, or the mapping of the radio sky. This is why no astronomer can devote his or her full time to searching. The fallow periods are too long for an active mind to tolerate. At the same time, I thought as I stole a glance at Carl and caught him looking out the control room window, there will always be a place in the search for the human operator. We'll always need an astronomer carefully studying the incoming data, to make judgments and to experience the thrill of the great moment when that moment finally comes.

Carl and I were not to experience the rush of discovery in our one hundred hours of observing stars of other galaxies at Arecibo.

Still, we came away from the experiment questioning our methods more than our results. After all, we had looked on only a few frequencies, and only for a minute or so at each star. We could easily have picked the wrong frequency or the wrong time. The negative outcome didn't settle anything. Nor did it show that our galaxy strategy was a poor one. In fact, Carl and I know we should expand and repeat our search, and someday we will. But in 1976, when we wrapped up our project, Arecibo went back to business as usual, and the question of whether the other galaxies were populated loomed as large as ever.

Right around that time, the Cyclops report, which was still circulating through the scientific community, reached a graduate student in astrophysics at Berkeley named Jill Tarter. She was pursuing theoretical research into invisible entities. One of her special interests was would-be stars that never successfully turn on their fires. (She named these "brown dwarfs.") She also sought the "missing mass"—the invisible, hypothetical material that many astronomers believe must lurk among the visible galaxies, as there doesn't appear to be enough matter to account for the gravitational attraction among clusters of galaxies. She enjoyed a reputation at the University of California as a person with a passion for hunting the hard-to-find. Undetected alien civilizations fit right into her view of the universe, and she immediately wanted to look for them.

It was brave of Jill, who was not only a young scientist but also a female scientist, to take up the search for extraterrestrial intelligence. Such a pursuit could have hurt her career more than it might have hurt someone else's. But Jill demonstrated her characteristic intellectual independence and followed her interest.

Jill's maiden name is Cornell, and she is distantly related to Ezra Cornell, the university's founder. His will stipulated that all his male descendants with the Cornell name would be entitled to attend Cornell University tuition-free. As the first female descendant to petition for the same privilege, Jill was roundly refused by the tough, tradition-bound university administration. On that very day, however, Procter & Gamble offered her an even better scholarship. It included textbooks and living expenses as well as tuition, enabling her to attend Cornell and take her undergraduate degree in engineering physics. Tall and strong-looking as well as pretty, she was the only woman in her class. But Jill, who had twirled a baton as a drum majorette in high school, was not the least bit self-conscious about choosing a traditionally masculine field.*

I was teaching at Cornell when Jill was a student there, but she never enrolled in any of my courses. I wish she had—and I wish I could take credit for recruiting her as a scientist who is today one of the foremost researchers in this field. But that honor belongs to Stuart Bowyer, an X-ray astronomer Jill worked with at Berkeley, who showed her the Cyclops study and subsequently shared her excitement over it. Bowyer had devised a new approach that would allow him to take up this line of work—without any funding or even any observing time of his own on a telescope.

He and Jill rounded up old, out-of-service equipment and rearranged it to ride piggyback on another telescope, which was being used for other purposes by other astronomers. They first tried this idea on the 85-foot radio telescope at the University of California's Hat Creek Radio Observatory near Mount Shasta. Bowyer and Tarter, with several other rash colleagues from Berkeley, hung a little black box at the back end of the telescope—a little spy that fed them all the same captured radio energy that the primary researchers received. (Once the incoming energy is amplified, it can be distributed to several receivers with no loss in the detectability of any signals that may be present.) With a donated computer that Jill programmed for their special purpose, they analyzed the borrowed data for intelligent signals. They called their effort Project Serendip.

As Jill tells the story, the system had to fend for itself at Hat Creek, since she and Bowyer had no real reason for being there, and nobody else had time to worry about their equipment. Sometimes the black box would malfunction by turning itself off, though no one noticed when this happened. A week or two might go by before she or Bowyer dropped around for a periodic check, only to discover that the machine hadn't listened to anything for days.

Serendip represented a whole new direction in searching—a "parasitic search mode," as Jill calls it. But it followed a very old

---

* Today Jill is frequently the only woman at specialized astronomy meetings—a situation she handles with great aplomb. Indeed, when I read Carl Sagan's novel *Contact*, I thought of Jill at every mention of the heroine, Eleanor Arroway, who directs the observatory where the first intelligent message of extraterrestrial origin is received.

course in human exploration—that of using any means available to break new ground. Columbus didn't wait for the invention of the jetliner before setting off to discover America. Neither Bowyer nor Tarter was going to wait for Cyclops. If Cyclops was too grand and too expensive—well then, there were other routes to the universal community of intelligent life.

Serendip stayed at Hat Creek for nine years, before moving on to Green Bank, where it was welcomed aboard the 300-foot telescope. After two years of smooth symbiosis between the giant instrument and the little black box, the telescope suffered its famed collapse, summarily ending Serendip II. As I mentioned in Chapter 2, the cause of the collapse was structural fatigue, but a few newspapers enthusiastically proclaimed otherwise: Angry aliens had trashed the telescope to stop Earthlings from monitoring their signals. Temporarily homeless, Serendip moved on to Arecibo, to help in a study of radio interference there, and later returned to Berkeley. A new generation, Serendip III, is about to go into continuous piggyback operation at Arecibo.

The name Serendip comes from a tale by Horace Walpole called *The Three Princes of Serendip*, about making desirable discoveries by accident. Later Jill turned it into an acronym, too: Search for Extraterrestrial Radio Emission from Nearby Developed Intelligent Populations.

Over the years, the Dolphins had evolved an acronym for the whole enterprise of exchanging radio signals across the galaxies. We called it CETI, for Communication with ExtraTerrestrial Intelligence. We pronounced it with a soft *c* (SETtee), as in Tau Ceti (the first star searched by Project Ozma, in the constellation Cetus, the Whale). Probably as early as the Order of the Dolphin meeting in 1961, CETI popped up as our shorthand way of referring to our efforts. And at the Byurakan meeting in 1971, our Soviet hosts gave us souvenir pins with the letters CETI forming an internationally recognized emblem.

By the mid-1970s, however, it occurred to us that using the word *communication* sounded rather arrogant, as we hadn't found anyone to communicate with. We were still *searching*. So we changed our acronym to SETI—Search for ExtraTerrestrial Intelligence. NASA adopted the new term first, to christen its growing involvement in search activities. Soon "SETI" was accepted in the international community as well—and not only in name, but also in new search projects undertaken at the Max-Planck-Institut für

Radioastronomie in Effelesberg, Germany, and the Westerbork Synthesis Radio Telescope in the Netherlands.

The Soviets had new projects in the works, too, and in 1981 they invited us to a second international meeting, this time in Tallinn, Estonia. The tone of the meeting, the living conditions, and the weather could not have been more different from our first, pleasant gathering in Byurakan. In December, Tallinn is a place where one could freeze to death. I recall that the Sun never rose before mid-morning, hovered near the horizon for a few hours, and set shortly after lunch. From 4:00 P.M. on it was pitch black, and the wind howled constantly. Looking out the hotel window at 9:00 A.M. or 5:00 P.M., in the dim glow of the few streetlights, I could see lines of Estonians trudging through the darkness on their way to or from work, bodies bent forward against the blowing snow.

The fact that the meeting was held in Tallinn, just a four-hour Soviet ferry ride from Helsinki, Finland, cut the travel costs greatly. I flew with a contingent of nine Americans, including Barney Oliver and Bob Dixon, to the meeting on a very limited travel budget. Carl was not part of our party, although I did bring along six copies of his book *Cosmos*. As a result, I had to wait while a Soviet customs agent checked through each page of each copy, and then examined every one of my several hundred slides. I think he was not really looking for spy material but maybe a young lady in a bikini.

We stayed in a relatively fancy hotel that had been built by the Finns, but there was no food to speak of in the restaurant. Food shortages already plagued the Soviet Union. The hotel kitchen staff apparently stole most of the better food to keep their families from starving, leaving the guests minimal provisions of poor quality.

Those were bleak days for Estonia. As visiting scientists, however, we Americans were treated royally in every way possible. When we commuted from our hotel to the meeting site each day in our private bus, for example, we had a police escort that shot ahead of us, stopping traffic at every intersection to give us clear passage.

We started out with only one woman in our contingent, Jill Tarter, but our Estonian bus came staffed with a Russian woman from Moscow introduced as our "interpreter." Within two minutes we discovered that she spoke almost no English. But she was astoundingly attractive, and dressed in a fur coat and fine clothes that simply weren't available in the local stores. She tried to attach herself to each of the men in our group, to no avail. When no one expressed any interest in her, she took a seat in the back of the bus, pouted, and ignored us all for the duration of the four-day meeting. She left the translation duties to a second (male) interpreter, who talked easily in both languages.

We were positively hounded by the Soviet press. Reporters nearly came to blows with each other in battling for our attention. For a group of astronomers in what folks back home regarded as a questionable discipline, this was a pleasant but unprecedented predicament. Television coverage of our visit included news spots and an hour-long program on prime time, during which I was interviewed by the Soviet cosmonaut Vitaly Sevastianov, who had flown in space three times.

I later learned that the local audience for such state broadcasts was limited. True, a giant television tower that transmitted all the Soviet state channels virtually dominated the landscape in Tallinn. However, I couldn't help but notice that all the television antennas on the rooftops were pointing not at this tower, but in the direction of Helsinki, just sixty miles away across the Gulf of Finland. The residents could all receive Western television this way, and their favorite show, they told us, was *Dallas*.

The meeting itself, truth to tell, was not very good. In fact, several of the Soviet papers were downright embarrassing. One proposed that we should send a message that said: $10^2 + 11^2 + 12^2 = 13^2 + 14^2$. Why? Because it was a "mind-catching" equation, and because the sums on each side of the equals sign totaled 365— the number of days in an Earth year. The same paper went on to suggest that extraterrestrials had perhaps adjusted the Earth's rotation to bring about this striking equality!

I remember the "evidence" presented, from photographs taken by the *Viking* spacecraft, for the existence of mammoth alien-made monuments on Mars. One scientist even espoused the idea that certain dying stars, known as "blue stragglers," were being kept alive by extraterrestrials: The aliens threw "logs" of hydrogen into the stars to stoke their nuclear fires.

Shklovsky, a vibrant presence at the meeting, as always, got up on the stage at one point and launched a tirade against his colleagues for the bad science they were doing. A shouting match ensued, with Shklovsky crying "False logic!" while his adversaries defended reports of UFOs sighted over Leningrad.

There were several excellent papers, too, offered by Shklovsky, Kardashev, Troitsky, and others. A key presentation from our group was Barney's talk about the possible high visibility of very slowly pulsed signals from extraterrestrials. And when Dixon described the Ohio State search program, details of the "Wow!" gave added emphasis to Barney's comments.

I brought up an idea I'd developed at Arecibo with a Cornell graduate student named George Helou. All through our years of searching for extraterrestrial signals, we radio astronomers had been on the lookout for extremely narrow-band transmissions. We fully expected intelligent signals to have a narrow bandwidth, to distinguish themselves as artificial. Nearly every natural radio emission, in contrast, has a broad bandwidth. What's more, narrow-band signals can be sent across great distances and still maintain their identity. The narrower the bandwidth of a transmission, the stronger the signal appears on its frequency and the more easily detectable it is.

The great expectation that extraterrestrial signals would be extremely narrow-band affected our equipment design. We were heading toward narrower and narrower channels, in the hope of capturing the most narrow-band, most detectable signals of all.

But Helou and I discovered that narrow-band signals get broader as they pass through moving clouds of free electrons in interstellar space. When radio waves of a single frequency pass through such an electron cloud, the motion of the cloud has a Doppler effect on them, changing their frequency. The waves then travel along separate curved and changing paths through space. As a result, a signal that starts out from a distant star as a single narrow-band frequency arrives at Earth over a small range of frequencies, having been spread out by its passage through the electron clouds. (Even radio signals find travel broadening!)

We had first noticed this effect during observations of the Crab Nebula. Single-frequency radio emissions from the Crab, wending their way through the electron clouds, would experience ever-so-subtle deflections from a straight line, finally to arrive at Arecibo over a period of several thousandths of a second instead of at the same instant. Such a minuscule but measurable effect was nevertheless enough to change significantly the signal's frequency and bandwidth.*

---

* Multifrequency, or broad-band, signals also arrive from space spread out in time by transiting electron clouds. The highest-frequency part of the signal arrives first, followed in succession by the middle and lower frequencies. A signal with a very broad bandwidth may take several minutes to complete its arrival.

The clouds thus put a lower limit on the narrowness of the bandwidth we can expect to receive from extraterrestrials. That natural restriction has since been named the "Drake-Helou Limit." It stipulates that no interstellar radio signal, no matter how narrow it is when transmitted, can reach Earth with a bandwidth narrower than a few hundredths of a hertz. If we build our receivers for bandwidths narrower than that, we'll actually *miss* the signals we're trying so hard to detect.

SETI researchers in the States, I told the gathering at Tallinn, were already taking these limiting factors into account in the design of new receiver systems.

The Drake-Helou Limit also hinted at a new region of the electromagnetic spectrum where we might logically search for extraterrestrial intelligence. We had been focusing our investigations in the region where the universe is darkest and quietest: the waterhole. Our choice "magic frequency" was the 21-centimeter line that Morrison and Cocconi had suggested in their pioneering paper and that I had selected for Project Ozma. Twenty years later, it still seemed reasonable to us that all technologically advanced civilizations would recognize the obvious advantage of exploiting that quiet region of the radio spectrum. That was where their beacons or other signals were most likely to stand out and be noticed. But now there was a new wrinkle. Those low frequencies of the waterhole region were the ones most likely to be affected by the electron clouds. Very-high-frequency signals would fare much better over interstellar distances. The higher the frequency of the signal at its source, the less it is spread out by electron clouds in space.

This is an observable fact. Extraterrestrials would not have to come up with theories to figure this out; they would see it, as we do, when pursuing ordinary research in radio astronomy. The implication is that the best way to keep a signal intact is to broadcast it at very high radio frequencies—many times higher than the frequency of the waterhole.

"If we want to be totally logical, in the style of Mr. Spock," I pointed out, "we have to take *both* phenomena into account: the universe's quiet zone *and* the Drake-Helou Limit. When you do that, you arrive at an optimum frequency of about seventy gigahertz. Here is where the most detectable signal can be created using the least power."

Everyone at the meeting suddenly went for coffee. I had dropped a bomb. The seventy-gigahertz region is inaccessible to Earth-based observers, literally blocked out by the oxygen in our atmosphere. If my reasoning was right, we might have to put an observatory in space—in low Earth orbit, or the far side of the Moon.

Even today, when I talk about this idea at meetings, it makes most astronomers want to put their heads in the sand. To the average person, not conversant with the technicalities or goals of SETI, such thoughts may appear impossibly arcane and farfetched. Why should we spend so much time figuring out what extraterrestrials might do? Where should such pursuits figure in a world full of starving children and diminishing natural resources? I know many individuals who would argue that we must tend first to the economic and political crises here on Earth. We need to remedy all the conditions, from the threat of global warming to the bloodshed of global terrorism, that menace our quality of life—even our very existence.

I agree that these issues could not be more urgent, and yet I do not believe that searching for extraterrestrial life is irrelevant or trivial by comparison. I maintain, in the spirit of the Cyclops report, that searching for other life in the universe is not an unnecessary luxury but an essential component of forging a better life for humankind.

In the 1960s and 1970s, the space program drew attention to the fragile beauty of our home planet. It was the sight of the Earth from space that shocked most of us into a true ecological awareness. Now, in the 1990s, the search endeavor promises to help position our lives against the backdrop of the universe at large, where other kinds of beings may share our plight, and expose us to an enormous wealth of shared facts and experiences that will enable us to gain new wisdom.

There is probably no quicker route to wisdom than to be the student of more-advanced civilizations. But just learning of the existence of other civilizations in space—even if they are no more advanced than our own—could catapult nations into a new unity of purpose. Indeed, the search activity itself reminds us that the differences among nations are as nothing compared to the differences among worlds. An implicit goal of interstellar communication is to draw together the residents of Earth, to make us recognize how intimately related we are compared to life-forms elsewhere.

In this tenor of global unity, the flag of Earth—with its simple colored circles depicting the blue planet, the white Moon, and the yellow Sun against the black field of space—flies at every observatory around the world involved in SETI activities. Part of the reason we search is to explore and confirm our common heritage.

To discover that we share the Galaxy or the universe with other sentient beings would upend our view of life and change our perspective of what it means to be human. I see it as an awakening, just like the one that followed Copernicus's revolutionary idea that the Earth was not the center of the universe. That revelation had tremendous social significance, and even figured as one of the key factors in the rise of democracy. The discovery of other life-forms would in turn cause us to understand human nature far better, and open our eyes to the fact that we have a variety of destinies from which to choose.

I fully expect an alien civilization to bequeath us vast libraries of useful information, to do with as we wish. This "Encyclopedia Galactica" will create the potential for improvements in our lives that we cannot predict. During the Renaissance, rediscovered ancient texts and new knowledge flooded medieval Europe with the light of thought, wonder, creativity, experimentation, and exploration of the natural world. Another, even more stirring Renaissance will be fueled by the wealth of alien scientific, technical, and sociological information that awaits us.

I can only guess what a civilization far more advanced than our own might teach us. Your speculation is as good as mine, but let me share one of my favorite "what ifs" with you: What if *they* are immortal?

I suspect that immortality may be quite common among extraterrestrials. By immortality I mean the indefinite preservation, in a living being, of a growing and continuous set of memories of individual experience. I think this might come about through the development of methods to eliminate the aging process, or to repair indefinitely the damage caused by aging.

Even we humans are closer to being able to do this than people realize. Most of us view the slow destruction of our bodily organs and our mental processes as an inevitable law of nature. But this is not true. There is nothing in the chemistry of life to require deterioration and death. The system of passing genetic information through the DNA molecule is an extremely robust one, with enormous protections against degeneration. We age and die because we have been programmed to do so, just as salmon suddenly grow old and expire within days of laying their eggs. Death is a way for one generation to make room for the next. But death can be outsmarted. Scientists have already located the gene that causes us to age. It lies on chromosome number one in human DNA. When that chromosome is removed from human cells in the laboratory, those cells cease to age.

Some aliens may already know how to transfer immortality from single cells to entire organisms. Or they may be able to transfer the inventory of memories of an old brain into a young brain—perhaps even the brain of a clone, or an exact copy of a being whose individuality is to be preserved. Death, in such a society, could only occur through the physical destruction of the individual in an accident, say, or by murder.

Although we can grasp some of the differences between our lives and those of immortal individuals, the totality of differences between us is surely beyond our comprehension. The immortals must have a fantastic obsession with safety, and every device and vehicle must be so constructed to present no lethal hazard under any circumstance. Speed limits would be nearly zero, to prevent any hazardous crashes, and because there would be no need to get anywhere in a hurry. Wars probably don't exist among immortals, who would not take the risk of fighting.

I think a civilization of immortals would be extremely active in detecting and communicating with other intelligent civilizations. Not only would they want to extend their resources for amusement beyond their own planetary system, but also communication would grant them the ultimate protection from harm.

Given their reverence for the preservation of individual lives, they would take every precaution against physical threats from other planets. They would appreciate the extreme unlikelihood of an interstellar visit or attack, but still they would want absolute assurance of safety. At first, it might seem to them that their best bet would be to try to conceal themselves—perhaps even prohibit transmission of radio signals that could be detected by other civilizations.

But a better strategy, I think, would soon occur to them, and that is to help other societies become immortal, too. Then they would never have to fret over the risk of hazardous military adventures, because the societies they instructed would inherit their same insatiable desire for personal safety. I therefore would expect the immortals to spread actively the secrets of their immortality among young, technically developing civilizations—and thus to change the lives of beings such as ourselves.

Sometimes, when I look at the stars twinkling in the sequined panorama of the night sky, I wonder if, among the most common interstellar missives coming from them, is the grand instruction book that tells creatures how to live forever.

CHAPTER 8

▲
▲
▲

The Case
for Intelligent Life
on Earth

*This is a present from a small distant world, a token of
our sounds, our science, our images, our music, our
thoughts, and our feelings. We are attempting to survive our time so we may live into yours. We hope
someday, having solved the problems we face, to join a
community of galactic civilizations. This record repre-
sents our hope and our determination, and our goodwill in a vast and awesome universe.*

—U.S. president JIMMY CARTER,
1977 *Voyager* spacecraft interstellar record

When you search for extraterrestrial life, when
you contemplate what frequencies might be the right frequencies
and what form an alien message may take, your thoughts turn
sooner or later to strategies for sending your own intelligible signals to "them."

I first caught myself thinking of this question soon after the
Order of the Dolphin meeting in 1961. That conference had given
such support to the concept of the search that communication
seemed almost at hand.

What would I say to an extraterrestrial? What precedent did I have for such an extraordinary cultural exchange? None, really. When I'd studied Russian in college, I balked at the idea of trying to establish a correspondence with a Soviet student studying English. There were just too many linguistic and political barriers. Yet the task before me now was infinitely more challenging—like writing a love letter to a woman I'd never met, who not only spoke a foreign language but also lived at an unknown address. She might not be able to read, or even to see. She might turn out to be not a woman after all—but a whale, perhaps, or a flower, or maybe a spider, or a virus, or something I simply could not imagine.

In my analogy, I was thinking of drafting an intentional message, devised for an extraterrestrial intelligence to decode with ease. But I recognized right away that *unintentional* messages were already being dispatched, on an almost continual basis, in the form of television programs. Thanks to television, we had become a readily detectable civilization years earlier, starting in the late 1920s. I knew very well that episodes of *I Love Lucy* and Uncle Miltie were spreading out to the stars, and the signals were becoming stronger every year as broadcast power increased. It was a sobering thought that the first sign of terrestrial intelligence might come from the mouth of Howdy Doody! But at the time, I wasn't worrying about our interstellar image. I was just trying to figure out what signals could be received at enormous distances by radio telescopes not much greater than our own. (Years later, in 1978, Woodruff Sullivan, professor of astronomy at the University of Washington in Seattle, would show with satellite studies that the strongest and most easily detected message from Earth, by far, is the action at the Super Bowl, which is broadcast from more transmitters than any other signal of this world.)

The format of television transmissions, if not the content, seemed to me to be the ideal medium for signaling extraterrestrials. We would be able to send unambiguous interstellar messages by transmitting pictures resembling ordinary television images. We could communicate with extraterrestrials in much the same way that we teach our babies to speak—by showing them pictures and naming the items in those pictures. *This is a human being. This is the planet Earth. This is our star, the Sun.* After all, we can go to another country where we don't understand the language, and from its television learn much—including, eventually, the language.

To send a picture across interstellar distances at the speed of light, the image should be as simple as possible. The clearer the information, I thought, the less it could get garbled en route. I decided that first messages should be all black and white, with no shades of gray. Black and white are more than adequate for sketching the prime characteristics of any image. What's more, a simple binary (two-color) image could be easily transmitted by any known communications system—as the alternating zeros and ones of computer talk, as the dots and dashes of Morse code, or as two tones of different frequencies that could be beamed into space by a radio telescope.

I began trying to construct a message in pencil on a sheet of graph paper. I colored some squares black and left others white. It took me a while to get used to drawing that way, without the luxury of curves. But I saw that a simple pattern of black and white spots could really tell a lot in a short space. I fit everything I wanted to say in a grid of 551 squares. I had a particular reason for choosing that peculiar number of squares, as I'll explain.

According to the conventional wisdom of scientific information theory, 551 characters should contain about the same quantity of information as 25 English words. But you know what they say about a single picture being worth 10,000 words. My message, with its 551 bits, contained a great deal more information content than I could have expressed in 25 words, no matter how carefully I had chosen those words. It expressed more because, first of all, it was a picture. I concede that it looked for all the world like a strange crossword puzzle from the Sunday newspaper, but it was still a picture. (See Figure 8.1.) And it had something else going for it, too: Its message was constructed with concepts of science that I knew were shared with the recipients. Our common language—call it radio-telescopese—guaranteed that we both understood physics and astronomy, and these concepts provided a ready shorthand for expressing some very big ideas.

I was able to squeeze into my 551 bits all of the following facts about the "extraterrestrial" me:

- A schematic drawing of my solar system, although its star was perforce square-shaped, and the nine planets admittedly boxy-looking.

FIGURE 8.1. A demonstration message.

- Crude diagrams of the oxygen and carbon molecules, to say something about my life chemistry.
- A rough self-portrait, showing that I stand with my head in the air and my two legs on the ground.
- Representations of the numbers one through five in binary code. (Since there's no reason to assume all life-forms have

ten fingers, I count by twos instead of by tens, using the simplest number system.)

- Three numbers—four billion, two thousand, and five— written in the binary code described. I drew a diagonal line (in boxes) from me to the largest number, which I placed next to the fourth planet from our sun, to show that there were billions of my kind living there. The second number, next to the third planet, was meant to indicate that a couple thousand of us had colonized that world. The third and smallest number, positioned near the second planet, was the news that we'd sent an exploratory party to check out the place.
- Under my picture was a symbol. It was different from the numbers because it had an even number of bits, whereas all the numbers were written with an odd number of bits to distinguish them as numbers. This, I hoped my interpreters would understand, was a word. It was four bits long, mak- ing my name "Four Bits." In future messages, I could refer to myself by this name and not have to draw my picture, which took up half the message space.
- A diagram on my left was meant to show my height: 31. You may well ask, "31 what?" But if you received the message via radio telescope, you would know that the only measure of length you and I have in common is the wavelength of the transmission, which, if it is somewhere near the middle of the waterhole, is ten centimeters. That makes me three hun- dred ten centimeters tall, or, in common American terms, about ten feet high.

This done, and feeling ten feet high from the exhilaration of it, I transcribed the picture into a long stream of zeros and ones. I didn't try to keep the digits arranged in the 29-by-19 grid I'd used in my drawing; I just typed them on a plain piece of paper, as many characters on a line as the margins would permit. (See Figure 8.2.) As a test, without any hints or explanation, I transmitted the message by mailing copies to all the members of the Order of the Dolphin with the following cover letter:

"Here is a hypothetical message received from outer space. It contains 551 zeros and ones. What does it mean?"

```
1 1 1 1 0 0 0 0 0 1 0 1 0 0 1 0 0 0 0 1 1 0 0 1 0 0 0 0 0 0 0 1 0 0 0 0 0 1 0 1 0 0
1 0 0 0 0 0 1 1 0 0 1 0 1 1 0 0 1 1 1 1 0 0 0 0 0 1 1 0 0 0 0 1 1 0 1 0 0 0 0 0 0 0
0 0 1 0 0 0 0 0 1 0 0 0 0 1 0 0 0 0 1 0 0 0 1 0 1 0 1 0 0 0 0 1 0 0 0 0 0 0 0 0 0 0
0 0 0 0 0 0 0 0 0 1 0 0 0 1 0 0 0 0 0 0 0 0 0 1 0 1 1 0 0 0 0 0 0 0 0 0 0 0 0 0 0 0
0 0 0 0 0 0 0 1 0 0 0 1 1 1 0 1 1 0 1 0 1 1 0 1 0 1 0 0 0 0 0 0 0 0 0 0 0 0 0 0 0 0
0 0 0 0 1 0 0 1 0 0 0 0 1 1 1 0 1 0 1 0 1 0 1 0 0 0 0 0 0 0 0 0 1 0 1 0 1 0 1 0 1
0 0 0 0 0 0 0 0 0 1 1 1 0 1 0 1 0 1 0 1 1 1 0 1 0 1 1 0 0 0 0 0 0 0 1 0 0 0 0 0 0
0 0 0 0 0 0 0 0 0 0 1 0 0 0 0 0 0 0 0 0 0 0 1 0 0 0 1 0 0 1 1 1 1 1 1 0 0 0
0 0 1 1 1 0 1 0 0 0 0 0 1 0 1 1 0 0 0 0 0 1 1 1 0 0 0 0 0 0 1 0 0 0 0 0 0 0 0 0
1 0 0 0 0 0 0 0 0 1 0 0 0 0 0 0 0 1 1 1 1 1 0 0 0 0 0 0 1 0 1 1 0 0 0 1 0 1 1 1 0
1 0 0 0 0 0 0 0 1 1 0 0 1 0 1 1 1 1 1 0 1 0 1 1 1 1 0 0 0 1 0 0 1 1 1 1 1 0 0 1
0 0 0 0 0 0 0 0 0 0 0 1 1 1 1 1 0 0 0 0 0 0 1 0 1 1 0 0 0 1 1 1 1 1 1 1 0 0 0 0 0 0
1 0 0 0 0 0 1 1 0 0 0 0 0 1 1 0 0 0 0 1 0 0 0 0 1 1 0 0 0 0 0 0 0 1 1 0 0 0 1 0 1
0 0 1 0 0 0 1 1 1 1 0 0 1 0 1 1 1 1
```

FIGURE 8.2. An example of a message that might be received from another civilization in space. It has a total of 551 zeros and ones. What does it tell us?

Thus the message wouldn't arrive as a picture but as a series of zeros and ones. The recipients would have to figure out that it was supposed to be a picture, and to set it up that way. Extraterrestrials would have faced the same problem if I'd sent it to them via radio telescope, because the information would have arrived from outer space as a series of bits, one bit at a time. To help them make this big conceptual leap, I had built into the message an important clue as to how to arrange the bits in the right format, so the picture would emerge.

The clue is that strange number, 551. It has to do with the concept of prime numbers—numbers that can be divided only by themselves and by the number 1. I had drawn the particulars of my alien life on a grid 29 squares high and 19 squares across. I picked that size because 29 and 19 are both prime numbers. Multiplied, they yield the product 551, which can be divided only by 551, 29, 19, or 1. So while 551 is not a prime number, it is the product of two prime numbers. The first obvious point about my message would be that it contained 551 bits of information. That number would be the only hard fact to go on, and they might safely assume it to have some special significance. Once the recipients recognized that 551 could be divided by 29 and 19—and by nothing else except 551 and 1—they might see that the message was two-dimensional, a still picture. The sequence of bits was meant to be laid out in 29 rows of 19 bits each, or 19 rows of 29 bits each. They would have to try both configurations to see which was right, but it shouldn't take more than a few moments to figure that out.

Or so I thought.

I received only one reply—only one successful solution. Back from Barney Oliver came a new sequence of zeros and ones. Prime numbers defined it. It was a very simple and inspiring message, containing a single image: a martini glass with an olive in it. Barney had caught my drift, but even he didn't entirely understand the message. The symbols that represented the numbers had totally eluded him. The message was just too difficult to decipher.

A little daunted by this realization, I tried sending the message to various other people, including a few Nobel prize winners. Not one of them achieved a successful solution. A most interesting interpretation, however, came from one scientist who saw the pattern of zeros and ones as almost the quantum numbers that describe the arrangement of the electrons in an iron atom. He was way off. Or rather, I was way off in the way I'd constructed the message.

About a year later, however, the message was included in a magazine for amateur codebreakers. Soon after it appeared, I got a letter from an electrical engineer in Brooklyn, who had deciphered it and actually understood the whole thing. He was the only person who ever interpreted it correctly. To this day, most people don't get it, even when they see it laid out as a picture. They understand the significance of the creature, all right, and they can see the solar system, but the rest of it is a jumble. So the experience taught me two things: (1) My message was too crowded and too confusing; and (2) On such a day as we actually receive an extraterrestrial message, we should be sure to involve enthusiastic amateur codebreakers in its interpretation, because their minds are uncommonly well prepared for seeing patterns, symbols, and abstractions.

Barney Oliver went on to improve on my attempt with a longer, less crowded message that depicted intelligent creatures of two

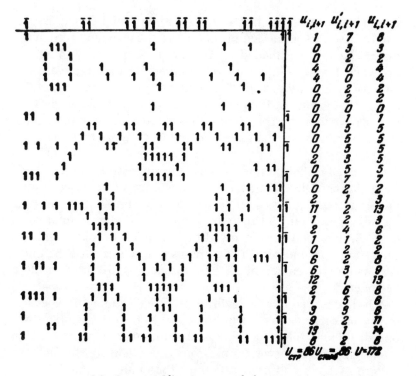

FIGURE 8.3. Barney Oliver's expanded message, showing adult creatures of different sexes with child between them.

sexes, with a child between them, showing that the creatures are not born full-size but develop from smaller versions of the mature ones. (See Figure 8.3.) This is the picture used in most textbooks that discuss the possibilities for interstellar communication.

Barney and I, though full of self-congratulatory sentiments, were not the first persons to entertain the idea of communication with extraterrestrials. As far back as 1820, Karl Friedrich Gauss, the great German mathematician and onetime director of the Göttingen Observatory, had proposed cutting a pattern into the forest of Siberia big enough for extraterrestrials to see. He wanted to plant an enormous field of wheat in the shape of a right triangle. Adjacent to each side of the triangle, like a living monument to Pythagoras, would be great square-shaped stands of pine trees. Viewed from far aloft, the pattern of vegetation would spell out the Pythagorean theorem: The square on the hypotenuse (the longest side of

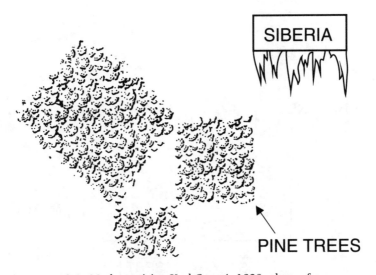

FIGURE 8.4. Mathematician Karl Gauss's 1820 scheme for announcing our existence to other planets of the Solar System.

the right triangle) equals the sum of the squares on the other two sides. (See Figure 8.4.) Gauss's father had been a gardener, which may have influenced the son's choice of message material. In any case, Gauss believed the contrasting crops would make themselves visible to powerful telescopes on the Moon or other planets. Aliens who spotted the symbol would know that there was intelligent life on Earth by the evidence of our mathematical prowess. But this proposal to signal extraterrestrials was never funded.

Twenty years later, in 1840, Joseph von Littrow, a Viennese astronomer, came up with a similar idea. He proposed digging big trenches in the Sahara desert, in the form of circles, triangles, and other shapes, perhaps twenty miles across. (See Figure 8.5.) He would then apply the very sophisticated technology of filling the trenches with kerosene and lighting them with a match, thus creating flaming geometric figures visible across the Solar System. His proposal was never funded, either.

The French physicist Charles Cros suggested in 1869 that an array of mirrors be used to reflect sunlight to Mars. The giant mirrors might be stretched across Europe in a pattern the extraterrestrials would recognize—the stars of the Big Dipper, say—and

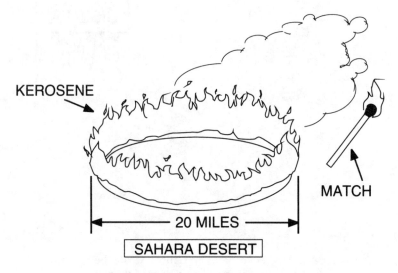

KEROSENE

MATCH

◄——— 20 MILES ———►

SAHARA DESERT

FIGURE 8.5. Physicist Joseph von Littrow's 1840 idea for interplanetary communication.

then "they" would also recognize the existence of intelligent life on Earth. (See Figure 8.6.) Cros couldn't raise the funds to put his idea into practice, however.

It was Nikola Tesla, an electrical engineer, who first succeeded in devising and sending an intentional radio message for extraterrestrial consumption, in 1899. J. Pierpont Morgan gave Tesla the funds to build an enormous radio transmitter in Colorado Springs. It contained a huge coil of wire—a transformer 75 feet high. When this was turned on, people for miles around found their hair standing on end. (See Figure 8.7.) Tesla also *received* signals on his device. These were strange, regular chirping noises that really sounded intelligent, and Tesla believed he had detected an alien civilization. He wrote of the experience, "The feeling is constantly growing on me that I had been the first to hear the greeting of one planet to another."

Today, knowing the frequencies at which Tesla's device could receive, we think he was probably intercepting a natural phenomenon called "whistlers." These are low-frequency electromagnetic waves caused by lightning flashes that propagate very slowly along

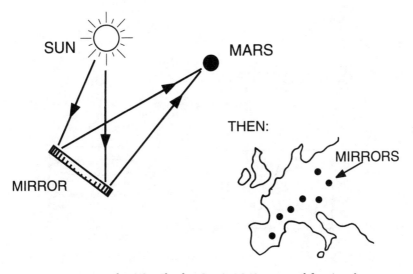

FIGURE 8.6. Physicist Charles Cros's 1869 proposal for signaling to extraterrestrials on Mars.

the magnetic lines of force around the Earth. They make a series of
warbling whistles—something like the sounds you hear after fireworks explode and start falling from the sky. Tesla was undoubt-
edly the first to hear whistlers, but he didn't explain their true
nature, so he never got credit for their discovery.

Guglielmo Marconi, the inventor of radio communications, also
listened for signals from outer space—and in 1922 he heard the
same chirping sounds that Tesla had described. Marconi intercepted these aboard his luxury yacht, the *Electra,* which he had
outfitted with radio apparatus and sailed to the middle of the
Atlantic Ocean, far from most man-made interference. (See Figure
8.8.) Like Tesla, Marconi also failed to recognize whistlers for what
they are.

As for my own designs on communicating with extraterrestrials,
I put them aside for the next several years—and saw them picked
up in works of fiction. Novelist James Gunn wrote *The Listeners,*
about a group of scientists at a big radio telescope in the tropics
who received an extraterrestrial message of the sort Barney and I
had concocted. That was followed by Robert Forward's *Dragon's*

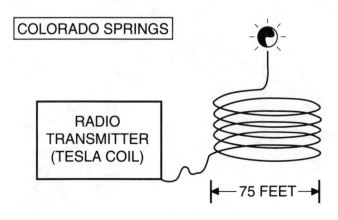

FIGURE 8.7. Electrical inventor Nikola Tesla's 1899 system for transmitting messages to extraterrestrials.

Egg, now a science fiction classic about life on neutron stars and which makes wonderfully irreverent references to me. In real life, however, Forward actually thanked me for giving him the idea by naming the main character in the book after my wife: Amalita Shakhashiri Drake. (Her real name is Amahl; the rest is correct.)

I got my first real-life shot at extraterrestrial communication in December 1969, when Carl Sagan and I attended a meeting of the American Astronomical Society that was held at a big resort hotel in San Juan, Puerto Rico. It's ironic that Carl and I were both on the Cornell faculty at the time, worked in the same building, and had lunch together often, but we had to travel all the way to Puerto Rico to have one of our most important talks, during a convention coffee break.

Carl had just flown in from NASA headquarters in Washington, and he was lit up with excitement when he collared me in the lobby of the San Jeronimo Hilton. He had been attending a meeting with his fellow project scientists working on *Pioneer 10*, a spacecraft that was soon to be launched on a mission to Jupiter and

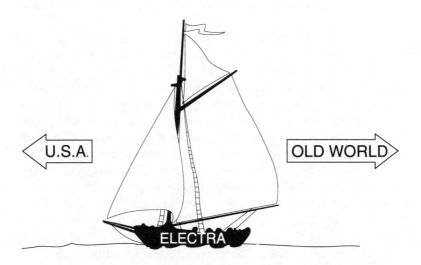

FIGURE 8.8. Cartoon showing inventor of radio communication Guglielmo Marconi's 1922 attempt to detect radio signals from other civilizations.

beyond. *Pioneer 10* was going to get near enough to make extensive observations of the planet and its moons, and relay thousands of photographs back to Earth. In the course of its maneuverings, *Pioneer 10* would approach Jupiter and gain enough velocity to leave the Solar System. Carl was especially excited over this point, because the significance of it had just hit home. As the first man-made object ever to escape the Sun's gravity, Pioneer would travel indefinitely among the stars on its own momentum. It would sail, perhaps, to the farthest reaches of the Galaxy.

Carl said that a writer for *The Christian Science Monitor*, Eric Burgess, and a planetarium lecturer named Richard Hoagland had made him appreciate this astounding fact. They had approached Carl, knowing his interest in exobiology, not to mention his important position as a planetary science experimenter. They expected him to be receptive to their idea: They thought that *Pioneer 10*, being the first interstellar emissary from Earth, should carry some message aboard. In that way, if any intelligent beings someday happened to intercept the spacecraft, they would receive greetings from its creators. And they figured that if anyone could convince the officials at NASA of the value of such a plan, that person would be Carl Sagan.*

Carl jumped at the idea, and had just gotten the official go-ahead from NASA to construct such a message when we bumped into each other in Puerto Rico. He had already given the matter some thought, and was envisioning an engraving on a metal plate. This made a lot of sense to me, because a metal engraving in a space environment would probably remain readable for a few billion years, at least. As for content, he wanted the message to express something of the nature of human life. It must also give the time and place, universally speaking, of the launching of *Pioneer 10*— our civilization's technological emissary in space.

Standing there in the lobby, Carl asked me to work with him on the message. The next session of the astronomical meeting was almost ready to begin. Participants bustled past us with empty cups and saucers, making their way to the scheduled talks. The "Yes, of course" wasn't even out of my mouth before the two of us started firing ideas at each other about what we would include. There was room on a metal plate of six by nine inches to crowd in as much as a hundred thousand characters' worth of information. We could draft a much more sophisticated message than the binary-code designs I'd traded with Barney Oliver. We could even make line drawings of human figures—and we immediately agreed to do so.

In the next moment, we hit on the idea of a galactic map that would pinpoint the location of the Earth in space. One possibility was to depict the Earth's position in relation to the Big Dipper and

---

* Recently, Hoagland has taken up a new cause—and one that is somewhat contrary to our purposes. He has become engrossed in the so-called Face on Mars. This is a Martian mountain, visible in spacecraft photos of the planet, that takes on a vague resemblance to a human face when the Sun hits it at certain angles. Like the Man in the Moon, the Face on Mars is just an accident of topography and photography. But Hoagland and his followers insist that the face is a message from extraterrestrials who are trying to attract our attention. There happen to be some rock formations near the Face that look vaguely like pyramids, which is enough of a coincidence to turn the Face into a cult figure for some people. A mythology has grown up around the Face, and whole books have been written about it. But most people find that a close study of the photographs—even a *casual* study, for that matter—shows the face to be just the side of a mountain.

several other constellations. Given the way constellations change over aeons, this plan would establish the launch date plus or minus ten thousand years. And given the distances of the constellations from the Solar System, the map would pin down the launch site to within twenty or thirty light-years. Not exactly latitude and longitude, but a start.

I thought I had a better idea. At that time I was actively involved in research on pulsars. It seemed to me that these rapidly pulsating radio sources offered a much more powerful approach to establishing our historic time and place. We could give the location of our Solar System with respect to a number of prominent pulsars, each of which had its own very characteristic and well-defined pulsing frequency. Because these frequencies gradually slow down, sometimes by as little as a fraction of a billionth of a second a day, they are timekeepers as well as place markers. The slowing of their periods can be very accurately measured. And to a civilization clever enough to intercept and interpret the *Pioneer 10* message, the amount of change in the pulsar frequencies between that shown in our engraving and that determined by them at the time of capture would tell them how much time had elapsed since the picture was drawn.

It was settled, then. We would use a pulsar map of the Milky Way. My job would be to create such a map—and quickly, too, because time was very short. Even though the launch date was a long way off, we had just a month to spend on the message. NASA would need the finished product in hand right away because even the little plaque we were designing would require a major reanalysis of much of the design of the spacecraft. The addition of the message plaque would change *Pioneer 10*'s center of gravity and its mass; those changes meant that the aim of the thrusters would have to be altered accordingly, to keep the spacecraft from tumbling in space. Unfreezing the spacecraft design in deference to the message plaque was a real nuisance for NASA, but the agency willingly took on the extra work once it recognized the popular importance of including extraterrestrial greetings.

My pulsar map came out looking something like a spider with too many legs. It was a starburst of fourteen straight lines, each line representing one pulsar. The proportional lengths of the lines indicated their distance from the central point, which was the Sun. Along each line I wrote the pulsar's period in binary numbers, using the radiation of the hydrogen atom as a universal unit of time and length.* These values must be well known to any sophisticated student of astronomy or physics, on any planet. To show the possible recipients of the message that the basic hydrogen line radiation was both the universal clock and the universal yardstick in the message—the source of the time and length units used—we put a graphic representation of the hydrogen atom as a key above the pulsar map.

Linda Salzman Sagan, then Carl's wife, was the artist who actually drew the picture for galactic exhibition. Her finished drawing, etched on a gold-anodized aluminum plaque, showed a nude man, with his hand raised in greeting, and a nude woman at his side. Linda depicted them of average height, and intentionally made their features a blend of various racial characteristics. The couple stood in front of the *Pioneer 10* spacecraft, drawn to the same scale, with the pulsar map beside them.

Along the bottom of the plaque Carl added the Sun and the planets, with their diameters given in multiples of hydrogen wavelengths. And skimming along a neat trajectory, starting out from planet number three, was a small schematic of *Pioneer 10*. It could be seen swinging up and out of the planetary lineup midway between the largest planet and the ringed planet. (See Figure 8.9.)

None of us was prepared for the reception the message got on Earth when news of its existence was released at launch time in March 1972. The trouble began the moment print and television news services *showed* the message, which depicted—eek!—naked people. The *Chicago Sun-Times* tried to airbrush out the offending organs. From the day's first edition to the last, the paper piecemeal eliminated one bit of sexual anatomy after another.

Then came the angry letters to the editor. The *Los Angeles Times* printed one that denounced NASA for spreading "smut" through

---

* The laws of quantum mechanics allow the hydrogen atom, with its single electron, to exist in only two possible states—one high-energy and one low-energy—and to jump from one state to the other. When the hydrogen atom makes the transition from the high- to the low-energy state, it releases energy in the form of a single photon. That photon has a specific wavelength and a corresponding frequency, or time interval from one peak of the wave to the next. In Earth terms, the wavelength is 21 centimeters and the frequency is 1420 megahertz—less than one billionth of a second. Other civilizations in space would, of course, use units other than centimeters, megahertz, and seconds, but the actual values of these fundamental measures of the hydrogen atom would be the same.

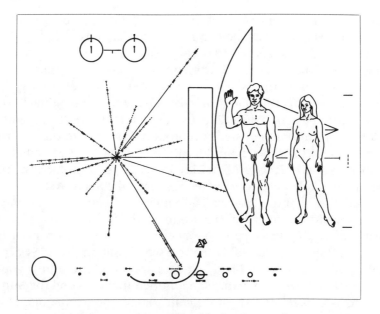

FIGURE 8.9. Message plaque aboard *Pioneer 10* and *Pioneer 11*.

space—and at taxpayers' expense! Feminists complained that the woman seemed subservient to the man. We were surprised to find that white people complained that the human figures looked too white, while black people felt they looked too black. Indeed, representatives of all races seemed to see themselves in the figures and to object to their appearance.

A crisis erupted at the Canadian Broadcasting Company when I described the message plaque on a morning talk show. Naked humans had never been shown on Canadian television before, but in fact, CBC received no complaints. Back at home, however, the caretaker of our own Space Sciences Building huffily branded our efforts "pornography."

Editorials in the British press lambasted us for keeping the composition task to ourselves, instead of assembling a large ecumenical group to create the message. This last impressed me as a legitimate gripe, except for the short time in which we had to work.

The furor over the *Pioneer 10* plaque made it a success, as far as Carl and I were concerned. We had already started to think of it more as a message *to* Earth than as a message *from* Earth. We had hoped it would hammer home the idea that we are not alone in the

universe, that others will learn of our existence someday, and that
some forms of contact and communication are possible.

For a while, the *Pioneer 10* message showed up everywhere, like
a symbol of the times. Graffiti artists copied it on walls. Cartoonists
made hilarious parodies of it. (One showed a group of "little green
men" examining the plaque, and one of them commenting, "I see
the Earthlings look just like us, except they don't wear any
clothes.") Entrepreneurs even reproduced the design on T-shirts.
And then NASA, too, reproduced the message—on the antenna
support struts of *Pioneer 11*, in May 1973. This craft was the twin of
Pioneer 10 and was also scheduled to leave the Solar System.

It may be that the Pioneers, although they now carry our message toward the stars, deliver it only to the people of *our* planet.
After all, neither *Pioneer 10* nor *Pioneer 11* was *aimed* at any particular star. Both spacecraft did their real work *inside* the Solar System,
taking photographs and relaying data back to Earth, until a gravitational boost from a giant planet hurled them beyond the Sun's
reach. The likelihood of either craft's landing on some planet of
another star is practically nil. Any alien being trying to retrieve a
Pioneer in a spaceship would have to be *very* clever—first to detect
it at all, then to pick it up, and, of course, to make any sense of it.
On Earth, on the other hand, it had a clear impact. And it paved the
way for more messages.

Indeed, the next official message-making opportunity arose in
1974, just a year after the launch of *Pioneer 11*. The Arecibo telescope had just been torn apart and put back together in a much
more powerful configuration, which would enable it to peer farther into space than ever before. I was busy planning new SETI
activities, in which we would scan the most distant stars we had
examined to date.

The telescope upgrading had taken three years of hard work and
major disruptions in our observation programs. Now the telescope
was so changed as to be virtually a new instrument, and deserved
to be rededicated with a gala celebration.

New ships are launched with a christening ceremony and a
bottle of champagne broken over the bow, but new national telescope facilities are usually inaugurated with ceremonial speeches
by astronomers and government dignitaries. As director of the
National Astronomy and Ionosphere Center (NAIC), which operated the Arecibo telescope for Cornell and the NSF, I was supposed
to be in charge of planning the ceremony. Fortunately for me, I had

a very capable administrative assistant, Jane Allen, who really knew how to throw a party and who took over the preparations. It was Jane who suggested we top off the ceremony by transmitting a radio message to extraterrestrials. It would be the first intentional radio communication sent into interstellar space. I was quick to agree and only too happy to take on the message as my project.

I started reworking the old zeros-and-ones model, determined to make a clearer message than my original attempt with the Order of the Dolphin. I also sent a memo to the whole NAIC staff, soliciting ideas to be included in the message. I didn't want to be the sole author of this one, because I remembered how the *Pioneer 10* plaque had been criticized as the work of a few elitists. As it turned out, only four graduate students took me up on my invitation. Despite my good ecumenical intentions, and their good suggestions, I wound up sitting down and writing the message by myself.

I followed the same basic plan of my Green Bank message, substituting our Solar System and a human-size Earthling for the 10-foot-tall extraterrestrial in the original. (See Figure 8.10.) And, of course, I stretched it out for clarity's sake, so the final picture consisted of 73 rows of 23 characters each, or a total of 1,679 bits. That was the upper limit for message length, because at a transmission speed of 10 bits per second, 1,679 bits would take just under three minutes to send during the ceremony. A longer message, I feared, might get boring for the dedication audience.

I started off the message with the binary counting system, showing the notations for the numbers 1 through 10. Then I used the numbers to draw and label diagrams of the molecules essential for life on Earth—hydrogen, carbon, nitrogen, oxygen, and phosphorus. I put in chemical formulas, too, for the components of our genetic material, DNA. I also drew a graphic representation of the double-helix shape of the DNA molecule, which ended right at the head of the human figure, suggesting a connection between them. Inside the double helix, an elongated block representing the number 3 billion indicated the complexity of our genetic material. (There are that many code bits in a molecule of human DNA.) To the human's right, another large number, 4 billion, gave our planetary census count.

The human appeared decidedly masculine, much to my chagrin. But when I tried to sketch a more unisex person with the limited number of bits, it came out looking more like a gorilla than a

FIGURE 8.10. Diagram of the Arecibo radio message transmitted toward the Great Cluster in the constellation Hercules (1974).

human. So I left it masculine rather than apelike. I may have been trying unconsciously to make it resemble me, as though I were beaming myself up *Star Trek* style. I admit I even noted the human's height (the number to its left) as 14. Given the wavelength of the transmission frequency, 12.6 centimeters, the human turned out to be 5 feet, 9 inches tall—just about my size. What a coincidence!

I lined up the Sun and planets under the human form, with the third planet from the Sun raised above the others, almost between the human's feet, to identify it as the inhabited world. Beneath the Solar System was a rough representation of a telescope, 1,000 feet wide, which would be recognized, I hoped, as the instrument sending the message.

I transmitted it first to Carl Sagan over lunch in the Cornell faculty club. Carl was the director of the university's Laboratory for Planetary Studies, not part of the NAIC, so he had not received my memo asking for message ideas. He figured out most of it quickly, which pleased me no end. He also had a few suggestions for modifications, which I incorporated. Of course, Carl's ready grasp of it was no guarantee that an extraterrestrial would have the same success.

I thought the message contained the information most relevant, most interesting, and most important to the creatures in space who might collect it someday. But I kept reassuring myself that the specific content, after all, was not the key point. The regular form of the message was a message in itself, which would be emphasized by periodic repetition. The broadcast power of the Arecibo transmitter was about half a million watts, but this would be concentrated into a beam with an effective radiated power of some twenty trillion watts. On its particular wavelength, the message would shine more brightly than the Sun. That ought to get someone's attention, I thought.

With Arecibo's new capability to make itself heard across vast interstellar distances, we could now pick a message target and be fairly certain of hitting it. It seemed we'd get the most mileage out of the message by aiming for a part of the sky where the stars were thickest. I looked at some sky charts and found that at about 1:00 P.M. on the day of the dedication, which was the time set for our ceremony, a dense cluster of some three hundred thousand stars (and possibly as many planets) would be nearly over our heads. That was our target, then: M-13, or the Great Cluster in the constellation Hercules. The fact that the cluster was twenty-four thousand light-years away did not dampen my enthusiasm in the least. This was a cosmic enterprise and could operate on a cosmic time scale. In the event that the message raised a reply, however, none of us would be around to hear it.

We managed to keep the message more or less secret until the day of the dedication, when the 250 guests and speakers arrived at the observatory. They sat under an open-sided party tent, within plain sight of the telescope's huge reflector bowl, its new aluminum surface shimmering in the midday sunlight.

For heightened effect, the staff had arranged to broadcast the sound of the transmission over the site through a loudspeaker at the same time as it was being beamed to M-13. When the speeches ended, a loud siren announced that the great suspended arm of the telescope was swinging into operating position. And then the two-pitched tones of the message filled the air, like the trilling of a strange musical theme played on a giant electronic synthesizer. The song, unique and full of yearning, affected us strongly. On that hot afternoon in the tropics, I saw women in sleeveless dresses rub chills from their arms. I saw the eyes of sober scientists fill with tears. And mine did, too.

Up in the control room, engineer Henry Cross found yet another dimension in the transmission that all of us had missed. Its first six sounds—four short beeps followed by two short beeps—formed a word in Morse code. The message started off saying, "Hi."

By the time the ceremony and the luncheon were over, when everyone had piled back on buses to leave the site, the message had reached the vicinity of Pluto's orbit. Already it was leaving the Solar System, not after a flight of years, as with a spacecraft, but after a journey only a few hours long.

News of its transmission reached Europe the next day, via press reports, where it provoked a serious outburst from Sir Martin Ryle, the astronomer royal of England. He sent the president of the IAU a letter full of outrage and anxiety, aghast that we had taken the hazardous step of revealing ourselves to the Galaxy in this way. He felt certain we had exposed humanity as a whole to extraterrestrials of possibly evil intent, who might now prey on us. So intent was he on making certain that no such message was ever transmitted again, he said, that he wanted the IAU's Executive Committee to condemn the activity in an official resolution.

Now, it's true that Ryle had a reputation among the astronomical community for being slightly crazy at times, and throwing real temper tantrums at scientific meetings. If, for example, some group of scientists gave observational results that his observatory *could* have discovered but had missed, he'd often go out in the hall, lie down on a couch, and cry. Nevertheless, for all his weirdness, Ryle was the astronomer royal. (Later that year he won the Nobel prize in Physics for developing important techniques in radio astronomy.) I couldn't simply ignore him.

I wrote to Sir Martin to tell him what I've already told you: It's too late to worry about giving ourselves away. The deed is done. And repeated daily with every television transmission, every military radar signal, every spacecraft command. I also told him my reasons for not worrying whether extraterrestrials know where we are: They're too far away to pose a threat. What's more, I don't believe they *will* pose a threat. I think that hostile tribes bent on war, be they terrestrial or extraterrestrial, destroy themselves with their own weapons long before they have any notion of how to attempt interstellar travel. The more peaceful nations, who study science and have perhaps cracked the secret of immortality, are more likely to be benevolent, shy, and wary of contact for their own good reasons. Ryle seemed satisfied with my rejoinder. In any case, I didn't hear back from him—in spite of the fact that the IAU never did issue a prohibition against interstellar messages.

Carl and I were thus free to try again. And in January 1977 we teamed up once more to plan the last of our interstellar missives. This one would ride as a passenger aboard the two Voyager spacecraft, to be launched the following August and September on a mission to Jupiter, Saturn (one Voyager also visited Uranus and Neptune), and out past the limits of the Solar System.

Again we met during a meeting of the American Astronomical Society, but in Honolulu this time, and in a much more premeditated fashion. Carl and his family had reserved a beautiful cottage at the Kahala Hilton Hotel, where I was invited to stay with them. Just outside the cottage was a picturesque lagoon inhabited by two trained dolphins. With our windows open, we could hear them playing together—swimming and breathing through their blowholes. They were definitely a source of inspiration to us human Dolphins inside the cottage.

As usual, time was short. We seriously considered sending copies of the *Pioneer 10* plaque rather than trying to create something new and meeting yet another round of criticism. But Carl had a song in his heart, so to speak. He wanted to send music this time. He felt strongly that our music was a real measure of our achievements. The challenge was to figure out how to do so. We considered a tape recording, but we didn't think the medium had the right stuff for interstellar communication. Tape was too flimsy. With longevity a prime prerequisite, we wanted materials that were as hardy as the metal plates of the *Pioneer 10* plaque.

I was still partial to pictures, and thought they must be part of the message. Carl felt as strongly about music. Then it struck me that we could send both kinds of messages—visual and auditory—on a phonograph record. After all, a phonograph record is an engraved plaque of sorts. We could make one out of metal. We could cut a record of the musical selections, and we could record images, too, on the same disc, in the form of television pictures.

Television pictures are transmitted as continuous signals over a wide range of radio frequencies. I was sure there must be a way to translate the picture frequencies into the much lower frequencies that are engraved on phonograph records. In that way we would be able to combine music, pictures, and miscellaneous sounds of Earth. We fancied we could even match pictures with appropriate sounds, such as a scene of Times Square with the automobile noise and other street sounds one would hear there. At the end we would package the record with its own special playback equipment, mount it on the Voyager, and send it on its way. Carl was thrilled at the prospect.

It was a good thing no one told us that the technology didn't exist to do what I proposed. There simply was no way to "record" television pictures on a phonograph record. However, blissfully ignorant as we were out there in our Hawaiian cottage, we covered sheets and sheets of hotel stationery with lists of picture ideas and the names of great works of music to be included in the message.

As things turned out, by the time Carl sold the record idea to NASA and assembled a group of experts to push through the actual production, someone had invented the machinery we needed. It was a special-purpose computer developed by Colorado Video, Inc. (CVI), in Denver. It could convert television-type signals to much lower frequencies for all sorts of applications, from recording them on phonograph records to sending them over telephone lines. It came along just in time, and we are eternally grateful to CVI for donating the use of the machine—and the services of its human operators—to the Voyager project.

At the outset, we thought we could include no more than ten pictures, because I imagined that each picture would take up about three minutes' space on our record. In practice, the clever CVI electronics system required just eight seconds of record time to capture each picture. We had room for more than one hundred photos, plus an hour and a half of music, spoken greetings, and other sounds of Earth, including the songs of the humpback whale, a kiss, a heartbeat, and the shock-wave boom of a *Saturn V* rocket at lift-off. The full information content of the Voyager interstellar

record weighed in at ten million characters—infinitely more infor-
mative than any previous message attempt.

It should have been easier to assemble this wealth of information
than it was to try to cram the essence of human existence into the
terse language of the *Pioneer 10* plaque or the Arecibo message. But
it wasn't. Having more room meant having more choices, and yet
the choices still had to be limited to fit the allotted space. Looking
back, I'm thankful that the technology for making videodiscs
didn't come along until after the Voyager launch. Although a
videodisc virtually lasts forever, it would have taken us forever to
fill it up because its capacity is so great—space for probably fifty
thousand pictures. I can't imagine how we would have dealt with
that volume of information potential. I fear the message might
never have gotten off the ground.

As it was, we had enough problems to cause enormous anxiety
and many sleepless nights spent working on the project. But many
talented people worked along with us to help solve problems as
they arose. I can't even begin to name them all here, but surely
novelist Ann Druyan (now married to Carl) collected most of the
sounds of Earth, from volcanoes and thunder to crickets, frogs, and
laughter. Artist Jon Lomberg gathered many of the pictures, and
science writer Timothy Ferris the musical selections with the help
of musicologist advisors. At one point, I recall, confusion over the
protocol for procuring greetings to the stars, in all of the many languages humans speak, nearly put the whole United Nations in an
uproar.

I was in charge of the picture selection. Our picture group decided
to send only information that extraterrestrials could not have
learned through their own activities. This meant that we didn't say
much about science, the universe, or mathematics. But we did go
on at length with images of flowers, trees, animals, oceans, deserts,
supermarkets, highways, houses, and humans engaged in all sorts
of ordinary and extraordinary activities. It was important to me to
show humanity with our foibles as well as our smoothly functioning technology. To that end, I chose one photo, taken on an Antarc-
tic expedition, of a giant tractor hopelessly snafued over a crevasse.

We also wanted to send pictures of nude humans, but which
ones? People who, to us, were the most glamorous and gorgeous?
Typical humans don't look like that, however. If we were to provide an honest portrait, we should show middle-aged people, with

paunches, slouches, and sags. In the end, this major philosophical decision was rendered meaningless, as NASA was intent on avoiding another brush with frontal nudity.

In the final photo selections we presented to the space agency for official approval, we included one that showed a nude man and a nude pregnant woman holding hands. It was part of a sequence on human reproduction—a tasteful expression of this aspect of life, and not the least bit prurient. But NASA, still remembering the *Pioneer 10* brouhaha, rejected it. They suggested in its place photographs of famous statues, such as Michelangelo's *David*. This gave me pause. I smiled to think how such images might be misinterpreted: Perhaps any Earthlings who removed their clothing turned to stone. As a compromise, we wound up creating a black-and-white silhouette of the hand-holding couple in diagram form, with a cutaway view of the baby inside the mother's body.

The finished record was pressed of copper and housed in an aluminum jacket. We had room on the aluminum cover to etch what you might call album or jacket notes. Here, in as much space as we once used for our entire communiqué, we drew top-view and side-view diagrams of how to set up the record, with its enclosed stylus and cartridge, for playback. (See Figure 8.11.) We also indicated how long it would take to listen to each side, using the hydrogen atom 21-centimeter time scale as our time unit again, as we had on *Pioneer 10*. In fact, there were two diagrams from the *Pioneer 10* plaque on the album cover: the energy jump of the hydrogen atom, and the pulsar map.

In case those were not enough to establish the date of our historic recording for an extraterrestrial audience, we also marked the cover with an ultrathin film of pure uranium-238. By its natural decay over the course of time, this tiny bit of radioactive material would provide one more clock for telling the age of the record.

The remaining diagram pointed out how the picture signals were to be translated from sounds into images. It's a tough diagram to understand. The extraterrestrials will have to discover something that's not at all obvious: When the record is spinning on a turntable with the stylus in the groove, variable voltage comes out of the stylus. They have to determine how to use that voltage—whether to make sound or pictures or what. This will take trial and error. They won't know that the voltage for making sound will actually make sound until they play it through an audio system. Even then it will be puzzling, because the music is rhythmic. It's

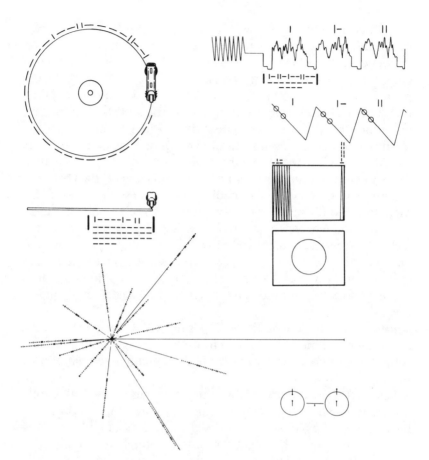

<small>FIGURE</small> 8.11. Cover of container holding audiovisual record aboard *Voyager 1* and *Voyager 2* spacecraft (1977).

got a beat. But the television pictures have a beat, too. If I could hum a few bars for you, the television pictures would sound like *click BUZZ click BUZZ click BUZZ.* There's a clicking sound followed by a noiselike buzz for each of the 512 lines that make up every picture.

With any luck, this part of the record will sound so different from the music, voices, and other recorded sounds that the aliens will realize they have to interpret the *click BUZZ* sequences in another way. That realization, of course, depends on whether they have the concept of music. If they do, they'll probably understand. But if they have no experience whatsoever with music, then the real music and the pictures will not seem that different from each other. And even if the aliens love music, I suppose theirs could be so different from ours that they just might prefer listening to the pictures! I can see them in their Walkmans now, happily snapping their tentacles to the pictures but finding the stuff we call music a puzzling, terrible noise. And I guess aliens with no concept of *sound* might try to make pictures out of everything. The actual pictures would come clear to them, while the music could approximate a Jackson Pollock painting. I hope they appreciate abstract art.

Seriously, here again the medium is the message, as Marshall McLuhan would say. Even if the record remains an inscrutable icon in some extraterrestrial world, it has to be seen as artificial, technologically advanced, and obviously of intelligent origin. Had we on Earth received a compact disc from some alien civilization at the time of the Voyager launch, I might not have known what to make of it, yet it would have been the answer to my fondest dreams.

Rushed as we were on the Voyager recording, we had to record the sounds and music separately from the pictures. How I wish we could have interlaced them as we had originally intended. If only we'd had more time.

I suspect the lament for more time is literally universal among civilizations who have not yet achieved immortality. Perhaps the recipients of the Voyager record will recognize our plight. They may size us up as having been smart enough to arrange this multimedia message but too harried to perfect it. They will rightly conclude that the senders' civilization didn't attach as much importance to the preparation of interstellar messages as to the spacecraft that carried them.

They may nod among themselves, or make whatever gesture passes for a nod among them, to recall knowingly their own civilization's childhood, when every project was a race against time. As they begin the leisurely task of interpreting our message—whether that task takes days or aeons—they may feel some compassion for the musicmakers of the record, now dead a billion years. Back then, their civilization, too, had been mortal. And rushed. And was not yet mindful of the benefits to be gained from contact with the community of galactic civilizations.

▲
▲
▲

CHAPTER 9

One Single
Little Blue Footstool?

*It is precisely because I believe theologically that there is
a being called God, and that He is infinite in intelligence, freedom, and power, that I cannot take it upon
myself to limit what He might have done.*

*Once He created the Big Bang . . . He could have
envisioned it going in billions of directions as it evolved,
including billions of life-forms and billions of kinds of
intelligent beings. . . .*

*As a theologian, I would say that this proposed
search for extraterrestrial intelligence (SETI) is also a
search of knowing and understanding God through
His works—especially those works that most reflect
Him. Finding others than ourselves would mean
knowing Him better.*

—THEODORE M. HESBURGH, C.S.C.,
University of Notre Dame

It was one of those days of conspicuous embarrassment and depression—a day when I wished I had stayed in
bed. It was Thursday, February 16, 1978, the day that Senator
William Proxmire awarded his "Golden Fleece of the Month
Award" to SETI.

Not to be confused with the much-prized Golden Fleece sought
by Jason in ancient mythology, Proxmire's Golden Fleece was his

own flashy way of bashing research projects and gaining publicity. He used "fleece" pejoratively, to mean cheating the government out of its gold.

Proxmire gave the Golden Fleece to studies he didn't like—or that sounded silly to him, whether he understood anything about them or not. He would scan long lists of projects funded by government agencies—from the National Institutes of Health to the National Science Foundation, as well as the armed forces—and hone in on those that seemed spoofable. Then he would cry out loud, complaining that Congress was frittering away citizens' tax dollars on foolish pursuits. The kind of attention Proxmire attracted often spelled doom for the research scientists, who then had to fight hard to get their grants renewed. Sometimes such a fate was well deserved. At other times, good work ground to a halt because of the way the senator spotlighted it in the press.

Invariably, Proxmire's targets were projects that could easily be made to look ridiculous to the lay public and therefore garner a lot of media attention. He naturally chose sex studies most often, and made his first attack on an attempt to explore the nature of human love. When Proxmire happened on SETI, he saw visions of little green men, not to mention headlines in the *National Enquirer*.

The shock came literally out of the blue, with no warning. The senator suddenly called a press conference in Washington to announce that NASA was riding the wave of *Star Wars* and *Close Encounters of the Third Kind* to find intelligent life in outer space. He wanted the project postponed for "a few million light-years," he said, apparently unaware of the fact that a light-year is a measure of distance, not time. One of his chief objections to the project was the fact that extraterrestrial civilizations might be a great deal older than ours.

"If we intercept messages sent from them," Proxmire said, "they could have been sent not only before Columbus discovered America or the birth of Christ, but before the Earth itself existed. The overwhelming odds are that such civilizations, even if they once existed, are now dead and gone."

Be that as it may, even if "they" *are* dead and gone, it would be stunning to have word of them. And to know the answer to one of the grandest questions in human philosophy: Are we the only intelligent life in the universe? Then, too, we still diligently study Dickens, the ancient Greeks, and, oh, yes, the Bible. A good message retains its importance long after its author perishes. I thought Proxmire had made a real fool of himself with that argument.

But Proxmire, unscathed, adroitly channeled all the laughs to SETI itself. He emerged as the people's champion, exposing a boondoggle.

I feared that the Golden Fleece would suffocate SETI. The project, which was finally gaining a firm toehold at NASA, might now get the boot as a result of this "award" presentation. My anxiety was well justified, as I'll explain later.

Proxmire blasted SETI as a NASA enterprise and never named me or any other individual in the citation. But I so identified myself with the search effort that he might as well have attacked me personally. I found it painfully embarrassing to have him poke fun at my work in public, even though I knew the ridicule was unjustified.

Frustrated and angry, I got busy right away devising an appropriate response. When the newspapers asked me for comment on the Golden Fleece, I said, tongue in cheek, that I was arranging a membership for the senator in the Flat Earth Society. I thought he'd find a lot of supporters there. I was astounded when one of his staff called my office to inquire earnestly whether Mr. Proxmire would receive a Flat Earth Society certificate or plaque suitable for framing and mounting on his office wall. As things turned out, he was to have neither.

The Flat Earth Society, originally founded in England, had moved its headquarters to Barstow, California, where the current society president lived and operated a gas station (in a place that did look rather flat). The society discounted the fact that astronauts had photographed a perfectly round Earth; its members even leveled charges of fakery at the space agency. Well, the president was outraged by my request to get Proxmire inducted. In fact, he rejected the senator's application for membership even before I could submit it.

"I know who you are, Frank Drake!" Flat Earth's president wrote in an angry letter. "I know what you're up to, too. You are using me to ridicule someone else, and I won't be part of it. I will not allow Senator Proxmire to be admitted as a member of the Flat Earth Society so that you can make fun of him and our organization." I found the letter refreshing in its honesty—and impressive, too. Even the president of Flat Earth could see the flaws in

Proxmire's logic! Despite the fact that the man was ignorant of the most fundamental facts of modern astronomy, I had to admit he stuck to his principles. I dropped the idea of retaliation altogether at that point, but Proxmire wasn't finished with his hatchet job on SETI.

Proxmire's Golden Fleece action had the sad effect I'd anticipated, and money grew scarce. Somehow, John Billingham kept hope alive through that grim period by funneling various discretionary funds into SETI research. He was able to get $500,000 one year and $1 million the next, to sustain NASA's big push to unite the Ames Research Center and the Jet Propulsion Laboratory in a joint project. Together the two centers would cooperate to develop hardware (multi*multi*channel receivers) and software (computer programs to analyze the received signals for intelligent patterns) for serious searching. When they had the wherewithal to approach the cosmic haystack, Ames would conduct a targeted search of about one thousand Sun-like stars, and JPL would survey the whole sky in a broad-brush approach.

The project promised such significant advances in signal-processing technology, and Billingham was so articulate in his appeals, that he continued to win approval at NASA for SETI activities. In fact, he gathered enough support within the space agency to put SETI on the federal budget proposal for fiscal year 1982.

The requested dollar amount was $2 million a year for the following seven years.* Proxmire, then the powerful chairman of the key Senate Appropriations Committee, became incensed. The fact that NASA had continued to work on SETI at all, despite his denigration of it, appeared to him to be an affront. Now they had the cheek to ask for more money!

"I have always thought if they were going to look for intelligence, they ought to start right here in Washington," Proxmire told the full Senate in his typical oratory style. "It is hard enough to find intelligent life right here. It may be even harder, I might say, than finding it outside our Solar System."

Nevertheless, he added, "If we continue to allow NASA to pur-

---

* That's a small amount for a NASA project, but truly big money for academic astronomy. To put it in perspective, space ventures typically run into the billions, while the whole 1981–82 operating budget of the National Astronomy and Ionosphere Center, for example, was $4 million.

sue this effort to intercept signals from some hypothetical intelligent civilization, we are sending exactly the wrong signal to the American taxpayer."

He proposed his own amendment to the appropriations bill under debate. His clause stipulated that "none of these funds shall be used to support the definition and development of techniques to analyze extraterrestrial radio signals for patterns that may be generated by intelligent sources." He characterized the search in clear, devastating, and rigid language as "a project that is almost guaranteed to fail."

Proxmire's amendment passed. It was small potatoes to the Senate—hardly worth anyone's using up political resources or favors to fight. SETI did have a few friends in Congress, including Senator Harrison "Jack" Schmitt from New Mexico, who had fond memories of walking on the Moon as an Apollo astronaut. SETI supporters tried to stop Proxmire's folly but failed. The suspension of funding put NASA's SETI project in imminent danger of extinction.

A few of my colleagues embellished the Drake Equation accordingly, with black humor. When they gave talks, they inserted a new factor, which I call f_g, for the fraction of planets that are governed only by scientifically wise elected officials. If every civilization has a Proxmire, you see, then $f_g = 0$ everywhere, and then $N = 0$, too. There could be no detectable aliens in space, since our experience shows that it takes only one Proxmire to strip a civilization of the means to communicate with its counterparts in the Galaxy.

Then Carl Sagan rode in like the cavalry for the first strong counterattack. Carl was probably America's best-known scientist, thanks in part to his book *The Dragons of Eden*, which had won the 1978 Pulitzer prize in General Nonfiction, and, of course, *Cosmos*, his television series with its best-selling companion volume. He was also president of his newly founded popular organization called The Planetary Society, made up of citizens committed to planetary exploration and the search for extraterrestrial life.

Carl was able to get an audience with Proxmire in Washington, and spent an hour educating him one-to-one on the true value and purpose of pursuing SETI. During that session, Proxmire finally grasped the implications of discovering advanced civilizations in space. He saw right away that if such societies had lived through their nuclear age, then we could, too—by their example, or perhaps their instruction. Even before Carl left the Senate Office Building, Proxmire had quietly changed his thinking on SETI. Now understanding, he was ready to stop deriding it as a financial fiasco and start seeing it as the script for a peaceful future. But he made no public announcement to that effect. He did what a good politician does in such circumstances: Instead of reversing his position and speaking in support of what he had once denounced, he just shut up.

Of course, the damage was already done. There was no money in the budget for SETI. Right after the Proxmire amendment passed in the summer of 1981, NASA gave John Billingham instructions to prepare a termination plan. It's NASA's way to phase out projects slowly, with minimal lawsuits, rather than abruptly. With a year to work, John came up with two plans: one for termination and one for revival of SETI. The revival plan so impressed NASA's two top administrators, James Beggs and Hans Mark, that they jumped hurdles to put SETI back on the budget proposal for the next fiscal year. Absent Proxmire's objections, SETI's funding was fully restored in fiscal year 1983 and has never been rescinded since, despite a few rather close calls engineered by Proxmire impersonators.

In the summer of 1990, for example, Representative Ronald Machtley of Rhode Island moved to eliminate the SETI project from NASA's budget for the 1991 fiscal year. He showed remarkable ignorance of our work, not to mention the course of science in general, when he commented in the *Congressional Record*: "We have no, and I repeat no scientific evidence that there is anything beyond our galaxy. . . . I would suggest that our constituents would agree that money ought not to be spent on curiosity. . . . If, in fact, there is a superintelligent form of life out there, might it be easier just to listen and let them call us?" (That is, of course, precisely what our project proposed to do.) In seconding the motion to terminate SETI, Silvio Conte of Massachusetts said, "Of course there are flying saucers and advanced civilizations in outer space. But we don't need to spend $6 million this year to find evidence of these rascally creatures. We only need 75 cents to buy a tabloid at the local supermarket. Conclusive evidence of these crafty critters can be found at checkout counters from coast to coast." Tremendous popular support helped turn the tide that time, especially the volume of mail that reached the Congress from elementary and high school science teachers. In the end, SETI's funding was not only restored, but also increased.

The following summer, in 1991, Senator Richard Bryan of Nevada proposed ending SETI support, and using the funds for scholarships at the University of Nevada at Las Vegas. Perhaps he thought this a clever method for recruiting a football team as good as the basketball team. But even in Las Vegas, Bryan's idea was viewed as crazy, and the local newspaper editorials said so. The Senate just ignored him.

In 1982 Carl sought more support for SETI by circulating a petition throughout the scientific community, gathering endorsements from some of the foremost researchers in the world. Signatories included seven Nobel laureates: David Baltimore; Melvin Calvin from the original Order of the Dolphin; Sir Francis Crick, who'd been at the Byurakan meeting; Manfred Eigen; Gerhard Herzberg; Linus Pauling (a two-time Nobelist, once in chemistry for his studies of molecular structure, and once in peace); and Edward Purcell, the physicist who relegated interstellar rockets to the back of the cereal box.* The petitioners constituted a veritable *Who's Who of Science;* they included, for example, Stephen Jay Gould, Stephen Hawking, Marvin Minsky, Lewis Thomas, and Edward O. Wilson. Among the seventy names Sagan collected were many staunch friends and supporters of SETI: Nikolai Kardashev, Iosif Shklovsky, and Vasevolod Troitsky from the Soviet Union; David Heeschen and Sebastian von Hoerner from Green Bank; and Philip Morrison, Barney Oliver, and Theodore Hesburgh, who'd been boosters since Project Ozma days. Carl and I signed, too, of course. (All the names are listed in Appendix C.)

The petition appeared as a letter to the editor, written by Carl, in *Science* in October 1982, with the signatories' names in alphabetical order in a footnote, and ending with these resounding words: "We urge the organization of a coordinated, worldwide, and systematic search for extraterrestrial intelligence."

The petition was gratifying and glorifying but looked a bit self-serving. Most of the university presidents, National Science medal-

---

* In the years since the petition appeared, another of the individuals who signed it has become a Nobel laureate in Physics: Subrahmanyan Chandrasekhar, an Indian-born astronomer and superb theoretician who studied at Yerkes Observatory under Otto Struve and who now teaches at the University of Chicago.

ists, and other eminent names in our camp had declared their support of SETI all along—even before we called it SETI. They were "the usual suspects." Perhaps for that reason, the petition did not have tremendous impact.

On the other hand, Carl's Planetary Society, which he co-founded with JPL director Bruce Murray, added great momentum to the positive course of events. The group took its grass-roots, nongovernmental monies and channeled them into worthwhile space objectives. It funded projects that NASA would not or could not support, including several SETI systems.

The Planetary Society attracted the attention of serious space enthusiasts who had been expressing their interest outside the realm of conventional science activities. Carl and his wife, Ann Druyan, recruited Steven Spielberg, whose fanciful *E.T.* furthered SETI's cause in 1982 by quickly achieving distinction as the most popular movie in history—and making "extraterrestrial" a household word. Spielberg offered Carl $100,000 to support a SETI project through The Planetary Society. How fitting that some of the box office receipts generated by *E.T.*, whose title character used radio to "phone home," would go to fund the radio search for the *real* E.T.

With momentum building, a particularly strong new endorsement of SETI sprang unexpectedly from the National Academy of Sciences, in a report commissioned to assess the needs of American astronomy. The authors of the report were a blue-ribbon panel of astronomers with no ties to SETI and no strong personal involvement in it. Yet, in their conclusions, they officially recommended that $20 million be spent on searching for alien signals in the 1980s—slightly more than NASA had requested from Congress. For the first time, SETI won laurels from total outsiders.

This 1982 report was the third in a series of such assessments, performed every ten years, to advise Congress on long-term goals and projects deserving of support. Agencies such as NASA and the NSF would swear by these documents when drawing up their budgets. Though the recommendations in the reports are not binding, they represent the consensus opinion of the foremost American astronomers and therefore carry considerable weight.

George Field, a distinguished astronomer and theorist who was then director of the Harvard Smithsonian Center for Astrophysics, headed the needs-assessment study group. Its members became known as the Field Committee, and the conclusions of their two-year collaboration the Field Report. Field had been a postdoctoral fellow at Harvard when I was a graduate student there. He had also served on the advisory committee for the NAIC when I was its director, so we had known each other well over a long period of time. George Field had put his John Hancock on the SETI petition, and I had served on an advisory panel to the Field Committee. In the end, however, it was neither Field nor Drake, but the full committee who endorsed this published appraisal of SETI:

"While the Committee recognized that this endeavor has a character different from that normally associated with astronomical research, intelligent organisms are as much a part of the universe as stars and galaxies; investigating whether some of the electromagnetic radiation now arriving at Earth was generated by intelligent beings in space may thus be considered a legitimate part of astronomy. Moreover, the techniques that can now be most effectively brought to bear on a SETI program for the 1980s are those of astronomy. . . .

"It is hard to imagine a more exciting astronomical discovery or one that would have greater impact on human perceptions than the detection of extraterrestrial intelligence."

My sentiments, exactly.

The victory in the congressional battle of the budget and the appropriation advised in the Field Report were indications of SETI's new legitimacy. There was enough awareness of nonsci-fi aliens now—and enough SETI activity going on—to warrant widespread attention, both positive and negative. Both were soon forthcoming.

Next, Michael Papagiannis, chairman of the astronomy department at Boston University, urged the IAU to make the search a worldwide goal. Papagiannis had never been a SETI experimenter himself, and hadn't really established a well-defined niche in astronomy before he took up this cause. But he declared himself bound and determined to create a new commission within the IAU that would be devoted to SETI and related subjects.

The IAU, the highest-ranking group of professional astronomers in the world, and which counts some seven thousand individuals among its elected members, is a working body with important legal authority. It names all the cosmic objects, from new moons in the Solar System to newly discovered features that spacecraft discover on the planets. It also establishes latitude and longitude coordinates on Earth, as well as their celestial counterparts, called right ascension and declination. Charged with the responsibility for monitoring civil time, the IAU decides when we need to insert a leap second into a year. And, in a Bureau of Standards–like capacity, the IAU defines cosmic units such as the parsec and the light-year.*

When Papagiannis began his campaign, the IAU had fifty commissions devoted to broad and familiar topics, such as the planets, galaxies, and interstellar matter. The new entity Papagiannis pushed for would be Commission 51—provided, of course, that he could convince the conservative European astronomers of the IAU's secretariat to consent to it. He began with a barrage of letters to these authority figures, then tried to impress them by organizing a special evening session on SETI at the IAU's 1979 meeting in Montreal. This was a general assembly—a marathon ten-day gathering of the full membership held once every three years, where official business gets conducted, special symposia are held, and famous scientists like Carl Sagan and Stephen Hawking give prestigious lectures.

I was thrilled to be one of the speakers at the Montreal SETI program. It turned out to be a huge success. We attracted an audience of more than a thousand conference attendees. The IAU president, general secretary, and full executive committee, who could aptly be described (with few exceptions) as a bunch of old fuddy-duddies, were so impressed with the content and the reception of this symposium that they gave another inch. They told Papagiannis he could put together a committee to plan his new commission. The only catch was that he would have to wait three years until the *next* IAU general assembly, which was scheduled for the summer of 1982, in Patras, Greece.

I served on that committee, along with Papagiannis, Jill Tarter, Nikolai Kardashev, Ron Brown from Australia, George Marx from Hungary, and other familiar SETI personalities. I remember we

---

* As a member of the IAU's commission on radio astronomy, I was once party to a lengthy debate over establishing the value of the "jansky," the aptly named unit of intensity for cosmic radio sources. (The suggested value, 10^{-26} watt per square meter per hertz, appeared an abomination to some commissioners because 26 is not neatly divisible by 3, as are the exponents in most scientific units!) I also recall a huge flap over the establishment of new galactic coordinates, after findings from radio astronomy research revealed the real center of the Milky Way to be far from the site that had been accepted for decades.

met in a hot, hot schoolroom for a whole hot day, without air conditioning. We staked out the new commission's purview and dubbed it "Commisson 51: Bioastronomy: Search for Extraterrestrial Life."

"Bioastronomy" was a word Papagiannis had coined. He defined it as the study of astronomical phenomena related to life. Commission 51 members would pursue such studies as planetary formation, the abundance of planetary systems, interstellar chemistry, the chemistry on planets, and, of course, the detection of extraterrestrial intelligence. Some of the people on the planning committee had pushed for the name "astrobiology," but we rejected that one because it put the emphasis on life instead of on astronomy. We SETI supporters were already once bitten on that score by the term "exobiology," which had long been ridiculed as a science without a subject. Bioastronomy, with its emphasis on astronomy, was something we could point our telescopes at.

When we presented our case, the executive committee voted to approve the new commission, and appointed Papagiannis its first president.*

Establishment of Commission 51 gave SETI the same status as the study of stars and galaxies in the eyes of the world's astronomers. There could no longer be any question that our pursuit was legitimate astronomical science.

Still, as SETI drew more accolades and aficionados, the detractors didn't disappear.

We had certainly known detractors from the earliest days of our activities. When Morrison and Cocconi first wrote their paper on the feasibility of searching for signals from extraterrestrials, they sent an advance copy to Sir Bernard Lovell for comment. Lovell was founder and director of the Jodrell Bank Radio Observatory in England, which boasted the biggest dish in the world at that time. Lovell was decidedly negative about detecting other civilizations, certainly with his own apparatus—or any other apparatus, for that

---

* I became the second president, in 1985, in New Delhi, followed by George Marx in 1988 and Ron Brown in 1991. Jill becomes president in 1994, at The Hague. Commission 51 now has three hundred members, making it one of the IAU's largest commissions. Since IAU members may serve on no more than three commissions, I am enrolled in Commission 51; Commission 40: Radio Astronomy; and Commission 16: Physical Study of Planets and Satellites.

matter. He said the odds of making such a discovery were so small that he couldn't see investing major resources in the attempt.

Lovell was probably speaking for one third of the scientific community when he argued that a full-fledged search would cost too much relative to its chance of success, since detecting other civilizations might prove so difficult. At least he didn't align himself with the segment—perhaps another third of all scientists—who considered such projects totally flaky. This contingent figured we had no chance of success at all, on the grounds that there just wasn't intelligent life out there to be found. Alas, Lovell did not count himself among the third who deemed the search enterprise truly worthy of support. (He later changed his mind, however.)

The ensuing two decades were witness to the milestone events already mentioned: the establishment of the NASA SETI program, the expedition to search for life on Mars with the Viking spacecraft, the endorsement of SETI in the Field report, and the creation of Commission 51. As a result, the validity of searching became acceptable, at least in principle, to scientists in every discipline in every country. Even those who did not support the idea of active searching had to concede that other life-forms must exist somewhere in space and that we might be able to detect them someday. They agreed with virtual unanimity that some search should be made, but left open the question of the magnitude—and cost—of the search.

By the late 1970s, perhaps 90 percent of the scientific community shared a belief in the existence of life on other planets of the Galaxy. Still, dissenters emerged from the remaining 10 percent, insisting that the cost of our curiosity was too high—or stubbornly maintaining that there was nothing to search for. Earth, these isolated individuals argued, must be God's little blue footstool— the single stronghold of life in all the vastness of the universe.

Enter Michael Hart of Trinity College, a physicist who began publishing "alone" arguments in the *Quarterly Journal of the Royal Astronomical Society*. Hart believed, first of all, that almost no planets were habitable, no matter where they were or what their nature. Earth was a fluke. He prepared computer models of planetary climates to prove his case.

The models showed that over the history of any star like the Sun, conditions would eventually make life impossible. Either life would be prohibited from arising in the first place, or it would evolve only to be destroyed. The proper weather forecast for a good life prognosis was a very iffy thing. Indeed, Hart argued that if the Earth's orbit had been just a few percent smaller or larger, there would be no life on Earth, either. Our ecosystem had missed not existing by a hairbreadth. And our planet was the only one supporting life.

I don't have to rip into Hart's logic, or give hand-waving arguments, because his computer models self-destructed. At first he failed to take into account the effect that clouds play in the climate complex, and when he inserted clouds into his later models, he had them perform opposite to the way we know they behave.* What's more, studies of ancient rocks show that the Earth's mean temperature has hardly changed at all, despite the fact that the Sun used to be 30 percent fainter than it is today. You would have expected the Earth's temperature to change a lot with the Sun's intensity, as Hart claimed, but in fact it has not. Even during the ice ages, the average global temperature dropped only about 5 degrees centigrade (9 degrees Fahrenheit)—instead of the 30 degrees Centigrade (54 degrees Fahrenheit) predicted by his model.

In another thrust, Hart offered the absence of colonists from other stars as evidence that we are alone. He argued, as in the Fermi Paradox, that as soon as an intelligent civilization starts colonizing other stars, it can colonize its entire galaxy within a few tens of millions of years, which is an eye blink on the cosmic time scale. In other words, if it could have happened, it should have happened already, and since it hasn't happened, we are the first, if not the only technological civilization.

Fermi had never taken the argument that far. He posed the question "Where are they?" but then decided we didn't know enough to answer it. When Hart took up the reprise, he reached a firm—negative—conclusion, although he didn't have any more hard information available to him than Fermi had.

Hart's line of reasoning, if you want to call it that, indicated that searching for other intelligent life was a waste of time. He was soon

---

* Even today, with far more sophisticated modeling systems than Hart had available to him, scientists still cannot model Earth's climate precisely enough to make meaningful predictions about pressing problems, such as the depletion of the ozone layer. We simply do not understand all the factors that contribute to climate change, or the identity and strength of the self-correcting mechanisms that affect climate. We do know, from all observations, that powerful factors are at work to stabilize the climate.

joined in this opinion by Frank Tipler, a mathematical physicist from Tulane University in New Orleans. Tipler's series of three articles appeared in the same publication, the *Quarterly Journal of the Royal Astronomical Society*, between 1980 and 1981. The heart of his hypothesis also depended on the assertion that other civilizations would colonize the Galaxy—not with creatures, but with robots.

Tipler's robots were the "universal constructors" first proposed by mathematician John von Neumann. I imagine von Neumann, who died in 1957, turning over in his grave at the notion of his theoretical machines being shanghaied for such a mission. He had originally proposed them as an exercise in logic, suggesting that it might be possible to build a machine, from a finite amount of material, that would contain enough information to reproduce itself. The crux of the von Neumann machine was its information content—almost like a genetic code and a memory bank rolled into one—that would be adequate to govern its self-duplication, using whatever materials were at hand (even inappropriate ones). However, the idea of building such a well-informed, ready-for-anything real machine stymies the inventive mind.

Suppose, for example, you were going to design a von Neumann machine to function in the Sahara desert. You would program it to understand that it had sand to work with. On its own, then, it has to build a silicon factory to make transistors. It has to mine ore and extract iron, or maybe titanium, for mechanical parts. And that's just the beginning of the challenge for a machine with a known goal. If you're planning to launch and dispatch it to some unknown planet in another star system, where the precise proportions of available materials are anybody's guess, the design problems quickly multiply.

Nevertheless, Tipler hypothesized that alien civilizations, if any existed, would colonize the Galaxy with von Neumann machines. Mean, nasty robots everywhere, devouring all the sand dunes. The obvious fact that this had not happened constituted his case for humanity's being the only extant technological civilization.

The obvious rebuttal to this sorcerer scenario is simply "Why? To what end?" Then again, who is to say that not once has there been a sorcerer in the Galaxy?

I argued back, not in person, as I've never met Tipler, but in the pages of the professional journal *Physics Today*, where a précis of his three-part series had been published. Even if we could overcome the fantastic difficulties of constructing the von Neumann machine, I countered, we would face the intractable challenge of sending it across interstellar distances to land in another star system (as discussed in Chapter 6). What's more, I could think of several scenarios that would explain the absence of an alien presence on Earth, while assuring that "they" were nevertheless out there to be found. To wit:

- They don't want to spend the money and expend the energy to attempt interstellar travel.
- They see no personal gain in creating a costly army of von Neumann machines.
- They are content to colonize their own star system and leave the Galaxy alone.
- They, like us, have found radio communication the more promising alternative, and are in fact engaged in it even as we debate the issue.

A student of mine at the time, Nathan ("Chip") Cohen, also took issue with Tipler's stand. In an ingenious letter, Cohen used Tipler's own brand of logic to prove, yes, that Tipler himself did not exist!

"Have you ever seen Frank Tipler?" Cohen wrote. "There are only 4×10^9 [four billion] people on this planet; surely an intelligent creature would find some direct way of making his presence known to at least a sizable fraction of the population.

"Perhaps we haven't seen Frank Tipler because we haven't looked hard enough. If we undertook a comprehensive and methodical search for him (in New Orleans?) then we may be able to make a definitive decision on his existence." By the same token, Cohen concluded, we will have to make a concerted effort to detect extraterrestrials before we decide whether *they* exist.

The existence of extraterrestrials is not an issue that can be determined on the basis of theory, no matter how compelling the arguments. SETI is by definition an experimental science. We can carry out reasonable experiments to discover whether any other civilizations may be trying to communicate with us. We can prove that they exist by making a discovery. But even in the worst case, if we make no such discovery, our failure still does not constitute proof that no aliens exist.

There are any number of scenarios in which life exists, even richly intelligent life, but it remains undetected. For example, if certain aliens used optical fibers for all communications on their world, then no radio waves would leak out and the civilization would be invisible to us. Thus we can never prove the nonexistence of life, intelligent or otherwise, in the universe. No amount of failure in SETI endeavors constitutes proof that we are alone. Only the existence of life is demonstrable.

For my part, I don't expect us to come out of the search empty-handed. All the physical processes we observe on Earth have counterparts elsewhere. The chance of any Earthly process being unique in the universe is surely the most unlikely of all possibilities. Other intelligent life-forms will differ greatly in appearance—they may resemble the creature in *E.T.* or startle us with their beauty—but life itself is common, I'm certain.

Tipler remains SETI's most vociferous critic in the scientific community. We are still entrenched in our differences. His latest tack is to brandish the controversial "Anthropic Principle," which holds that the universe was made exactly the way it is so we may exist. Or, put another way, we exist only because the universe is the way it is. This is actually a straightforward and reasonable statement of fact. We recognize that the physical constants of our universe—the velocity of light, the charge on the electron, etc.—have to be pretty much exactly as they are for us to exist here. Had they been even slightly different, there would be no intelligent life. There would probably be no life at all. In Tipler's view, however, the Anthropic Principle also implies that the universe is so finely tuned as to hold just one intelligent species: us.

I, and most other scientists, disagree. Our universe may allow for only carbon-based life, but that condition puts almost no limitations on what form life may take. On this planet alone, carbon constitutes everything from sulfur-eating worms at deep-sea vents to redwood trees and us. I think our universe allows for countless types of intelligence. Our universe also contains numerous energy sources in the tremendous variety of stars, many of which last long enough to allow intelligent life to evolve.

The nature of our universe promotes the existence of numerous civilizations within it. More than that, its very structure suggests a multitude of other, separate universes, ever invisible to us. Some of these may also harbor living beings.

Physicist John A. Wheeler of Princeton University and the University of Texas, who has considered the Anthropic Principle in great depth, was the first to note that our universe is uncannily uniform. True, in recent years we have found that there are lumps, sheets, walls, and voids in the distribution of galaxies, but overall there is a remarkable smoothness. This uniformity is very hard to understand unless we assume that our universe started out as a small piece of something much larger and more turbulent. In the first fraction of a second after the big bang, Wheeler proposed, this larger something split into a multitude of separate universes. The traditional view of the big bang has the initial glob of energy transmuting itself eventually into the stars and galaxies we see around us. But Wheeler's theory changed the big bang to an even bigger bang—a megabang that gave rise to some 10^{50} individual universes (zillions and zillions of them).

We can never observe any of these universes to determine what conditions prevail there. Most of the others must have different laws of physics from ours, and different forces operating in them. Imagine, for example, a universe where the physical forces conspire to make all the matter fall together into one massive object. Now change the physical laws and forces slightly to form another universe, where there is nothing but dark dust. Or planets, but no stars. I can imagine alternative universes that do not even have electromagnetic radiation. In most of these universes, circumstances make the development of life impossible. I'm quite content with the idea that there may be only one universe, ours, that is just right for life. And that is exactly why we exist. But in our universe, where we *know* life arose once, I think we can safely assume that it arose *more* than once among all its 10^{22} stars.

I had barely finished responding to Tipler's early attacks in 1981 when astronomer Robert Rood and physicist James Trefil came out with their mildly anti-SETI book, *Are We Alone?* They concluded, from solid scientific reasoning, that we don't have sufficient evidence to make strong claims for the existence of life elsewhere in the Galaxy. Their publisher secured them several talk-show appearances, as I discovered when I was invited to debate Rood on *Good Morning, America.* This was, to the best of my knowledge, the first televised presentation of the Drake Equation. I don't know which side came out the winner to the viewing audience, although I like to think I did.*

---

* Not long ago, Cable News Network ran a short segment about SETI and asked viewers to call in their answers to the question "Do you think there is intelligent life in space?" Fully 86 percent of the callers voted "Yes."

Later, in a far more clever attack, Bob Rood came up with SETI-type equations and arguments to prove that unicorns existed in medieval France, where they inspired much speculation and search activity. Indeed, unicorns served important purposes. They proved the validity of certain passages in the Bible and kept numerous artists and writers employed—not to mention the sellers of unicorn horn (probably taken from narwhal or rhinoceros), which was supposed to be a universal antidote to poison. People *needed* the idea of unicorns, Rood argued, and the idea served their psyches. Much the same could be said about ideas of extraterrestrials today, he concluded—namely, that they may be the embodiment of modern wishful thinking.

I applauded Rood in this analogy, not only for the wit of his approach but also for his meticulous research. I actually enjoy a good argument, as long as it has intellectual integrity. Science thrives on skepticism, after all, and anyone who has an informed opinion about SETI is welcome to try to make me look all wet. I get upset only when the objections are unfounded, biased, or specious—especially if the person with the objection has power over federal purse strings.

Rood and I have always very much respected each other, as we find ourselves pitted against each other regularly in symposia on questions of other civilizations, interstellar travel, and related tantalizing concepts. Recently he has become a SETI researcher himself, conducting an ongoing search program at Green Bank with Tom Bania of Boston University. Even though Rood thinks it unlikely that we'll detect advanced extraterrestrial civilizations, he believes that we ought to look for them. He knows that theorizing alone cannot prove (or disprove) the existence of extraterrestrial life; only observations can do that.

Most of the dissenters I've mentioned so far questioned the very existence of aliens, and therefore the wisdom of searching for them. But SETI also has some critics who believe we are *not* alone, yet still decry the search for extraterrestrial life.

The great Harvard anthropologist and paleontologist George Gaylord Simpson is perhaps the most eminent person ever to have misunderstood totally the foundations of SETI. Simpson wrote a paper called "The Nonprevalence of Humanoids," published in *Science* in 1964, in which he first missed the basic concept. He later played out the idea in his famous book *This View of Life*. People still quote the paper and the book today, and perpetuate Simpson's misunderstanding. What he failed to grasp was the nature of the extraterrestrial.

Simpson thought we were looking for humans elsewhere in the cosmos. He took great pains to demonstrate how the sinuous course of evolution could never produce the anatomical duplicates of human beings on two or more planets. This is true, and is universally accepted. I don't know any SETI researcher who is expecting to hear from duplicates of humans, or humanoids, or even hominids. (We would fire anyone who entertained such Earthist ideas!)

In truth, the existence of humanoids on Earth is the result of pure chance. But intelligence itself, in all probability, can and will evolve in any number of guises. Sixty-five million years ago, a dinosaur that had about the same height and weight as we do was well on its way to developing intelligence. Paleontologists call this creature saurornithoides, which means reptile with feet like a bird. The saurornithoides stood on their hind limbs, using the front ones to catch food. Their "hands" had the equivalent of an opposable thumb, permitting a precision grip.

Most interesting of all, the saurornithoides possessed rather large braincases. Their brain mass was not the few grams typical of other dinosaurs, but on the order of one hundred grams—just a little smaller than that of a human infant. If the saurornithoides had had another ten million or twenty million years, they could well have become the first intelligent creatures on Earth. But that was not to be. Before they became intelligent enough to preserve themselves from catastrophe, a catastrophe occurred. An asteroid struck the Earth, wiping out the large reptiles and leaving the planet to the small mammals that eventually evolved into our kind.

The saurornithoides are an example of creatures that could have led to a decidedly nonhuman species of intelligent life on the Earth. In time, they might well have mastered technology with their intelligence.

Simpson, however, apparently couldn't understand how any creature other than a humanoid could build a radio telescope. He assumed we were looking for our twins, and therefore derided our goals. Simpson never said that there could be no other intelligent beings in the universe, though people commonly attribute that sentiment to him. When SETI critics use Simpson's writings as ammunition, they assume "nonprevalence of humanoids" means the nonprevalence of thinking beings, but they're only compounding Simpson's original mistake.

George Wald, a Harvard University biologist and Nobel laureate in physiology, picked a different bone with us. Wald believes in the existence of extraterrestrials and expects them to be extremely different, but once felt we shouldn't search. Why? Because it would be very depressing for us to detect a more advanced civilization. It would give us a planetwide inferiority complex, he said. Therefore he would pull the plug on any radio telescope that might detect intelligent life. Robert Sinsheimer, the eminent molecular biologist and former chancellor of the University of California at Santa Cruz (he's now a friend of mine), used to hold the same belief.

For fifteen years, up until the time I met Wald at a Los Alamos symposium in 1988, he had been publishing his belief that encountering a superior culture would cause our whole civilization to sink into the depths of despair. Now the two of us were head to head as invited speakers on a panel titled "Unsolved Problems in the Science of Life." During one of the discussion periods, I gave Wald an analogy that swayed his thinking. We have all been exposed to minds and accomplishments greater than our own, I said. In fact, for most of us that is a continual experience, beginning with our parents and teachers. But the result is more often inspiration rather than depression. It's a challenge, because we know that if we work hard enough, we can be as good as they are. And the impact of SETI on human civilization is likely to follow that same pattern.

I don't believe the human brain is limited in any fundamental way. I think it can emulate the power of any intelligence we may find in the universe. And I expect the discovery of extraterrestrial life to bear me out on this account soon.

Of all the discouraging words said about SETI, the ones that puzzled me most came from Iosif Shklovsky, the great SETI pioneer who seemed to undergo a massive change of heart a few years before his death in 1985.

Shklovsky, who had spurred the search for extraterrestrial life, suddenly took a dim view of the chances for establishing radio contact with alien civilizations. I very much wanted to question him on the matter, but we were out of touch during those years. He had suffered a heart attack and was no longer making trips abroad.

On my own, I guessed he'd put several pessimistic numbers in the Drake Equation and lost the faith.

Recently I learned the real story from Nikolai Kardashev, who had been Shklovsky's student and remained close to him all his life. Indeed, Shklovsky had taken a new view of the answer to the Drake Equation. He did not doubt the abundance of planetary systems or other astronomical or biological factors we had established. Rather, he questioned the value of L—the longevity of intelligent civilizations.

Shklovsky had become depressed by the global political situation, Kardashev said, and concluded that nuclear war was inescapable. Superpower leaders seemed too weak and ignorant to avoid an imminent nuclear holocaust. If we were destined to destroy our world, which seemed likely to him, then it was likely that intelligent aliens had quickly destroyed their worlds, too. Technological civilizations must be short-lived phenomena, and we might as well abandon hope of ever finding any.

For Shklovsky it was a political, not a scientific, calculation.

Had he lived just a few more years, he would have seen *glasnost* and a wave of peace sweeping the world, with a backing away from nuclear weapons. I am sure he would have changed his mind again, and signaled, with his characteristic smile and shake of the head, his renewed enthusiasm for SETI.

CHAPTER 10

▲
▲
▲

No Greater Discovery

As our metal eyes wake
to absolute night,
where whispers fly
from the beginning of time,
we cup our ears to the heavens.
We are listening

on the volcanic rim of Flagstaff
and in the fields beyond Boston,
in a great array that blooms
like coral from the desert floor,
on highwire webs patrolled
by computer spiders in Puerto Rico.

We are listening for a sound
beyond us, beyond sound,

searching for a lighthouse
in the breakwaters of our uncertainty,
an electronic murmur,
a bright, fragile I am. . . .

—DIANE ACKERMAN,
from *Jaguar of Sweet Laughter*

Because I was a white-haired senior scientist from my earliest days as an astronomer, I fell into two roles I never expected to play in my career. One was as a "father figure" at the observatories where I worked.

▲ 213

Astronomers, fleeing light pollution and radio interference, are always being shipped off to isolated places where they confront overwhelming questions about the shape of space, the nature of matter, and the origin of the universe. This is sheer pleasure for most of us, or for all of us most of the time. Still, combined with the normal demands of life—hungry, growing families, financial worries, obnoxious neighbors, you name it—the passion to pursue astronomy can create a strain, or even precipitate an internal crisis. On numerous occasions over the years, I found myself trusted with the secret, searing content of these crises. To listen attentively was often the best help I could give. Several times, though, I had to act—quickly. Once, I took a loaded gun out of someone's hand.

After these experiences, I sought training as a crisis intervention counselor in Ithaca. I was no longer willing to trust anyone's welfare to my instincts alone. In return for the excellent instruction I received, I worked the all-night shift at Tompkins County [New York] Suicide Prevention one or two Fridays a month for the next ten years. I still consider those anxious nights on the telephone with strangers to be some of the most important work of my life. I had the satisfaction of helping a lot of people who never saw my face, let alone the color of my hair. I turned tears to laughter, and that is the best thing anyone can do.

I owe my other unexpected role, as a "founding father" in the search for extraterrestrial intelligence, to the combined effects of my white hair and the amount of time that has elapsed since Project Ozma. At scientific meetings now, I am the one asked to discuss the history of SETI. This is mildly disconcerting—evidence, perhaps, of some professional consensus that I'm at the point in life where I can look only backward. I take it as good-naturedly as I can, however, and the more perspective I offer on the past, the more people listen to me when I talk about the future; for the point of explicating SETI's history is to show that we have only just begun to search.

So many individuals I meet seem to think that we have already searched the sky completely and continuously over the past thirty years. The deed is done, they assume. And since we found nothing out there, to search further is to beat a dead horse. But in fact, the combinations of frequencies and places to look have hardly been touched.

In my historical analysis, the search for extraterrestrial intelligence divides itself into four eras. The first dates back at least three thousand years, to the time when people started contemplating the universe, without any hard scientific data or scientific method. Instead, they applied the principles of philosophy, especially pure logic, to the task of deducing the structure, nature, origins, and history of the universe—and of life itself. Lucretius, who lived in the first century B.C., spoke of a "huge supply of atoms" (a word coined by his predecessor Democritus) and "a force" that drove the atoms hither and thither, shaping them into "other parts of the universe with races of different men and different animals." This belief that what had happened on Earth must also have happened elsewhere was a philosophical deduction. The idea appealed to many who discussed and debated it. They could not test it, though. Millennia passed during which people wondered if there was extraterrestrial life to be found but who knew well that they lacked the means to detect such life.

I trace the start of the second era to the coming of the Copernican Revolution in the sixteenth century. That was when astronomers such as Kepler and Galileo, who used a real telescope, recognized that some of the other objects in the Solar System were planets similar to the Earth. Scientific observations could now support the philosophical argument in favor of other life in the cosmos—and perhaps even within the Solar System.

Also during this second era, in the early 1800s, the first hands-on proposals for signaling our planetary neighbors emerged (as I described in Chapter 8). The physics employed by early searchers, including Gauss and Cros, was right, but only in a qualitative way. None of these scientists, not even the electrical engineers among them—Tesla and Marconi, who lived well into the twentieth century—had any idea of the power levels or sensitivities required to transmit or detect signals traveling from one world to another. And so their experiments, although on the right track, were very ill-conceived—really wild shots in the dark.

The third era began in 1959–60, when scientists first employed quantitative measures to compute the strength of possible signs of life crossing interstellar space. In other words, we made precise calculations of the detectability of alien signals, and acted on them. Projects—beginning with Morrison and Cocconi's proposal to search for radio waves and my strategy for Project Ozma—sprang from a greater knowledge of the universe and a real sense of the numbers involved. For the first time, SETI embodied philosophical, qualitative, *and* quantitative elements. Scientists conducted some sixty "third era" extraterrestrial searches in the 1960s, 1970s, and 1980s. Most of these, however, were low-budget productions, done with leftover funds in borrowed time on equipment built for other purposes.

The fourth era, which starts now, is not only quantitative, it is also, finally, *thorough*. The projects of the 1990s represent the most exhaustive probing to date of the cosmic haystack. Here I am referring especially to the NASA SETI project that was almost killed by Senator Proxmire but that is now humming along at last.

It is always a thrill for me to present my historical overview from the pioneer's perspective at large gatherings where substantial numbers of people are talking seriously about SETI. I gave it for the first time in the summer of 1991, at the U.S.A.-U.S.S.R. SETI conference at the Santa Cruz campus of the University of California, where I teach astronomy and astrophysics. This marked the third in what is now a series of such gatherings, beginning with Byurakan in 1971 and Tallinn in 1981. In the audience were veterans of those earlier meetings, from both countries, as well as several members of the original Order of the Dolphin. But seated next to them, in front of them, behind them, and filling row upon row in the lecture room were many more young scientists with new ideas and great talent, who had only recently joined the effort.

One of the Soviet delegates to this international meeting was Vladimir Kotelnikov, a distinguished vice president of the Soviet Academy of Sciences and a former chairman of the Russian Republic. Academician Kotelnikov arrived in a gray suit and white shirt, befitting a man of his position and age (eighty-two). But he immediately traded in his dress shirt for a whimsical conference T-shirt decorated with the university's mascot—a smiling banana slug, with radio telescopes in place of ordinary slug antennae to help it tune in to the Milky Way.

For me, the highlight of the meeting came the last night, when my family and I were able to host the Soviet visitors and a few other conferees at a buffet dinner in our backyard. It was a delightful evening, with unusually balmy weather, good food, and a warm sense of camaraderie. My two daughters, Nadia, age eleven, and Leila, age nine, who had joined in the conference preparations by coloring a banana slug on everyone's name tag, entertained the visitors. Leila pretended to be a Saturnian, much to their delight, and Nadia discussed the quite elegant paper she'd recently written about the temperature of Venus. The girls also distributed a wonderful assortment of gifts that Amahl had assembled for the children and grandchildren of our guests. I remember thinking that if, after all those years, I could really have Nikolai Kardashev, Vladimir Kotelnikov, Yury Pariisky, and their colleagues at my home among the redwood trees, then we could surely find other friends in the cosmic forest, as we had so long dreamed of doing.

I take up the role of SETI historian not from the dispassionate distance of a scholar but as a person who has lived through so many of the pivotal events and known all the key players intimately. Still, SETI is just beginning in earnest, and there is more history to make than to recount. I know I have a better chance now than at any time in the past to take part in the greatest historical event of all.

My involvement in SETI activities has actually increased over the years, because SETI itself has grown so much. It occupies more people than ever before, and demands more of their time. Jill Tarter, for example, is the first astronomer to work full-time as a SETI scientist. When she isn't fully engaged in her role as project scientist, the senior scientific position in the NASA SETI project, she is in Washington, explaining the project to congressional representatives. Paul Horowitz runs a close second in activity. Despite his teaching duties at Harvard, Paul has had one search or another in progress since 1977. In some years he devotes nearly 100 percent of his time to these efforts—masterminding a new project and then personally soldering the thousands of joints that hold the equipment together.

Paul met me before I met him, when I returned to Harvard to give the Loeb Lecture in the fall of 1969, and he attended the talks. My topic, fitting for that year, was pulsars. However, I did sneak in one lecture on the likelihood of extraterrestrial life and the methodology for detecting it. Paul had already distinguished himself in the physics department as both a genius at theory and a hands-on electronics enthusiast who liked nothing better than to build equipment in the laboratory. Like Barney Oliver, Paul embodied the very broad combination of skills that SETI demands of its researchers. Most important of all, the scent of extraterrestrials stirred him like no other topic had before. He later told me he got genuinely excited listening to my lectures. Since his mentor at Harvard was Edward Purcell, the Nobel prize–winning physicist who had attended all the astronomy colloquiums in my graduate-student days, Paul met no resistance when he meandered across the borders between physics and astronomy.

Just the year before, in fact, in 1968, Paul had worked with other physicists at Harvard to produce a beautiful light curve of the pulsar in the Crab Nebula. A light curve is a description of the way a star's light intensity changes with time. Astronomers had used light curves to deduce a great deal of information about other types of variable stars, and it was hoped that a well-executed light curve for a pulsar would yield clues to its emission mechanisms. Many leading astronomers attempted the difficult measurement, but Paul and his band of gung-ho physicists achieved the best results, even though they were using a crummy little old telescope in cloudy Massachusetts.

One mildly unpleasant thing about my Loeb lectureship sticks in my memory, and that is that my hotel key was stolen one afternoon from the office where I'd left my sport coat. The thief— probably Harvard-educated!—ransacked my room while I held forth, oblivious, about signals from stars. I had nothing of value at the hotel worth stealing—just some clothing—and nothing was taken. In retrospect, even if I had lost cash, credit cards, and my watch, I would still have come out ahead that week—with Paul Horowitz now on the team.*

I finally got my turn to meet Paul in 1977, when he was already a full professor of physics at Harvard. He had such a youthful appearance, such exuberance, and such an abundance of dark hair that I could easily have mistaken him for one of his students. He said he wanted to "look for life in Puerto Rico," which was his way of requesting observing time at Arecibo to detect intelligent signals from space. I was NAIC director then, and helped him plan a search for extremely narrow-band signals, as no one had done this before. The bandwidths Paul selected were of the size stipulated by

---

* The chance to win brilliant converts is the best reason for giving lectures, as far as I'm concerned. I recruited Woodruff Sullivan this way, too, at a much more tender age, when he took a summer program for gifted high school students at Texas A&M University. I remember I had to lecture at six o'clock in the morning, because the classrooms had no air-conditioning, so lectures had to be done early in the day. Woody still has the diary he kept as a teenager, and recently read me the entry about my talk. On that day he decided to become a radio astronomer.

my work with George Helou—the Drake-Helou Limit of a few hundredths of a cycle per second.

A short time later, thanks to Jill's influence, Paul accepted a 1981–82 NASA Ames fellowship, which enabled him to work on SETI at the Ames Research Center and at Stanford University. He joined the Ames-Stanford group trying to create a SETI machine that could analyze a huge number of separate channels—128,000 of them, more than anyone had ever been able to monitor simultaneously. With this work, Paul was continuing the great expansion of SETI hardware that Oliver and Billingham started in the 1970s. It was the necessary nuts-and-bolts prelude to the "fourth era" of SETI.*

The sheer number of channels in this multichannel analyzer was a big advance in itself, but Paul also made the components portable, so they could be packed up in three small boxes and hand-carried to any observatory, anywhere in the world. The system, which he dubbed "Suitcase SETI," traveled first to Arecibo. After examining 250 stars with it, Paul took it back to Harvard in 1983. He hooked it up to the same telescope I had partially built and calibrated in my student days—the one I had used to observe the Pleiades for my doctoral thesis. Suitcase SETI's rambling days were over at that point. Portable though it was, it never ventured out of Harvard's Oak Ridge Observatory again. A new name, Project Sentinel, recognized the fact that Paul's multichannel analyzer was now connected to a dedicated telescope, with funding from The Planetary Society to run a permanent SETI facility.

In time, Sentinel begat "META-SETI"—the Megachannel ExtraTerrestrial Assay—which boosted the number of channels from 128,000 to more than 8 million. (This was the project *E.T.* paid hard cash for, via Steven Spielberg and The Planetary Society.) Paul needed the extra channels, he said, to respond to a new concept put forward by Phil Morrison, who had reminded him in a letter that everything in the universe is in motion.

"Look at this letter from Phil Morrison." Paul waved it proudly at a recent SETI gathering, as though it had just arrived in the mail. "It's so much like a talk with Phil in person. It starts off organized

---

* Paul has codified his enormous knowledge of electronics in a superbly articulate, readable textbook, *The Art of Electronics*. It is the most widely used textbook on the topic in America.

and typewritten, but by the time he's finished it, he's gotten more new ideas, so the page is scattered with little symbols and stick drawings in purple Magic Marker."

Not only is each part of the universe flying away from every other part as the universe expands, but also the stars orbit the centers of their galaxies, moving toward us and away from us as they do so. Given the way "things zip around out there," Paul said, extra channels would help sort out the confounding effects of stellar motion and concomitant Doppler effects.

Intelligent radio signals from distant civilizations could be expected to arrive shifted in frequency, just as the starlight from distant suns is shifted toward the red or the blue end of the optical spectrum by stellar motions. There was no way to predict which way a signal's frequency would shift without knowing how its home star was moving. Thus a message transmitted on the hydrogen frequency could wind up far above or far below that frequency by the time it reached a radio telescope on Earth.

With META, Paul could scrutinize myriad frequencies in the vicinity of the hydrogen line and sift through them, narrow bandwidth by narrow bandwidth, on millions of channels at once to detect the displaced signals.

In 1991 Paul set up a second META, also financed by The Planetary Society, called META II, in the Southern Hemisphere, at the Instituto Argentino de Radioastronomia in Villa Elisa, Argentina. This allowed Argentinian astronomers led by Raul Colombo to observe the portion of the southern sky that's not visible from Cambridge. META II opened up very important new regions of the Milky Way as well as a clear line of sight to the two galaxies that are the Milky Way's nearest neighbors: the Magellanic Clouds. Now, with META and META II thriving, Paul is already dreaming of BETA. This would be a new system ("It'll be *betta* than META," he promises), with one hundred million channels.

Paul has obviously done more searching, with more sensitivity, than anybody who preceded him, so it shouldn't be too surprising to learn that he's actually heard things through his systems. Indeed, Paul has records of about sixty signals that are all excellent candidates for being the real thing. But Paul's searches run themselves, automatically. By the time he recognizes the candidates in the recorded data, hours or days later, it's too late to check them. Looking for them later proves fruitless, as they are no longer where they were. No doubt the civilizations are still there—if that's what made the signal—but they've stopped talking, at least for the moment. Maybe intermittent fan beam messages that sweep our way for just a few moments a year, as I discussed in Chapter 7, are responsible. If only Paul's strategy included a human operator who could double-check the signals on the spot! However, Paul has severe budget constraints, and I know that he can't afford to pay someone to sit there through the long nights and wait.*

The new NASA SETI Microwave Observing Project will change all that, because I'll be sitting there myself. Or Jill will, or some other radio astronomer who will be able to react immediately to chase down a candidate signal the moment it appears. This project, which has been in various stages of planning and development since 1978, is just now beginning its methodical hunt. Because of its great power and sensitivity, it outstrips all previous search activities combined. Three days' operation can accomplish more than was done in the preceding three decades. Indeed, it gives me a strange chill to acknowledge that it takes this new setup only one one-hundredth of a second to duplicate what Project Ozma did in its full two hundred hours.

Before I say another word about this long-awaited endeavor, I have to apologize for its unfortunate acronym, MOP—although I played no part in its selection. I guess NASA was hoping to mop up the heavens with this one, but the word is hopelessly out of keeping with our sense of exploration and discovery. This project's official start-up date, in fact, coincides with the five hundredth anniversary of Columbus's discovery of America. I had pushed for the name AURORA, which is a pretty word that means the dawn and could have stood for All Universe Radio Observations of Rational Activity. I admit that's a fairly tortured acronym, but overall it would have been more acceptable than MOP. As it is, nobody uses MOP; we all call the project "NASA SETI" to avoid sounding silly.

What does NASA SETI have that no other search had? The short answer is "everything." It has everything the early searches had, and everything we could think of that had never been done before.

Like Ozma, NASA SETI scrutinizes a group of relatively close, Sun-like stars for signs of intelligent life. But where Ozma had only two targets, NASA SETI has one thousand. This much more exten-

---

* Recently, Paul has altered META's control system so that it automatically takes a second look when a big signal is received. This is a major step in the right direction.

sive "targeted search," however, is still only half the mission. The other half is an "all-sky survey" that repeatedly scans the whole grand volume of outer space for alien signals from any star, anywhere. Our dual search strategy deals with two alternate possibilities for our cosmic neighbors: Either the easiest aliens to detect are right nearby (targeted search), or they are very far away but very bright (all-sky survey and targeted search).

Like the Ohio State project, NASA SETI is an ongoing endeavor that will run for years. But unlike the low-cost efforts that preceded it, this project fought for and won a total of more than $100 million in federal funding. While other searches started up and faded out without so much as a nod from NASA, this one enjoys the same position as a mission to send a small spacecraft to another planet. Mission status means that SETI is supported all through NASA management, right up to the topmost level.

Like META and META II, NASA SETI spans the globe and the heavens. It utilizes at least five telescopes—at Arecibo, Green Bank, the Observatoire de Nançay in France, the Goldstone Tracking Station in California, and an identical NASA tracking station at Tidbinbilla, Australia. It is the first truly global cooperative effort to search for interstellar signals.

Unlike Project Serendip and Suitcase SETI, NASA SETI is no backseat or part-time visitor. It constitutes the largest single program running at Arecibo and will soon dominate a fully dedicated telescope at Green Bank. It employs more than one hundred people, including a rotating team of radio astronomers who stand ready to respond to candidate signals in real time.

Most American searches until now have sought narrow-band signals on magic frequencies, such as the hydrogen line. We call them "magic" because they seem to have some real rationale for being logical channels of communication. Part of their magic is that they occupy quiet regions of the electromagnetic spectrum. What's more, the hydrogen line, considered the most magical frequency of all, is such a fertile field for making general discoveries in radio astronomy that scientists of all civilizations probably keep close tabs on it. Thus, a signal on that particular frequency should have the greatest chance of being detected. The hydrogen line is the frequency Morrison and Cocconi suggested in their original paper, and the actual frequency searched in Project Ozma.

The word "magic," though it carries the connotation of "perfect" or "ideal," really embraces mysticism, too. Some of our magic frequencies hark back to the numerology of Pythagoras, as when we designate the harmonics, or multiples of the hydrogen frequency as additional places to search. All of Paul Horowitz's efforts have focused on the hydrogen (1420 megahertz) and hydroxyl (1612, 1665, 1667, and 1720 megahertz) lines of the waterhole, as well as the first harmonic of the hydrogen line (2840 megahertz). These three regions are but a tiny fraction of the full radio spectrum, however. Even with 8 million channels, META has devoted itself to the hydrogen region and left the vast majority of other possible frequencies totally unexamined.

Magic frequencies have special appeal, but even human beings disagree as to which ones are best. Kardashev's positronium line enthralls the Soviets, and the waterhole attracts most Americans, but there are half a dozen other magic frequencies that some investigators find equally compelling. The point is, any search based on a magic frequency assumes first of all that extraterrestrials are broadcasting on a chosen frequency, and furthermore that we can know what that frequency is.

The NASA SETI project makes no such assumptions. It scans most of the frequencies in the waterhole that penetrate the Earth's atmosphere. This means we'll have a much greater chance than ever before to detect a message, whether the aliens choose a frequency for convenience' sake or some numerology of their own. Our new equipment frees us from the need to select just one or two frequencies from among the vast field of possibilities.

I would like to point out here that the Arecibo message of 1974 was *not* broadcast on a magic frequency. We used what we had available, which was the broadcasting frequency of the Arecibo radar transmitter at that time (2388 megahertz). To do otherwise would have cost millions of dollars.

This frequency was one arbitrarily assigned to radiotelemetry— for communicating instructions to our own spacecraft. It was thus a frequency of convenience, with no connection to any profound universal truth. Some radio astronomers got very upset on hearing that we had used the available frequency band instead of a magic frequency. It seemed as though our group at the NAIC had violated the Golden Rule of extraterrestrial communication: "Transmit to others as you would have them transmit unto you." Detection of that message by an alien civilization might thus spawn scores of doctoral dissertations on this question: What was the profound and mysterious logic behind the choice of that particular frequency? (Watch it turn out to be the height of *their* Great Pyramid divided by pi! If so, their version of the *National Enquirer* will be the first to report this amazing fact!)

Whereas other searches depended on preexisting equipment, NASA SETI demands special hardware. Part of the NASA support has gone to pay for these new additions. At Arecibo, the prime observing site, a second major upgrading includes installation of a dish-shaped Gregorian feed, which can intercept the whole range of radio frequencies. The old line feeds, in contrast, were quite frequency-specific. Any time you wanted to observe a frequency outside their range, you had to design and build a new feed, at a cost of about $100,000—or run out and buy a TV antenna, as I did during the pulsar craze. With the Gregorian in place, flipping from one frequency range to another becomes almost as simple as pushing a button. The Gregorian also increases the overall sensitivity of the telescope by an average factor of three—a 300 percent improvement. I had begun pushing for a switch to this type of feed when I was still NAIC director, so I'm delighted to see one installed at last.

META set a world's record with 8 million channels, but NASA SETI has 28 million. At the core of its hardware is a device called a multichannel spectrum analyzer (MCSA in NASA's beloved alphabet soup), which divides the incoming radio noise into 14 million narrow-band channels. The MCSA also combines the signals from several adjacent channels to create another 14 million broader bandwidths, just in case the extraterrestrials use them.

The MCSA relies on ultra-advanced software to make sense out of the millions of data points pouring in every second. Software analyzes the data, looking for patterns that reveal intelligence—and that could not possibly be intercepted as fast or as well by human intelligence. The human operator, whose presence is so important to me, steps in *after* computers sound the alarm that a candidate signal has just been detected.

In the past, Americans traditionally focused their efforts on detecting continuous-wave signals, while the Soviets geared up to find pulsed signals (as explained in Chapter 5). But NASA SETI casts a wide net. Any kind of signal—continuous, pulsed, polarized, even drifting signals that appear in different channels at different times—can be intercepted by this system.

The man who came up with all these sophisticated ways of "looking" at data via software has never seen any signal's signature, or anything else, for that matter—not even his own face. He is Kent Cullers, a blind physicist whose favorite childhood memory is of his father telling him astronomy stories at bedtime. Kent knocked on our door, eager to put his expertise in signal processing to work for SETI, after his wife read him the whole text of the Cyclops report. (This was a labor of love that took twenty-four hours.) Now Kent is signal-detection team leader for NASA SETI.

When I attend Kent's talks, I marvel at the way he anticipates the needs of his sighted audience with slides and view graphs that he manages to present in correct order while reading his notes in Braille. Once, when we traveled to a meeting together in Hungary, I familiarized him with his hotel room, explaining the operation of the unusual hand-held shower and other novelties, and placing his hands on key controls. As we were walking out to dinner, without thinking I led him over to the corner by the door and said, "Here's the light switch. It will be to your right when you return to the room." He reminded me gently then, "Thanks, Frank, but I won't need the light switch."

Kent is a full-time NASA employee at Ames, assigned to the SETI project. But many of the other scientists working closely with him, including Jill Tarter, come from outside NASA. The space agency has a manpower limit, mandated by Congress, to keep it from growing into some great bureaucracy. As a result, the actual NASA scientific manpower is about one tenth the number of people who work on NASA projects. The rest are provided under contract to NASA. The crews who run the launchpads and staff the tracking network for spacecraft missions, for instance, were actually employees of commercial firms such as the Bendix Corporation. On the research side, NASA gets most of its contractors from university faculties, though universities typically charge high fees for "overhead" that can deplete budget reserves in short order.

Faced with this problem in the NASA SETI budget, and with encouragement and advice from Barney and John Billingham, I took steps to found a nonprofit corporation, the SETI Institute. This was a way to provide talented subcontractors to NASA and avoid high overhead charges so we could channel the maximum amount of money to science instead of administrative costs. The institute started its life in November 1984, chartered to support any research associated with life in the universe. Our prime mission was, and is, to help NASA SETI find good people and accomplish its scientific goals. We took over personnel searches and paper-work, yet our institute overhead charges are only about a fifth of those charged by some local universities.

At first the SETI Institute operated with three employees out of the corner of a trailer at Moffett Field. One of them, Thomas Pierson, a burly young Oklahoman with an imposing build and an extremely gentle manner, has since become our executive director—and a master at navigating the incredible complexities of NASA bureaucracy. By 1989 we were handling $2 million worth of contracts a year for NASA, and our activities had grown to include nineteen other projects, such as investigations of archaebacteria—strains of bacteria that date back to the origin of life on Earth. It was time to move into our own headquarters, so we rented office space in nearby Mountain View. Through the years, the Institute staff and projects have been shored up more times than I can count by Vera Buescher, whom we refer to as our "utility infielder" because she always jumps in to fill any special need that arises. (When the first data analysis program was con-structed to operate the MCSA, it was named Vera in her honor because, like her, it could do anything.)

The SETI Institute has become my favorite organization, and serving as its president one of the most enjoyable positions I have ever held. (The four scientists—myself and three others—who serve as the board of directors are unpaid for this task.) One of our largest ongoing efforts is an education project that produces cur-riculum materials for elementary and middle schools, using extra-terrestrial life as a magnet to attract students' interest in the SETI-related sciences—chemistry, physics, astronomy, planetary science, biology, and evolution. NASA SETI, of course, remains our chief activity.

In the course of gushing about the great power of NASA SETI compared to any and all of its predecessors, I've dropped several huge numbers, referring to everything from frequencies and sensi-tivities to dollars and cents. That said, do I really need one more quantitative comparison to make my point? Would it really clarify things further to say that NASA SETI is a ten-millionfold improve-ment over past efforts? Maybe not. Maybe the more important thing to say now is that the magnitude of our current efforts creates so much promise that we find ourselves contemplating what we should do when we actually receive signal evidence of extraterrestrial life. When and how do we inform the people of Earth?

John Billingham has probably given more thought to this delicious dilemma than anyone else. Working with other members of the SETI committee of the International Academy of Astronautics (IAA), he has drawn up a "Declaration of Principles Concerning Activities Following the Detection of Extraterrestrial Intelligence." It lists all the steps to be taken to verify the authenticity of a signal and inform the proper authorities that extraterrestrial word has been heard.

This document has been approved or endorsed by every major, international, professional space society, including the IAA, the International Institute of Space Law, the Committee on Space Research, Commission 51 of the International Astronomical Union, and Commission J of the Union Radio Scientifique Internationale. In essence, Billingham's protocol says, *Make sure you've got something; then tell EVERYBODY*.

I've spoken at some length about how one goes about checking a candidate signal for authenticity—how to establish extraterrestrial origin, and how the special hallmarks of artificiality can distinguish a signal as being of intelligent design. But to announce to the world at large that you've made the greatest discovery in the history of astronomy—perhaps in history, period—takes an even wider margin of certainty.

On the NASA SETI project, you probably can't ask another observatory to help you verify your findings. If the long-awaited signal is intercepted at Arecibo, and it is weak, which is the most likely possibility, then no other observatory in the world could make the desired verification. This is because Arecibo has the greatest collecting area of any telescope, as well as the Gregorian feed and other specialized equipment. Even the other participants in NASA SETI, in France and Australia, will not match Arecibo's wide range of frequency coverage. And if the signal did fall within their frequency range, they might lack the sensitivity to hear it. Arecibo is so much more sensitive than the others—ever so much more capable of picking a faint, fragile *"We are here!"* out of a welter of cosmic noise.

In lieu of interobservatory checks and balances, the people at Arecibo (I hope I'm one of them when this happens) will have to spend several days checking and rechecking their data, locating the signal, if possible, a second, third, and fourth time rather than risk setting off a false alarm. After several days, however, repeated observations would build up a chink-free wall of evidence that would justify going public.

"Couldn't a clever enough character pull off a convincing hoax?" a Hollywood producer asked me a couple of years ago. "Isn't there a way to foil the system and fool the astronomers into thinking they had an E.T. signal when they were just being hoodwinked?" The producer thought I was the perfect person to figure out such a hoax. He was willing to pay me a lot of money to come up with the plan, and then he was going to plot it into a screenplay. I took on the assignment, not just for the lark or the money, but because I was worried about the hoax possibility, just like everyone else at NASA SETI. I thought and thought about how to go about it. Finally I determined that it couldn't be done. There really is no way to make a fake signal that appears to emanate from a source moving consistently with respect to the stars. You could probably make it look convincing for an hour or so, but no longer. (Having thus failed to sketch the central scenario for the filmmaker, I did not expect, and did not receive, my consultant's fee.)

Hard upon detection of an intelligent signal, there follows the delicate matter of a reply to the civilization that sent it. I've thought a lot, of course, about what to say in that happy situation. I have waited a lifetime for the opportunity, and the waiting has not diminished my confidence or my enthusiasm. I can't be specific about it, though, because when you really think about it, the only answer to the question "What do you say?" is "It depends."

It depends on the nature of the signal and what it's telling us. It depends on the world's reaction. It depends on the distance the message traveled, because we couldn't establish true dialogue with civilizations far removed from us—only lengthy monologues, crossing each other eternally in the interstellar mail. It depends on whether we can understand it. Certainly no stock reply, prepared in advance and stashed in someone's file cabinet, could match more than one of the infinite possibilities for the message's content. Certainly any reply should be crafted on a worldwide basis, and only after lengthy deliberation by knowledgeable individuals.

I have a recurring dream in which we receive our much-anticipated intelligent signal from across the Galaxy. The signal is unambiguous. It repeats over and over, allowing us to get a fix on its source, some twenty thousand light-years away. The signal is circularly polarized, apparently dense with information content. It is so full of noise, however, that we can't extract any information from it. And so we know only that another civilization exists. We cannot decipher the message itself.

If this dream becomes real, such documented detection of alien signals will, of course, be big news in itself. It will be a call to action, too, beckoning us to do whatever is required—build a much larger radio-telescope system, for example—to obtain information about that civilization, to learn whatever secrets the extraterrestrials will share with us.

Indeed, our response to a message from an alien civilization may thus be a response to the *situation* instead of an actual reply to the senders. We will tell the world at large what has happened, and that we're taking the next step by building better equipment to understand the message we've received. How I would love to have to go to Congress with a budget request for that project. I don't imagine I'd encounter much opposition.

At some point in the not-too-distant future, no matter what the outcome of current searches, we will still need to build a giant telescope. If we fail to find signals, we'll need to move to a bigger system to improve our sensitivity and therefore our chances of detecting them. And if we succeed, we'll need the larger instrument to gather more signal and less noise. So you see, it isn't too soon to start planning the next step. We could build it on the ground, Cyclops style. We could also build it in space, using the space shuttle to carry components aloft, where astronauts would assemble a network of several huge dishes, shielded by screens that shut out man-made radio transmissions. The Russians already have such a scheme in the works.

Personally, I think the most desirable spot of all for a grandiose new telescope is on the far side of the Moon. That is the only place in the entire Solar System that is not bombarded, at one time or another, by signals from Earth. Because of the way the Moon keeps the same face turned toward us as it rotates around us, its far side is a natural "radio quiet zone."

On the Moon, where gravity is only one sixth that of the Earth, we could use conventional materials—steel and aluminum—to build an Arecibo-style telescope thirty miles wide. The real Arecibo is one fifth of one mile wide, so the Moon version would be one hundred fifty times bigger in diameter, making it several thousand times larger in energy-collecting area. What faint signals such a system could detect! We could plop it into the bottom of a big crater, and hang the platform and feeds from the crater's rim on lightweight cables. There'd be no wind to budge or bounce the structure in any direction. The installation of this particular instrument hinges, of course, on the presence of a preexisting manned Moon base, but such a base is already a defined NASA goal.

In the realm of ultimate cosmic dreams, the Sun itself could serve as the best telescope of all. It is by nature a "gravitational" lens that provides a detailed view of the entire universe. But, like Archimedes boasting that he could move the world if he but had a place to stand, astronomers need to send spacecraft far beyond the limit of our present capabilities to exploit the lens of the Sun.

Egging us on is the knowledge that the Sun's enormous mass promises magnification powers and image sharpness that surpass our largest telescopes by almost unbelievable amounts.

The gravitational lens is elegantly simple in its design. Rather than bringing rays of light to a focus by bending them in a lens of glass, or reflecting them with a high-tech mirror, the Sun focuses light by bending *space.*

The concept of the gravitational lens stems from the work of Albert Einstein. In his theory of general relativity, Einstein proposed that the presence of mass bends space. The Sun, being a massive object, warps the space it occupies. As a result, light traveling past the Sun from distant stars is deflected from a straight-line path and is actually pulled in toward the Sun.

This particular aspect of Einstein's theory has been directly observed. The great physicist Arthur Stanley Eddington, one of the few people to grasp general relativity immediately, suggested a way to test the theory with the aid of a solar eclipse. He would photograph the sky during totality—when the Moon blocked out the Sun's light and let the stars appear in midday. Also, months later, he would shoot another photograph, with the same telescope, of the same area of the sky where the eclipse had taken place—but when the Sun was on the other side of the world, and the same stars would be visible *at night.* Comparing the two photographic plates, the stars that had stood closest to the Sun during the eclipse should appear to have changed position from one photo to the other: the Sun's proximity would have bent their light in the eclipse photo.

Eddington himself led one of the expeditions to conduct this experiment in 1919, when he set off for the total eclipse at the island of Príncipe, off the western coast of Africa. He and his party had to stay there for five months, so they could photograph the exact same patch of sky with and without the Sun. (And this was after Eddington made a previous attempt in Brazil in 1912, when the foul weather foiled his observation efforts.) With considerable difficulty, Eddington's group in Príncipe measured the deflection of starlight at the limb, or edge, of the Sun to be one second of arc. On a photographic plate, that distance shows up as less than one one-hundredth of a millimeter. The observations appeared to agree with Einstein's prediction but were not precise enough to confirm it. A later expedition of astronomers from the Lick Observatory (my present home) traveled to Australia, where they witnessed a spectacular eclipse that brought 140 stars into view, and measured enough deflections to prove Einstein's theory conclusively.

Nowadays, radio telescopes can make such comparisons quickly, easily, and more accurately, too, without the need for any special conditions such as a total solar eclipse. We no longer harbor any lingering doubts that the Sun is an extraordinarily powerful lens.

The starlight passing the Sun is deflected, or bent, toward an imaginary line running between the center of the Sun and the center of the source star. Now, after considering how much hard work went into proving that fact, picture yourself relaxing at day's end, contemplating the setting Sun. In addition to the Sun's orange glow at that hour, and the sunset colors that paint the sky, there is a great flood of faint, deflected starlight from all over the universe, invisible to you, but nonetheless streaming past you from all around the rim of the sun, to be focused into perfect, sharp images far behind your back.

How far behind your back?

About 51 billion miles.

For convenience, astronomers describe the distance between the Earth and Sun as one astronomical unit, instead of the more unwieldy figure of 93 million miles. In these terms, the distance to the Sun's enchanted focal point is about 550 astronomical units. That's very far out in space—farther than any of our spacecraft has ever traveled. It is well beyond the orbit of Pluto, 40 astronomical units away, though only the smallest fraction of the way to the closest star, which is 300,000 astronomical units from the Sun.

If we could send a receiving device to that far region of space, we would indeed have a window on the universe. We would find there, not just the image of one star at one focal point, but a sphere of myriad focal points creating images of every star whose light passes the Sun. Every star of every galaxy is represented here. It is as though the Sun were surrounded by a great celestial sphere studded with superbright pictures of distant objects. The images appear this clearly because their light has been focused by the giant lens of the Sun. And as a telescope lens, the Sun is equal to about 10,000 times the collecting area of Arecibo. What's more, the Sun functions equally well collecting and resolving any form of electromagnetic radiation. It's an optical telescope, a radio telescope, an infrared telescope, a gamma-ray telescope, and an X-ray telescope all rolled into one.

The Sun performs as an oddly shaped lens to be sure—a thin ring that measures more than 900,000 miles in diameter. Its resolution, or ability to clarify images, is about 1 million times superior to the best resolution achieved when using several big telescopes together. That means that the Sun could project images of distant stars *with* their planets, giving us the best means imaginable for detecting extrasolar planets. What's more, thanks to the remarkable resolving power of the gravitational lens, we could even see certain large surface features on those planetary surfaces—entities the size of a Grand Canyon, say, or a Mississippi River.

Throughout my account of the history of SETI, I've been talking about the need for big collecting areas to detect faint signals, such as Cyclops would have provided. But even Cyclops is *tiny* compared to the solar gravitational lens. In terms of SETI's goals, the Sun's enormous collecting area can pick up radio signals sent by transmitters as small as walkie-talkies from clear across the Milky Way.

"I know perfectly well that at this moment the whole universe is listening to us," Jean Giraudoux wrote in *The Madwoman of Chaillot*, "and that every word we say echoes to the remotest star." That poetic paranoia is a perfect description of what the Sun, as a gravitational lens, could do for SETI. I wonder if other worlds are watching us and listening to our every word with their great stellar lenses.

We are just beginning to recognize the power of the gravitational lens phenomenon. We have not tried to utilize it. Indeed, it's hard to estimate how much technological *savoir-faire* stands between our present capabilities and the launching of a spacecraft to orbit the Sun at 550 astronomical units. But if we could put one there, we would need to equip it with only a small antenna—perhaps 30 feet in diameter, or even as small as 3 feet in diameter—to mine the vast wealth of sights and sounds awaiting us in that realm.

All things considered, we'd need to put the spacecraft a bit farther still. Right at 550 astronomical units, where the light passing over the rim of the Sun is focused, we'd encounter a lot of distortion from the Sun's atmosphere and corona. But starlight that passes not quite so near to the Sun, a little farther from the rim, is also brought to a focal point—a little farther out in space, where all the pristine images of the universe remain visible. There is in fact an infinite number of celestial spheres, starting at the radius of 550 astronomical units and then spreading out through space like the ripples around a stone dropped in a pond. Each of these spheres bears its own true likeness of the universe. At a distance of 1,000 astronomical units from the Sun, the seeing conditions should be ideal.

The Jet Propulsion Lab is already looking at the feasibility of a mission to that region, 1,000 astronomical units from the Sun, because it lies in the Oort Cloud, a breeding ground for comets that surrounds the Solar System. The JPL hopes to measure the cloud's particles and magnetic fields, and maybe even try to photograph comets at close range. If I'm still around when that mission flies, I'll be sure to suggest they mount a small radio telescope on the spacecraft, too.

My sense is that by then we will have already received an extraterrestrial signal. Buoyed by the sense of galactic companionship it engenders, we'll be looking for still more signals that are fainter and farther away—because detecting one civilization will prove there are many others to be found. I do not wonder *whether* this will happen. My only question is *When?*

The silence we have heard so far is not in any way significant. We still have not looked long enough or hard enough. We've not explored a large enough chunk of the cosmic haystack. I could speculate that "they" are watching us to see if we are worth talking to. Or perhaps the ethic exists among them that rules, "There is no free lunch in the Galaxy." If we want to join the community of advanced civilizations, we must work as hard as they must. Perhaps they will send a signal that can be detected only if we put as much effort into receiving it as they put into transmitting it. NASA SETI is the beginning of the first truly meaningful effort to demonstrate the sincerity of our intentions.

Thus, the lesson we have learned from all our previous searching is that the greatest discovery is not a simple one to make. If there were once cockeyed optimists in the SETI endeavor, there aren't any now. In a way, I am glad. The priceless benefits of knowledge and experience that will accrue from interstellar contact should not come too easily. To appreciate them, we should expect to devote a substantial portion of our resources, our assets, our intellectual vigor, and our patience. We should be willing to sweat and crawl and wait.

The goal is not beyond us. It is within our grasp.

Epilogue

I do not know what I may appear to the world, but to myself I seem to have been only a boy playing on the seashore, and diverting myself in now and then finding a smoother pebble or a prettier shell than ordinary, whilst the great ocean of truth lay all undiscovered before me.

—SIR ISAAC NEWTON

So much has happened in the thirty-plus years since SETI began—all of it good. We have seen clear evidence of the unrelenting metamorphosis of cold and barren interstellar clouds into rich planetary systems. We have seen stars do the timid dance by which they reveal that their partners are, indeed, planets. The corps of dancers seems countless. And, as thirty years ago, it is still in the realm of microwave radiation where the universe is darkest and quietest. Here the glimmer of the faint beacons of intelligent life may overcome the darkness and still be detectable amid the cacophony of unintelligent signals from the objects of the mechanical universe.

Here on Earth we have seen two major developments. Through the near magic of the explosion in computer technology, our power to search for extraterrestrial intelligent life has doubled about every 235 days. And no end is in sight. Of equal importance, surprising numbers of our most brilliant scientists have turned their talents and committed their careers to SETI. Both of these advances were required if we were to have the ability to mount a search that was equal to the task of sifting through all the grains of sand on a vast beach in search of a few rare and barely visible treasures.

To use Newton's words, our efforts up till this moment have but turned over a pebble or shell here and there on the beach, with only a forlorn hope that under one of them was the gem we were seeking. Now we have the sieve, the minds, the hands, the time, and, particularly, the dedication to find those gems—no matter in which favorite hiding place the children of distant worlds have placed them.

Additional Information

Additional information about the search for extraterrestrial intelligence is available from the following organizations:

The SETI Institute
2035 Landings Drive
Mountain View, California 94043

The Astronomical Society of the Pacific
390 Ashton Avenue
San Francisco, California 94112

The Planetary Society
65 North Catalina Avenue
Pasadena, California 91106

Bibliography

Ashpole, Edward. *The Search for Extraterrestrial Intelligence*. London: Blandford, 1989.

Asimov, Isaac. *Asimov's Biographical Encyclopedia of Science and Technology*. Garden City, N.Y.: Doubleday, 1972.

Billingham, John, ed. *Life in the Universe*. Cambridge, Mass.: MIT Press, 1981.

Blum, Howard. *Out There*. New York: Simon & Schuster, 1990.

Bova, Ben, and Byron Preiss, eds. *First Contact*. New York: New American Library, 1990.

Bracewell, Ronald N. *The Galactic Club*. Stanford, Calif.: Stanford Alumni Association, 1974.

Cameron, A.G.W., ed. *Interstellar Communication*. New York: W. A. Benjamin, 1963.

Cohen, Nathan. *Gravity's Lens*. New York: John Wiley & Sons, 1988.

Drake, Frank D. *Intelligent Life in Space*. New York: Macmillan, 1962.

Forward, Robert. *Dragon's Egg*. New York: Ballantine, 1980.

Goldsmith, Donald. *The Quest for Extraterrestrial Life*. Mill Valley, Calif.: University Science Books, 1980.

————, and Tobias Owen. *The Search for Life in the Universe*. Menlo Park, Calif.: Benjamin/Cummings, 1980.

Gunn, James. *The Listeners*. New York: Charles Scribner's Sons, 1972.

Hey, J. S. *The Evolution of Radio Astronomy.* New York: Neal Watson, 1973.

Lilly, John C. *Man and Dolphin.* Garden City, N.Y.: Doubleday, 1961.

McDonough, Thomas R. *The Search for Extraterrestrial Intelligence.* New York: John Wiley & Sons, 1987.

Mamikunian, Gregg, and Michael H. Briggs, eds. *Current Aspects of Exobiology.* Pasadena, Calif.: Jet Propulsion Laboratory, 1965.

Morrison, Philip, John Billingham, and John Wolfe, eds. *The Search for Extraterrestrial Intelligence,* NASA Report SP-419. Washington, D.C.: U.S. Government Printing Office, 1977.

Oliver, Bernard M., and John Billingham, eds. *Project Cyclops,* NASA Report CR-114445. Moffett Field, Calif.: NASA/Ames Research Center, 1973.

Overbye, Dennis. *Lonely Hearts of the Cosmos.* New York: Harper-Collins, 1991.

Papagiannis, Michael D., ed. *Strategies for the Search for Life in the Universe.* Boston: Reidel, 1980.

Ponnamperuma, Cyril, and A.G.W. Cameron, eds. *Interstellar Communication.* Boston: Houghton Mifflin, 1974.

Rood, Robert, and James S. Trefil. *Are We Alone?* New York: Charles Scribner's Sons, 1981.

Sagan, Carl. *Contact.* New York: Simon & Schuster, 1985.

————, ed. *Communication with Extraterrestrial Intelligence.* Cambridge, Mass.: MIT Press, 1973.

Sagan, Carl, et al. *Murmurs of Earth.* New York: Random House, 1978.

Shklovsky, Iosif. *Five Billion Vodka Bottles to the Moon.* New York: W. W. Norton, 1991.

————, and Carl Sagan. *Intelligent Life in the Universe.* San Francisco: Holden-Day, 1966.

Sullivan, Walter. *We Are Not Alone: The Search for Intelligent Life on Other Worlds.* New York: McGraw-Hill, 1964.

Swift, David W. *SETI Pioneers.* Tucson: The University of Arizona Press, 1990.

White, Frank. *The SETI Factor.* New York: Walker, 1990.

Glossary

alt-azimuth mount A telescope support structure that has a horizontal axis and a vertical axis. By rotating the telescope around these two axes, usually under computer control, an observer can point it and simultaneously compensate for the Earth's rotation.

angular momentum The momentum of a rotating body around the axis of spin.

antimatter Matter made of negatively charged protons and positively charged electrons—the charges opposite of those found in ordinary matter. Very little antimatter exists in nature, as it is destroyed soon after its creation.

Archimedes Greek mathematician and engineer (287–212 B.C.), considered the greatest scientist of ancient times, who worked out, among many other things, the principle of the lever.

astronomical unit (AU) The average distance between the Sun and the Earth, or 93 million miles.

bandwidth The difference in frequency between the lowest and highest frequencies in a radio channel; the range of frequencies covered by the channel. If the range is small, the signal is said to be narrow-band; if large, broad-band. In general, natural emissions from cosmic objects are broad-band, while intentional signals are narrow-band. In a radio transmitter or receiver, bandwidth refers to the width of the channel the equipment can transmit or receive. Modern SETI equipment consists of receivers with millions of narrow-band channels.

beam   The portion of the sky from which a radio telescope collects signals, or to which it sends signals, at any given time.

BETA   Billion-channel ExtraTerrestrial Assay.

binary code   A message coding system in which only two characters are used. These could be, for example, dots and dashes, zeros and ones, or two different tones.

binary star   Two stars orbiting a common center of gravity. They may be so close together as to appear as a single star to an observer on Earth. If they periodically obscure each other from sight, they constitute an eclipsing binary.

black hole   A collapsed star or other object so dense that nothing, not even light, can escape its strong gravitational pull.

Bracewell probe   Hypothetical unmanned spacecraft that travels to other planetary systems and monitors them for signs of intelligent life, as suggested by Ronald Bracewell.

broad-band   Wide in frequency range. In tuning an ordinary radio, the hissing background noise is broad-band, while the individual stations are narrow-band signals.

Caltech   The California Institute of Technology, Pasadena.

CERN   Centre Européen Recherche Nucleaire (European Center for Nuclear Research), Geneva, Switzerland.

CETI   Acronym for Communication with ExtraTerrestrial Intelligence.

Copernican revolution   The change in thinking that followed the posthumous publication of a book by Nicolaus Copernicus, a Polish astronomer (1473–1543), postulating that the Sun, not the Earth, was the center of the Solar System.

cosmic haystack   A metaphor for the universe as it appears to those who search for extraterrestrial intelligence, since their mission has been compared to finding a needle in a haystack.

cosmic rays   High-energy nuclear particles from the Sun and sources in outer space; Earth's atmosphere protects us from many of them, but they pose a threat to astronauts on interplanetary missions.

Crab Nebula   Crab-shaped gas cloud in the constellation Taurus (the Bull) distinguished for its strong radio and X-ray emissions.

Both the cloud and the pulsar within it are remnants of a supernova that exploded in 1054.

CSIRO   Commonwealth Scientific and Industrial Research Organisation, Sydney, Australia.

CTA-102   Radio source first cataloged by Caltech scientists, later identified as a quasar, and mistaken for a Type III civilization by Soviet scientists in 1965.

Cyclops (also called Project Cyclops)   A proposed array of up to fifteen hundred radio telescopes, dedicated to SETI activities, that was designed under NASA auspices in 1971 but never built.

declination   The celestial equivalent of latitude for establishing positions of planets and stars. The celestial equator (0 degrees) and north and south poles are projections on the sky of their counterparts on Earth.

Doppler effect   The effect of a source's motion on the waves it emits. Austrian physicist and mathematician Christian Johann Doppler (1803–53) first described the relationship between the pitch of a sound and the motion of its source toward or away from a listener: The pitch rises when the source is approaching and drops when it is receding. The same phenomenon is observed with electromagnetic radiation from stars: Light is shifted in color, and radio waves in frequency, by the motion of their source.

Drake Equation   Formula for estimating the number of advanced intelligent civilizations in space.

Dyson sphere   An enormous artificial shell that advanced extraterrestrial civilizations might build around a star to capture its energy for their use; first proposed by Freeman Dyson.

electromagnetic radiation, or electromagnetic spectrum   Energy in the form of packets of electrical and magnetic energy called photons. The electrical and magnetic energy fields in these photons vibrate at a frequency that characterizes the radiation. Electromagnetic radiation, starting from the longest wavelengths and slowest vibrations, includes radio, infrared, visible light, ultraviolet light, X rays, and gamma rays.

equatorial mount   *See* polar mount.

exobiology   The study of extraterrestrial life.

feed   The antenna at the focal point, or focal line, of a radio telescope's collecting area. It captures the energy collected by the telescope, or radiates the radio energy if the telescope is used to transmit radio signals.

Fermi, Enrico   Italian-born physicist (1901–54) who won the 1938 Nobel prize for his work in nuclear physics that laid the groundwork for nuclear fission and the first atomic pile or nuclear reactor.

Fermi Paradox   The seeming disparity, probably not significant, between the likelihood of the existence of other civilizations and the lack of evidence that they have ever visited Earth.

frequency   The number of radio waves transmitted or received per second. Signals of short wavelength (as measured crest-to-crest) have high frequencies; those of long wavelength, low frequencies.

Fresnel, Augustin-Jean   French physicist and civil engineer (1788–1827) who fathered the theory of refraction and conducted much important work in optics.

Galileo Galilei   Italian astonomer (1564–1642) who advocated the ideas of Copernicus and made observations to support them. He first used a telescope to discover mountains on the Moon, the phases of Venus, and the four large moons of Jupiter, called the Galilean satellites in his honor.

gamma rays   Electromagnetic radiation of extremely short wavelength—even shorter than X rays.

gigahertz (GHz)   *See* Hertz, Heinrich.

globular cluster   Spherical group of several hundred thousand very old stars, orbiting around their common center of gravity, found in the outskirts of galaxies.

gravitational lens   Any star or other massive celestial object that bends light and other electromagnetic radiation, in accordance with the laws of General Relativity, focusing it to a point or several points in space.

Green Bank   A hamlet in Pocahontas County, West Virginia, in the Allegheny Mountains at the eastern edge of the state, near the Virginia border. It is the home of the NRAO and often used as an informal name for that observatory.

habitable zone   The region around a star where conditions may be favorable for the development of life-forms.

Heisenberg, Werner   German atomic physicist (1901–76) who won the 1932 Nobel prize for his formulation of the uncertainty principle, which points out the impossibility of determining both an object's precise position and its velocity at the same time.

Hertz, Heinrich   German physicist (1857–94) who discovered radio waves. The standard unit for measuring radio frequency is named for him: One hertz (Hz) = one cycle per second. Also, one megahertz (MHz) = one million cycles per second, and one gigahertz (GHz) = one billion cycles per second.

Hubble, Edwin   American astronomer (1889–1953) who classified the galaxies and showed that the universe was expanding.

hydroxyl radical   The union of one atom of oxygen and one atom of hydrogen. An additional atom of hydrogen turns the hydroxyl radical into a molecule of water.

IAU   International Astronomical Union, Paris, France.

infrared   Region of the electromagnetic spectrum between optical and radio waves. Most infrared rays from space do not penetrate the Earth's atmosphere and must be observed from satellites or high-flying aircraft.

IRAS   InfraRed Astronomy Satellite, launched in 1983 to observe infrared emissions, with unexcelled sensitivity, from the entire sky.

Jansky, Karl   Bell Telephone Labs physicist (1905–50) who first detected radio noise coming from outer space. The unit of intensity for cosmic radio sources is called the jansky.

Jodrell Bank   Site of the 250-foot radio telescope built in England in the 1950s.

Kardashev civilization types   *See* Type I, II, and III civilizations.

Kelvin   Lord Kelvin, whose name was William Thomson (1824–1907), was a Scottish mathematician and physicist; the absolute temperature scale, one of his many achievements, is called the Kelvin scale in his honor.

Kepler, Johannes German astronomer and mystic (1571–1630) who believed in Pythagoras's "music of the spheres," yet determined that the planets traveled in elliptical orbits around the Sun and who formulated other laws of planetary motion.

laser An acronym (Light Amplification by Stimulated Emission of Radiation) that refers to the production of narrow-band, single-color beams of light by electrically exciting the atoms in certain substances, such as ruby or argon.

light-year The distance light travels in a year, or six trillion miles.

Lowell, Percival American astronomer (1855–1916) who fancied he saw evidence of an advanced civilization on Mars.

magic frequency Radio frequency assumed by scientists to be a possible favorite of intelligent creatures as a result of some logical argument, and thus a reasonable choice to search for extraterrestrial signals of intelligent origin.

magnitude The brightness of a celestial object, described on a scale that gives low or minus numbers to very bright planets and stars, and high numbers to dim ones.

maser Acronym (Microwave Amplification by Stimulated Emission of Radiation) referring to the enhancement of radio signals by excited atoms, as in a laser.

Maxwell, James Clerk Scottish mathematician and physicist (1831–79) who made many contributions to astronomy. He showed that Saturn's rings must consist of thousands of small bodies. He was the first to construct a correct theory of electromagnetic radiation.

META Megachannel ExtraTerrestrial Assay.

meteor Commonly called a shooting star, a meteor is the streak of light seen in the sky when a piece of interplanetary debris strikes the Earth's atmosphere and is heated to incandescence.

meteorite Fragment of a meteor that survives its very hot trip through the atmosphere and reaches the ground.

meteoroid Piece of interplanetary debris, such as ice or rock, that does not enter the Earth's atmosphere.

NAIC The National Astronomy and Ionosphere Center, Ithaca, New York, and Arecibo, Puerto Rico.

narrow-band Limited in frequency range. Intelligent signals are expected to be narrow-band to distinguish them from broadband noise. Narrow-band signals, because of their concentrated power, can be detected farther and more clearly than broad-band ones can.

NASA The National Aeronautics and Space Administration, Washington, D.C.

nebula An object with a cloudlike appearance, either dark or light, in deep space. The Milky Way Galaxy contains many nebulae in the form of clouds of gas and dust. Some of these may contain stars being born, such as the nebula in Orion's sword. Others, called planetary nebulae, are gas clouds ejected from dying stars. Galaxies were called nebulae before astronomers determined them to be distant groups of billions of stars accompanied by their own gas and dust clouds.

neutron Uncharged particle found in the nucleus of the atom; its discovery came long after the discovery of the positively charged proton in the nucleus and the negatively charged electrons orbiting the nucleus.

NRAO The National Radio Astronomy Observatory, headquartered in Charlottesville, Virginia, with primary observing stations at Green Bank, West Virginia; Socorro, New Mexico; and Tucson, Arizona.

NSF The National Science Foundation, Washington, D.C.—the U.S. government agency that sponsors much of the astronomical research in this country.

Order of the Dolphin Informal association of scientists interested in communication with extraterrestrial life, formed at a November 1961 meeting in Green Bank, West Virginia.

Ozma (also called Project Ozma) First modern radio search for extraterrestrial signals of intelligent origin, staged at Green Bank, West Virginia, in 1960.

parametric amplifier Device that greatly improves the receiving sensitivity of a radio telescope. An early, experimental one was used in Project Ozma.

parsec   A measure of astronomical distance equal to 3.26 light-years.

photon   *See* Electromagnetic radiation.

***Pioneer 10* and 11**   U.S. spacecraft that traveled through and beyond the Solar System, adorned with message plaques designed for extraterrestrials.

polarized emissions   Electromagnetic radiation in which the waves are all vibrating in the same way. Polarization is a characteristic of intelligent signals; the waves in most natural signals, in contrast, are jumbled and scattered.

polar mount   Telescope support structure that has one "polar" axis, parallel to the Earth's axis, and a second axis at a right angle to the first. It can track a celestial object if the polar axis is rotated at a speed of one revolution per day, opposite to the rotation of the Earth.

positronium line   Magic frequency proposed by Nikolai Kardashev for use in SETI activities. It is a radio spectral line emitted from an atom consisting of one positive and one negative electron orbiting around their common center of gravity.

primordial soup   The chemical composition of the oceans and lakes of the Earth at the time the first living creatures arose.

protected frequency   Radio frequency barred from use by terrestrial transmitters because of its importance in radio astronomy research.

pulsar   The remnants of a dying star that has exploded as a supernova, leaving its magnetic field greatly strengthened and its core collapsed to neutron-star density. It spins rapidly, emitting pulsed bursts of radiation.

Pythagoras   Greek philosopher (582–497 B.C.) who believed in a mathematical foundation for the universe and taught that the Earth was round. He demonstrated that the square on the hypotenuse of a right triangle equals the sum of the squares on the other two sides.

quasar, or quasi-stellar object Extremely distant celestial object that looks like a star because it appears so compact, but is in fact the nucleus of a turbulent galaxy releasing prodigious amounts of energy, possibly as a result of matter falling into a central black hole.

relativistic rocket Hypothetical spacecraft that travels at an appreciable fraction of the speed of light.

right ascension The celestial equivalent of longitude for describing stellar and planetary positions, measured in hours, minutes, and seconds to the east from the point at which the plane of the Earth's orbit crosses the celestial equator.

sensitivity The acuity of a radio receiver. The greater its power and sensitivity, the better its ability to detect faint signals.

SETI Acronym for Search for ExtraTerrestrial Intelligence.

sky survey SETI research strategy that scans the whole sky, or as much of the sky as a given telescope can see, as opposed to examining specific targets.

solar wind The steady stream of atomic particles flowing out from the upper atmosphere of the Sun.

spectral lines Bright and dark lines that appear in the spectra of objects such as stars, planets, galaxies, and radio sources. They occur all through the electromagnetic spectrum. They can be used to determine the chemical composition of the object, as well as its velocity and temperature.

spectrum The intensity of electromagnetic radiation (usually) from an object over all observed wavelengths.

Struve, Otto Distinguished astrophysicist (1897–1963) who was among the first to suggest that billions of other stars had planetary systems that might harbor life. As director of the NRAO in 1960, Struve helped initiate the search for extraterrestrial intelligence.

supercivilization Advanced extraterrestrial civilization, as in Type III.

supernova A rare stellar explosion in which a massive star ejects its outer shell, appearing remarkably luminous for a short time. During the explosion, it may emit more light than all the other stars in its galaxy combined.

synchrotron radiation Blue-white light and other emissions given off by charged atomic particles, usually electrons, when they orbit in magnetic fields.

targeted search SETI search strategy of examining specific stars or galaxies, as opposed to scanning the whole sky.

transit instrument Radio telescope that cannot move to counter Earth's rotation. Such telescopes usually move around a horizontal, east-west axis only. This motion, plus the Earth's rotation, allows them to point at a given target once a day.

Type I civilization In Nikolai Kardashev's classification scheme, a civilization using only the energy available to it from natural sources on its planet, such as oil and water power. Ours is a Type I civilization.

Type II civilization More advanced than a Type I civilization, a Type II civilization utilizes all the energy radiated by its star.

Type III civilization The most advanced postulated, capable of tapping the full energy output of its home galaxy.

Viking U.S. spacecraft, first to land on Mars in 1976 and sample the red soil for evidence of microscopic extraterrestrial life-forms.

Voyager 1 **and** *2* Two U.S. spacecraft that explored and then left the Solar System, carrying the Voyager interstellar record—a message to extraterrestrials in sounds and pictures.

waterhole Dark, quiet region of the electromagnetic spectrum considered to be a likely frequency band for extraterrestrial communication.

Zeeman effect The changes created in the spectra of electromagnetic radiation by magnetic fields. The measurement of the Zeeman effect is a prime way to measure the strength of magnetic fields in interstellar space.

Appendix A: SETI Folk

The original Order of the Dolphin, 1961

Dana Atchley, Jr.	Philip Morrison
Melvin Calvin	Bernard M. Oliver
Frank D. Drake	J. Peter Pearman
Su Shu Huang	Carl Sagan
John C. Lilly, M.D.	Otto Struve

Participants, CETI conference, Byurakan, Soviet Armenia, 1971

Viktor Ambartsumyan	Y. K. Khodarev
Boris Belitsky	Y. I. Kuznetzov
S. Y. Braude	Richard Lee
B. Burke	William H. McNeill
Francis Crick	B. E. Markarian
E. M. Debai	E. S. Markarian
Frank D. Drake	M. Y. Marov
Freeman Dyson	George Marx
K. Flannery	Marvin Minsky
Lev Gindilis	E. Mirzabekian
V. L. Ginzburg	L. V. Mirzoyan
Thomas Gold	V. I. Moroz
David Heeschen	Philip Morrison
Sebastian von Hoerner	L. M. Mukhin
David Hubel	Bernard M. Oliver
G. M. Idlis	Leslie Orgel
S. A. Kaplan	L. M. Ozernoy
Nikolai Kardashev	B. I. Panovkin
V. V. Kazutinsky	Yury Pariisky
Kenneth Kellerman	Rudolph Pesek
E. E. Khachikyan	N. T. Petrovich

J. R. Platt   Gunther Stent
R. K. Podolny   B. V. Sukhotin
Carl Sagan   M. L. Ter-Mikaelian
V. A. Sanamyan   G. M. Tovmasyan
Iosif Shklovsky   Charles Townes
V. I. Siforov   Vasevolod Troitsky
Viacheslav Slysh

American Participants, SETI conference, Tallinn, Estonia, 1981
Robert Dixon   Philip Morrison
Frank D. Drake   Bernard M. Oliver
George Gatewood   A. Schwartzmann
Paul Horowitz   Woodruff T. Sullivan III
Jonathan Lomberg   Jill Tarter
(Among the more than 200 Soviet participants were Nikolai
  Kardashev, Iosif Shklovsky, and Vasevolod Troitsky.)

Participants, U.S.A.-U.S.S.R. SETI conference, Santa Cruz, California, 1991
Valery Altunin   Leonid Litvinenko
Peter Backus   Jonathan Lomberg
Tom Bania   Geoffrey Marcy
Gregory Beskin   Lori Marino
Albert Betz   Philip Morrison
John Billingham   Bernard M. Oliver
Stuart Bowyer   Edward Olsen
Nathan Cohen   Ehud Pardo
James Cordes   Yury Pariisky
Kent Cullers   Karl Rebane
Laurance Doyle   John Reykjalin
Frank D. Drake   Georgy Rudnitsky
Jay Duluk   Carl Sagan
Freeman Dyson   Viacheslav Slysh
Michael Garyantes   David Soderblom
Lev Gindilis   Paul Steffes
Samuel Gulkis   Vladimir Strelnitsky
Paul Horowitz   Woodruff T. Sullivan III
Nikolai Kardashev   Jill Tarter
Michael Klein   Alexander Tutukov
Vladimir Kotelnikov   Daniel Wertheimer
Steve Levin   George Zimmerman
Sergey Likhachev

Appendix B: SETI Projects in Summary

A Compendium of Search Activities, Compiled by Jill Tarter

YEARS	PARTICIPANTS	OBSERVATORY	ACTIVITY
1960	Drake ("Ozma")	NRAO	Searched 2 stars
1964–65	Kardashev, Sholomitsky	Crimea Deep Space Station, USSR	Searched 2 quasars
1966	Kellerman	CSIRO, Australia	Searched Galaxy 1934–63
1968–69	Troitsky, Gershtejin, Starodubtsev, Rakhlin	Zimenkie, USSR	Searched 11 stars and Galaxy M-31
1968–82	Troitsky	Gorky, USSR	All-sky search
1969–83	Troitsky, Bondar, Starodubtsev	Gorky, Crimea, Murmansk, and Primorsky regions	All-sky search for sporadic pulses
1970–72	Slysh, Pashchenko, Rudnitsky, Lekht	Nançay, France	Searched 5 OH masers
1970–72	Slysh	Nançay	Searched 10 nearest stars
1971, 1972	Verschuur ("Ozpa")	NRAO	Searched 9 stars
1972	Kardashev, Popov, Soglasnov et al.	Crimea	Searched galactic center
1972–74	Kardashev, Gindilis, Popov, Soglasnov, Spangenberg, Steinberg et al.	Caucasus, Pamir, Kamchatka, Mars 7 Spacecraft	"Eavesdropping" search for pulses
1972–76	Palmer, Zuckerman ("Ozma II")	NRAO	Searched 674 stars

YEARS	PARTICIPANTS	OBSERVATORY	ACTIVITY
1972–76	Bridle, Feldman ("Qui Appelle?")	Algonquin Radio Observatory, Ontario	Searched 70 stars
1973–present	Dixon, Ehman, Raub, Kraus	Ohio State University Radio Observatory	All-sky search
1973–74	Shvartsman et al. ("MANIA")	Special Astrophysical Observatory, USSR	Searched 21 peculiar objects for short pulses of light
1974	Wishnia	Copernicus satellite	Searched 3 stars for ultraviolet laser lines
1975, 1976	Drake, Sagan	NAIC	Searched 4 galaxies for Type II civilizations
1975–79	Israel, De Ruiter	Westerbork Synthesis Radio Telescope, Netherlands	Searched 50 star fields
1976–85	Bowyer et al. ("SERENDIP")	Hat Creek Radio Observatory, University of California at Berkeley	All-sky survey
1976	Clark, Black, Cuzzi, Tarter	NRAO	Searched 4 stars with high-frequency resolution
1977	Black, Clark, Cuzzi, Tarter	NRAO	Searched 200 stars
1977	Drake, Stull	NAIC	Searched 6 stars
1977–present	Wielebinski, Seiradakis	Max-Planck-Institut für Radioastronomie, Germany	Searching 3 stars for pulsed signals
1978	Horowitz	NAIC	Searched 185 stars
1978	Cohen, Malkan, Dickey	NAIC, Hat Creek, CSIRO	Searched 25 globular clusters
1978	Knowles, Sullivan	NAIC	Searched 2 stars
1978	Makovetskij, Gindilis et al.	Zelenchukskaya, RATAN-600, USSR	Examined Barnard's Star for pulsed signals
1978–80	Harris	*Pioneer Venus* and *Venera 11* and *12* spacecraft	Studied 54 gamma-ray bursts for skidmarks in space

YEARS	PARTICIPANTS	OBSERVATORY	ACTIVITY
1978–present	Shvartsman et al. ("MANIA")	Special Astrophysical Observatory	Searching 93 objects for optical signs of Type II or III civilizations
1979	Cole, Ekers	CSIRO	Searched nearby solar-type stars
1979	Freitas, Valdes	Leuschner Observatory, University of California at Berkeley	Looked for interstellar probes near Earth-Moon system
1979–81	Tarter, Clark, Duquet, Lesyna	NAIC	Searched 300 stars
1979–82	"SERENDIP"	JPL, University of California at Berkeley	Parasitic search using spacecraft-tracking operations
1980	Witteborn	NASA, University of Arizona, Mount Lemon	Searched 20 faint stars for Dyson spheres
1980–81	Suchkin, Tokarev et al.	Nirfi, Gorky, Gaish, Moscow	Looked for radar reflections from artifacts in Earth-Moon system
1981	Lord, O'Dea	University of Massachusetts	Searched for signals along Galaxy's axis of rotation
1981	Israel, Tarter	Westerbork	Searched 85 star fields
1981–88	Biraud, Tarter	Nançay	Searched 343 stars
1981	Shostak, Tarter ("Signal")	Westerbork	Searched for pulsed signals from galactic center
1981	Talent	Kitt Peak National Observatory	Searched 3 stars for spectral evidence of nuclear waste dumping
1981–82	Valdes, Freitas ("SETA")	Kitt Peak	Searched for discrete artifacts in Earth-Moon and Sun-Earth systems

YEARS	PARTICIPANTS	OBSERVATORY	ACTIVITY
1982	Horowitz, Teague, Linscott, Chen, Backus ("Suitcase SETI")	NAIC	Searched 250 stars and then 150 stars on magic frequencies
1982	Vallee, Simard-Normandin	Algonquin	Searched for strongly polarized signals from galactic center
1983–85	Horowitz ("Sentinel")	Oak Ridge Observatory	Automated all-sky survey
1983	Damashek	NRAO	Searched pulsars
1983	Valdes, Freitas	Hat Creek	Searched 92 stars for signs of fusion technology
1983–present	Gulkis	NASA Deep Space Network, Tidbinbilla, Australia	Sky survey of Southern Hemisphere
1983–88	Gray	Small SETI Observatory	Sky survey conducted by amateurs
1983–88	Stephens	Hay River	Northern sky survey, amateur observatory
1984	Slysh	*Reliikt* satellite	All-sky search for Dyson spheres
1985–present	Horowitz ("META SETI")	Oak Ridge	Sky survey with 8 million channels
1985–present	Bowyer, Wertheimer, Lampton ("SERENDIP II")	NRAO	Automated search piggybacking radio astronomy observations
1986	Mirabel	NRAO	Searched galactic center and 33 nearby stars
1986–present	Colomb, Martin, Lemarchand	Instituto Argentino de Radioastronomia	Searching 80 solar-type stars in Southern Hemisphere

YEARS	PARTICIPANTS	OBSERVATORY	ACTIVITY
1986	Arkhipov	Molonglo Survey Catalog of Radio Sources	Examined radio sources near solar-type stars as signs of extraterrestrial industrial activity
1987	Tarter, Kardashev, Slysh	Very Large Array, New Mexico	Examined infrared source near galactic center for Dyson sphere
1987	Gray	Oak Ridge	Searched for source of "Wow!" signal
1992 et seq	NASA SETI Microwave Observing Project	NAIC, NRAO, Nançay, Goldstone, Tidbinbilla	All-sky and targeted searches over 15 million channels with global network and response capability

Appendix C: Signatories to the SETI Petition*

Carl Sagan
  David Duncan Professor of Astronomy and Space Sciences;
  Director, Laboratory for Planetary Studies, Center for Radio-
    physics and Space Research, Cornell University
David Baltimore
  Professor of Biology, Massachusetts Institute of Technology
    Nobel Laureate in Physiology and Medicine
Richard Berendzen
  President, American University
John Billingham
  Chief, Extraterrestrial Research Division,
    NASA Ames Research Center
Melvin Calvin
  Professor of Chemistry
  Former Director, Chemical Biodynamics Division,
    Lawrence Radiation Laboratory, University of California at
    Berkeley
  Nobel Laureate in Chemistry
A.G.W. Cameron
  Professor of Astronomy, Harvard University
  Former Chairman, Space Science Board,
  National Research Council/National Academy of Sciences

---

* Individuals are listed with the titles they held when the petition was printed
in *Science* on October 29, 1982.

M. S. Chadha
  Senior Researcher, Bhabha Atomic Research Centre,
    Bombay, India
S. Chandrasekhar
  Morton D. Hull Distinguished Service Professor of Physics and
    Astrophysics, University of Chicago
  National Medal of Science
Francis Crick
  Distinguished Research Professor, Salk Institute
  Nobel Laureate in Physiology and Medicine
Robert S. Dixon
  Assistant Director, Ohio State University Radio Observatory
T. M. Donahue
  Professor of Atmospheric Sciences, University of Michigan
  Chairman, Space Science Board, NAS/NRC
Frank D. Drake
  Goldwin Smith Professor of Astronomy, Cornell University
  Former Director, National Astronomy and Ionosphere Center
Lee A. DuBridge
  President Emeritus, California Institute of Technology
  Former Presidential Science Adviser
Freeman J. Dyson
  Professor of Physics, Institute for Advanced Study, Princeton
    University
Manfred Eigen
  Director, Section on Biochemical Kinetics,
  Max Planck Institute for Biophysical Chemistry,
    Göttingen, German Federal Republic
  Nobel Laureate in Chemistry
Thomas Eisner
  Jacob Gould Schurman Professor of Biology, Cornell University
James Elliot
  Associate Professor of Earth and Planetary Sciences
  Director, George R. Wallace, Jr., Astrophysical Observatory,
    Massachusetts Institute of Technology
George B. Field
  Professor of Astronomy, Harvard University
  Former Director, Harvard/Smithsonian Center for Astrophysics
Vitaly L. Ginzburg
  Senior Staff Member, Lebedev Physical Institute, Moscow
  Lenin Prize Laureate

Thomas Gold
  John L. Wetherill Professor of Astronomy
  Former Director, Center for Radiophysics and Space Research,
    Cornell University
Leo Goldberg
  Former Director, Kitt Peak National Observatory
  Past President, International Astronomical Union
Peter Goldreich
  Lee A. DuBridge Professor of Astrophysics and Planetary
    Physics, California Institute of Technology
Richard J. Gott III
  Professor of Astrophysics, Princeton University
Stephen Jay Gould
  Professor of Geology
  Adjunct Professor in Biology and in the History of Science,
    Harvard University
Tor Hagfors
  Director, National Astronomy and Ionosphere Center
  Professor of Electrical Engineering, Cornell University
  Former Professor of Electrical Engineering, University of
    Trondheim, Norway
Stephen W. Hawking
  Lucasian Professor of Mathematics, Cambridge University,
    United Kingdom
David S. Heeschen
  Former Director, National Radio Astronomy Observatory
Jean Heidmann
  Professor of Astrophysics, University of Paris
Gerhard Herzberg
  Distinguished Research Scientist, National Research Council of
    Canada
  Nobel Laureate in Chemistry
Rev. Theodore M. Hesburgh
  President, University of Notre Dame
Paul Horowitz
  Professor of Physics, Harvard University
Fred Hoyle
  Former Plumian Professor of Astronomy and Experimental Phi-
    losophy
  Director of the Institute of Astronomy, Cambridge University

Eric M. Jones
Staff Member, Los Alamos Scientific Laboratory
Jun Jugaku
Professor of Astronomy, University of Tokyo, Japan
N. S. Kardashev
Director, Samarkand Radio Observatory, Institute for Cosmic Research, Soviet Academy of Sciences, Moscow
Kenneth I. Kellerman
Senior Scientist, National Radio Astronomy Observatory
Michael J. Klein
Senior Scientist, Jet Propulsion Laboratory, NASA
Richard B. Lee
Professor of Anthropology, University of Toronto, Canada
Per-Olof Lindblad
Professor of Astronomy
Director of the Stockholm Observatory, Stockholm, Sweden
Paul D. MacLean
Chief, Laboratory of Brain Evolution and Behavior, National Institute of Mental Health
Matthew Meselson
Thomas Dudley Cabot Professor of the Natural Sciences
Professor of Biochemistry and Molecular Biology, Harvard
Marvin L. Minsky
Donner Professor of Science
Former Director, Artificial Intelligence Laboratory, Massachusetts Institute of Technology
Masaki Morimoto
Director, Nobeyama Radio Observatory, Tokyo, Japan
Philip Morrison
Institute Professor, Massachusetts Institute of Technology
Bruce Murray
Professor of Geological and Planetary Sciences, California Institute of Technology
Former Director, Jet Propulsion Laboratory, NASA
William I. Newman
Assistant Professor of Planetary Physics and Astronomy, University of California at Los Angeles
Bernard M. Oliver
Vice President for Research and Development (Ret.), Hewlett-Packard Company

J. H. Oort
  Professor of Astronomy, Leiden University
  Former Director, Leiden Observatory, Netherlands
  Past President, International Astronomical Union
Ernst J. Opik
  Senior Scientist, Armagh Observatory, Armagh, Northern Ireland
Leslie E. Orgel
  Research Professor, The Salk Institute
  Adjunct Professor of Chemistry, University of California at San Diego
Franco Pacini
  Director, Arcetri Observatory, Florence, Italy
Michael D. Papagiannis
  Chairman, Department of Astronomy, Boston University
Linus Pauling
  Former Chairman, Division of Chemistry and Chemical Engineering, California Institute of Technology
  President, Linus Pauling Institute for Science and Medicine
  Nobel Laureate in Chemistry
  Nobel Peace Prize Laureate
  Lenin Prize Laureate
  National Medal of Science
Rudolf Pesek
  Czechoslovak Academy of Sciences, Prague, Czechoslovakia
  Vice President, International Astronautical Federation
W. H. Pickering
  Professor of Electrical Engineering Emeritus, California Institute of Technology
  Former Director, Jet Propulsion Laboratory, NASA
  National Medal of Science
Cyril Ponnamperuma
  Professor of Chemistry
  Directory, Laboratory of Chemical Evolution, University of Maryland
Edward M. Purcell
  Gade University Professor, Harvard University
  Nobel Laureate in Physics
  National Medal of Science

David M. Raup
    Chairman, Department of Geophysical Sciences, University of Chicago
    Former Dean of Science, Field Museum of Natural History
    Former Professor of Geology and Paleontology, University of Rochester
Grote Reber
    Inventor of the radio telescope, Tasmania
Martin J. Rees
    Plumian Professor of Astronomy
    Director of the Institute of Astronomy, Cambridge University, United Kingdom
Dale A. Russell
    Chief, Paleobiology Division, National Museums of Canada, Ottawa
Roald Z. Sagdeev
    Institute for Cosmic Research, Soviet Academy of Sciences, Moscow
Claude E. Shannon
    Former Research Mathematician, Bell Laboratories
    Donner Professor of Science Emeritus, Massachusetts Institute of Technology
    National Medal of Science
I. S. Shklovsky
    Chairman, Astrophysics Division, Institute for Cosmic Research, Soviet Academy of Sciences, Moscow
Jill Tarter
    Research Astronomer, University of California at Berkeley
Lewis Thomas
    Chancellor, Memorial Sloan-Kettering Cancer Center
    Professor of Medicine, Cornell University Medical School
Kip S. Thorne
    William R. Kenan Professor of Theoretical Physics, California Institute of Technology
V. S. Troitsky
    Scientific Director, Radiophysics Research Institute, Gorky, U.S.S.R.
Sebastian von Hoerner
    Senior Staff Member, National Radio Astronomy Observatory

Edward O. Wilson
  Baird Professor of Science and Professor of Biology, Harvard
    University
Benjamin Zuckerman
  Professor of Astronomy, University of Maryland

Index